Noverr & Ziewacz, Sport History

Selected Reading Lists and Course
Outlines from American Colleges
and Universities

Sport History

edited by Douglas A. Noverr
and Lawrence E. Ziewacz
Michigan State University

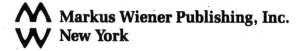 Markus Wiener Publishing, Inc.
New York

ISBN 0-910129-58-4

Library of Congress Cataloging-in-Publication Data

Sport history.

(Selected reading lists and course outlines from
American colleges and universities ; vol. 15)
    Includes bibliographies, filmographies, and index.
    1. Sports--History--Study and teaching. I. Noverr,
Douglas A. II. Ziewacz, Lawrence E. (Lawrence Edward)
III. Series.
GV571.S57 1987   796'.09   86-28993
ISBN 0-910129-58-4

Printed in America

TABLE OF CONTENTS

INTRODUCTION

It is safe to say that ten years ago the following extensive and varied collection of course materials on sport history would have been impossible to compile, or at least would have been so attenuated so as not to justify publication. However, a number of important factors have contributed to the development of sport history and its vital expansion beyond its historical locus in departments of physical education, which themselves encompass such areas as recreation, human performance, leisure, etc.

Sport history has indeed steadily moved toward increasing acceptance and recognition as a legitimate field of academic endeavor. This is not to say, however, that those involved in sport studies have had an easy time of it in claiming legitimacy for their efforts. For those in the health and physical education, sport history, as such, was a relatively minor area because they focused their research on matters they knew best and utilized quantitative methodologies they were trained to employ in the interests of better performance, skills development, conditioning, etc. For those researchers in the areas of history, literature, philosophy, psychology, sociology, their early efforts to apply a particular discipline's analytical tools and methodology to the study of sport and its relationship to society may well have been met with disbelief or even ridicule. Such traditional academicians might be suspected of becoming adulatory "jock sniffers" or selling themselves out to gain preferential treatment by athletic departments in the matter of choice seats in the stadium or basketball arena. Books, articles, and professional papers on sport would count, of course; however, in a field such as history, a sport researcher's colleagues might wonder why the individual did not pursue more prestigious fields like intellectual, political, or diplomatic history. Sport history could be too readily dismissed as scores, statistics, and standings--a welcomed diversion and entertainment on the weekend but hardly the stuff of serious study during the week, let alone full consideration as a course in the classroom. Well entrenched assumptions about "highbrow" and "lowbrow" culture and literature served to further reinforce such attitudes.

One of the main factors in the establishment of sport studies as a vital enterprise was, of course, the pioneering work of a number of individuals who not only surveyed the territory but also formulated key questions and showed how the approaches of various disciplines could begin to illuminate the complex reciprocal relationships between sport and culture. It is impossible to cite all the significant pioneers. However, the names of John R. Betts, Frederick W. Cozens and Florence Scovil Stumpf, Foster Rhea Dulles, Jennie Holliman, John Allen Krout, Herbert Manchester, Robert B. Weaver, and A.S. "Doc" Young certainly deserve mention. One particular native sport, baseball, has richly been documented and analyzed through the separate three-volume accomplishments of Harold Seymour and David Quentin Voit. More recently, the local and period studies of sport have been enriched by the work of Dale A. Somers, Stephen Hardy, Benjamin Rader, Steven A. Riess, Donald Mrozek, and others too numerous to cite. Our purpose here is not to create a pantheon of researchers but merely to show how progress depends on the interplay and exchange of research. Even those researchers who find faults or limitations in others' work benefit from the work criticized. Later work becomes more sophisticated, inclusive, balanced, and corrective as the methodology becomes more clearly articulated and more convincingly verified.

Another impetus to the research in and teaching of sport studies has been the establishment of such diverse academic journals as the Canadian Journal of Sport History (established 1970), Journal of Sport History (1973), Journal of Sport and Social Issues (1977), Journal of Sport Behavior (1978), and the Journal of Sport Psychology (1979). The American Quarterly and the Journal of Popular Culture have also published articles on sports or even published a special issue on sports as the Journal of Popular Culture did in its Fall, 1974 issue. One of the oldest and best established journals is the Research Quarterly for Exercise and Sport and its antecedent title that goes back to 1930, and one of the most recently founded journals is Arete: The Journal of Sport Literature, established in 1983. These journals signal the development of significant research, much of it resulting from courses taught at the undergraduate and graduate level. In these journals serious and spirited debates are conducted about definitions of sport, theoretical frameworks, the dynamics of the interrelation between sports and culture and culture and sports, methodology, assumptions and conclusions. More traditional journals in history, sociology, literature, and education have started to feature articles on sport. What all of this suggests, of course, is that one who is interested in developing and teaching a sport centered course has a rich and substantial body of research and literature to digest. Much of that literature is identified and cited in the course materials reproduced in this volume. The increasing quantity of material does not, of course, necessarily always imply quality, and one must keep up with reviews and with scholarly review articles of the emerging field.

What can be said is that many disciplines have contributed to the advancement and sophistication of sport study. Sport has clearly become another window through which we can view American culture and society.

Sport studies provide a means of examining such crucial topics as ethnicity, immigration, social-sexual as well as racial roles, urbanism, mobility, major movements such as progessivism, business and entrepreneurship, as well as legal and labor history. Our country's social history is enriched through the exploration of new avenues of understanding our society's dynamics in such a way that our history becomes more inclusive and more representative. In examining human physical activity--organized or unorganized, amateur or professional, individual or group--sport study provides an ingress to our values, aspirations, ideals, and deepest needs. Sport study is, then, a way of examining much of what we mean as a culture as well as what is happening in our society.

It is axiomatic that progress in a field of study should inform and enrich the teaching of courses. College age students are active students who participate in and watch diverse kinds of sporting and recreational pursuits. One can say that their interest in sports is both culturally conditioned as well as naturally instinctive. Sport studies courses can capitalize on their interests and direct them to a more thoughtful and perceptive understanding of sport and its complex social interconnections. Issues such as competition, individualism and cooperation, social and sexual conditioning, the meaning of physical and mental health, exploitation of athletes, violence, drugs, and many other ethnical and philosophical considerations can be explored through sports history. History imvolves a perspective and an understanding of how present day phenomena have evolved and changed in the context of conditions. Such courses provide intellectual rigor and substantial content and can be interdisciplinary in addition to providing a grounding in a particular discipline, whether it is history or sociology. Clearly, the challenges of teaching such courses are substantial, but they are also revitalizing and energizing.

This text has been compiled with the goal of providing those teaching sport courses, or those interested in teaching one, with representative samples of courses and learning materials. Some observations should be made about particular challenges and considerations in teaching such courses. The illustrative courses come from five different departments, with the majority coming from history and physical education. One of the major challenges of teaching any sport history course is the location and combination of the right texts. Instructors frequently must require students to read assignments on library reserve reading or must provide handouts. The increasing availability of a number of good textbooks in sport history, both primary and secondary sources, will soon lessen this problem. Since students may well have the false impression that a course dealing with sports might be an easy and undemanding course, instructors can offset this by presenting a thorough and detailed syllabus with a clear explanation of course objectives and requirements, grading system, and extent of reading assignments. The materials contained in this text illustrate how demanding and academically rigorous sport studies courses are, whether they are formulated for majors or students who take the course as an elective. Further, since most students are unfamiliar with sources, they need extensive help in bibliography and guidance in doing research and locating project materials. This illustrates the point that sport history teachers have to be actively and extensively involved in the students' learning experience. Since students have experiences with sports as well as attitudes and viewpoints, these should be brought into the course, as many of these course syllabi illustrate with their provisions for class discussion, panel or group presentations, or other forms of direct involvement. A last observation that can be made points to the value of writing and research projects in sport history courses. Many topics can be formulated that will give students the excitement of doing some original research and looking at primary source documents. Teachers can also capitalize on student interest by focusing on the history and heritage of sport at their particular institution as well as explore student attitudes about eligibility, athletic scholarships and "perks" for athletes, pressures on athletes and coaches, and a range of current problems facing intercollegiate sports.

Finally, we would like to thank all of our contributors for their involvement in this project. These contributors represent some of the best known researchers and scholars in the field, many with well-known books to their credit, as well as some of the strongest physical education programs in the country. All the contributions represent the commitment and energies of individuals who take sport history and studies as serious enterprise that brings its own rewards. The field is an exciting and promising one, and these materials indicate the emergence of a rich diversity of new courses and approaches. Further, we would like to thank Dr. Markus Wiener, our publisher and editor, for his support and belief in this project. We hope that this work contributes, in whatever ways it can, to the expansion of sport hsitory study and to the further development of a substantial body of established course offerings and curriculums.

Douglas A. Noverr   Michigan State University

Lawrence E. Ziewacz

I. TEACHING SPORT HISTORY:

RATIONALE, METHODOLOGY,

AND MATERIALS

David L. Porter
William Penn College

"The Significance of Sports in American History"

Historians traditionally have concentrated relatively little on the development of American sports. With the notable exception of some large universities, few History Departments have offered courses on American Sports History. At the present time, there are hardly any scholarly textbooks devoted primarily to the development of American sports.

My paper will show how sports have played a significant, often neglected, role in American history. Sports have reflected significant patterns and trends concerning socio-economic class, urbanism, immigration, technology, business-labor relations, and social movements.

Sports have reflected increasing socio-economic class mobility. During the nineteenth century, sports were enjoyed primarily by the upper classes. Elite classes often spent leisure time watching horse racing, baseball, and other sports, while other Americans were to preoccupied with struggling for survival. In the present century, sports have become more accessible to all socio-economic classes. Shorter working hours, coupled with vastly improved wages, gave Americans more time and financial resources with which to enjoy recreational activities.

There is a significant correlation between the development of sports and the tremendous growth of American cities. The movement of Americans from rural to urban areas encouraged the growth of professional sports, including baseball in the post-Civil War and football and basketball in the twentieth century.

Sports also have reflected immigration patterns. During the nineteenth century, numerous Irish immigrants settled in eastern cities. Irish immigrants not only enjoyed watching professional baseball and college football games, but often were participants.

There is a significant correlation between the development of American sport and the dynamic growth of technology. Changes in transportation and communications enabled Americans to travel more extensively and to learn more about contemporary events. The automobile and mass transit systems enhanced considerably attendance at sporting events, while the newspaper, radio, and television have provided wider coverage of athletic contests.

Sports have reflected changing relations between business and organized labor. Until the New Deal, big business prevailed in the American economy forcing workers to toil long hours for low pay and few benefits. Professional sports owners likewise controlled players, paying them low wages, providing them few benefits, and fining them for violating team rules. Since the New Deal, organized labor has increased enormously in power, securing lucrative contracts for workers. Athletes also have wielded more influence, signing very generous contracts and having more tolerant management.

There is a significant correlation between the development of American social reform movements and sports. Following World War II, the civil rights and women's rights movements burgeoned in hopes of eliminating political, economic, and social discrimination against blacks and women. After being denied entrance into organized team sports for over half a century, blacks in the late 1940's began participating in professional baseball, football, and basketball. Jackie Robinson, Willie Mays, Hank Aaron, Jimmy Brown, O.J. Simpson, Bill Russell, Wilt Chamberlain, and others have made a dynamic, often dramatic, impact on sports. Considerably more women now are participating in both amateur and professional sports, most notably involving tennis, golf, and basketball. Prominent women athletes in the 1970's include Billie Jean King, Chris Evert Lloyd, Nancy Lopez, and Ann Myers, most of whom have participated on professional teams.

Sports thus have played a significant role in American history and mirrored major patterns in American society. Historians consequently should devote more attention to researching the development of sports and, if their departments have not already done so, seriously should consider offering courses in American Sports History. Such courses provide an interesting, more innovative way of examining American history and, in this sports-minded era, probably would attract considerable student following.

David L. Porter
William Penn College

"The Teaching and Significance of American Sport History"

Until the last two decades, the historical profession largely ignored the development and significance of American sports. History departments, textbooks, journals, and associations did not give serious attention to this topic, regarding popular culture and especially sport history as too insignificant or non-traditional to include in academic curricula.[1] Within the last two decades, however, this scenario has begun to change. History departments, textbooks, journals, and associations are concentrating much more on the historical development and significance of American athletics. Several sport history textbooks, including the very fine The Saga of Ameri-Sport by John Lucas and Ronald Smith, have been published.[2] Sport historians have formed professional groups, most notably the North American Society for Sport History and the Society for American Baseball Research. These societies, which have grown considerably in membership, publish valuable research journals and hold annual conventions at which informative scholarly papers are presented.[3] Nevertheless, I believe that many more schools should offer courses in American Sport History and that far more interested historians should research athletic history.

Since sport history is a relatively new academic discipline, I will attempt to accomplish two objectives today. I will discuss how I teach my sport history course, indicating how I use the lecture method, debates, and guest speakers. Sport history is one of the most popular of the nearly dozen different courses I teach and consistently draws at least 35 students at a small liberal arts college with only 600 students. Second, I will attempt to explain some of the significance of sports in American history and indicate why colleges and universities should offer a sport history course.

5

I devote about three-fourths of my course to traditional lectures and class discussion on the historical development and significance of American sport, dividing the time equally between pre-twentieth and twentieth century. Although stressing how athletics grew, I also analyze why sports developed the way they did in the colonial period, nineteenth and twentieth centuries. During the first few sessions, I discuss colonial sports and stress the surprising abundance of sports in Puritan New England, the highly developed Indian game of lacrosse, and the significance of horse racing in the Middle Atlantic and Southern colonies. Students are surprised to learn that the incredibly talented Benjamin Franklin was considered America's first great swimmer and was sought after as a swimming coach. Some colonial sports, including cock fighting and wrestling, unfortunately were less civilized. Wrestlers, for example, bit noses, pulled hair, occasionally plucked eye sockets, and otherwise mauled opponents.[4]

For several weeks, I examine the historical development and significance of nineteenth century team and individual sports. Team sports examined include baseball, football, and basketball, while the individual sports covered include boxing, horse racing, foot racing, tennis, and bicycling. With the exception of basketball, American team sports evolved from other sports; baseball developed from town ball and football from soccer-rugby. After debunking the myth that Abner Doubleday invented baseball, I describe how New York City surveyor Alexander Cartwright drafted the early baseball rules and field dimensions. In addition, I show how baseball shifted from a leisurely upper socio-economic class amateur sport played on weekends by the New York Knickerbockers to a professional sport with the National Association and National League. Students enjoy hearing about the Cincinnati Red Stockings, who went undefeated in the 1869 season, and the individual contributions made by Harry and George Wright, Albert Spaulding, and Cap Anson.[5] I trace how intercollegiate football began to evolve from a very dangerous sport to a more structured one, emphasizing the formative role of Walter Camp.[6] Basketball originated in the United States, being founded by Dr. James Naismith of the Springfield, Massachusetts Y.M.C.A. Training School to keep football players in good physical condition over the winter months. The major roles of black slaves like Tom Molineux and Irishmen like John L. Sullivan in boxing, the classic North-South matches in promoting horse racing, and the impressive long distance running feats of American Indians are also stressed.[7]

During the last few weeks of the course, I lecture and conduct discussions on the development and significance of twentieth century sports. I concentrate on baseball, featuring the contributions of Ban Johnson, Ty Cobb, Kenesaw Mountain Landis, Babe Ruth, and Jackie Robinson. I relate how the Chicago Black Sox scandal of 1919 nearly destroyed baseball and how Babe Ruth and the New York Yankees helped revive the sport. In addition, I describe how blacks excelled in the Negro Leagues and how the signing of Jackie Robinson by the Brooklyn Dodgers enabled many talented black athletes eventually to enter modern organized sport. Robinson was the first black to play organized major league baseball since the National Association barred the Walker brothers after the 1884 season.[8] I relate how intercollegiate football, after being nearly outlawed in the Theodore Roosevelt era, developed into a highly structured, strategy oriented, popular sport by the 1920's. Pop Warner, Jim Thorpe, Amos Alonzo Stagg, Knute Rockne, and Red Grange particularly played crucial roles in developing intercollegiate football. Professional football, by contrast, struggled during the early twentieth century, but George Halas, Paul Brown, Vince Lombardi, and others helped build the sport into one that has surpassed baseball in popularity.[9] Other units trace the development of twentieth century basketball, boxing, golf, tennis, the modern Olympics, and black and women athletes. Particular attention is given to the significance of Jack Johnson, Jack Dempsey, and Joe Louis in boxing, Jesse Owens in track, Bobby Jones in golf, and Bill Tilden in tennis. The role of the very talented Babe Didrikson Zaharias, who was voted the greatest woman athlete of the first half of the twentieth century, is also stressed.[10]

For background reading, I assign four required books. Besides using the excellent Lucas-Smith work as the basic text, I use Lawrence Ritter's The Glory of Their Times, Robert Creamer's Babe: The Legend Comes to Life, and James Michener's Sports in America as supplementary texts. Ritter's work is a fascinating oral history vividly describing the life of professional baseball players both on and off the field in the early twentieth century, while Creamer's book is perhaps the finest sports biography to date detailing the life and impact of Babe Ruth. Michener's work describes and discusses several recent great issues confronting American sport.[11]

Six-eight sessions each semester are devoted to classroom debates, with each student expected to participate once. Controversial debate topics are selected from the Michener book and have included the following samples: Is competition emphasized too much in children's sports? Do colleges and universities spend too much money on sports programs? Is there too much emphasis on winning in amateur sports? Should the reserve clause be removed from all professional team sports? Are professional athletes paid too much? Is there too much violence in sports?[12] Students are required to do extensive library research on both the affirmative and negative cases and write a paper presenting and defending both sides. During the actual classroom debate, each student will defend one side for five minutes and then give a two minute rebuttal of the arguments used by the opposition. The debate process helps make students better researchers, more effective writers, more confident and fluent speakers, more careful listeners,

8

and better critical thinkers, enabling them to learn through doing. College
and university students too often are content to listen to the talking teacher
rather than directly participating in the learning process.

For one or two sessions, I invite former professional athletes or
current sports writers to talk informally with the class. Since 1974, guests
have included former baseball players Rip Coleman, Billy Harrell, Dale
Long, Bob Oldis, Birdie Tebbetts, Hal Trosky, and Bill Zuber, football player
Jack Kemp, one-time mile record holder Glenn Cunningham, and noted journalists
Will Grimsley and Colman McCarthy. Besides sharing fascinating anecdotes,
they usually make candid, perceptive comments on sports past and present.[13]

I must turn now to the significance of sport history and the rationale
behind teaching sport history. Sports are a mirror of American life and
values and consequently provide an excellent way for studying major historical
developments and movements.[14] Sports furnish an excellent mechanism for
examining significant patterns concerning socio-economic class, urbanism,
immigration, technology, business-labor relations, leadership, minority
groups, and social movements. Similarly, socio-economic class, urbanism,
immigration, technology, business-labor relations, leadership, minority
groups, and social movements profoundly influence the development of
American sport.

Sports, for example, often have reflected increasing socio-economic
class mobility in American society. Before the twentieth century, upper
classes were the main spectator in sports. Elite classes often spent
leisure time watching horse racing and other sporting events, while other
Americans usually worked long hours struggling for the basic essentials of
life - namely adequate food, clothing, and shelter. Since 1900, sports have
become far more accessible to all socio-economic classes. Shorter work

hours, coupled with vastly improved wages and benefits, have given Americans more time and financial resources with which to enjoy recreational activities.[15]

Second, there is a significant correlation between the development of sports and the tremendous growth of American cities. The movement of Americans from rural to urban areas in the late nineteenth century encouraged the growth of professional sports, particularly baseball teams, in the northeast and midwest. Since 1900, the rapid development of cities led to the expansion of professional baseball, football, basketball, boxing, and other sports.[16]

Sports also have reflected immigration patterns, most notably among Irish-Americans. During the nineteenth century, Irish immigrants settling in eastern cities often became rabid sports fans and furnished many premier athletes. Irish immigrants enjoyed attending professional sports contests and cheering ethnic heroes like baseball player Mike "King" Kelly and boxer John L. Sullivan. Kelly became the subject of a popular song, "Slide, Kelly, Slide" and was noted for both a vigorous lifestyle and short-circuiting bases when the umpires were not looking.[17]

Fourth, there is a significant correlation between the expansion of American sport and the rapid growth of technology. Transportation systems, most notably the railroad, automobile, and mass transit, enabled Americans to travel greater distances and attend more athletic events. The mass media, including newspapers, radio, and more recently television, spread the coverage of and stirred American interest in sporting contests. Newspapers promoted horse racing and boxing before 1900, while radio publicized professional baseball, intercollegiate football, and boxing in the early twentieth century. Television played a very dynamic role in the expansion and rising popularity of football, basketball, golf, tennis, and the Olympic games.[18]

Sports have reflected the changing historical status of big business and organized labor. Until the 1930's, big business prevailed often forcing American workers to toil long hours for low pay and few benefits. Professional baseball and football owners rigidly controlled players, paying them low salaries, providing them few benefits, and owning exclusive rights to their services. During the last half century, however, organized labor has become very powerful securing lucrative wage and benefit contracts for workers. Athletes now wield much more influence over management, threatening to become free agents if owners do not comply with their salary demands. Professional baseball players now average $130,000 annually and basketball players an even higher amount.[19]

Sixth, sports often have provided the nation with symbolic heroes. During the 1920's, the nation refused to consider as heroes Presidents like the scandal-prone Warren Harding and colorless Calvin Coolidge and found them instead in sports figures Babe Ruth, Knute Rockne, Red Grange, Jack Dempsey, and Bobby Jones.[20] The nation likewise could not find its heroes in Washington politics in the 1970's and instead turned to sports figures Muhammad Ali, Hank Aaron, Reggie Jackson, O.J. Simpson, Earl Campbell, and Kareem Jabbar.

Finally, there is a significant correlation between sports and social reform movements. Historically both black and women athletes suffered considerable discrimination. Many qualified blacks were barred from organized baseball because of race and were treated as second-class citizens in the Negro leagues. Few women had the opportunity to enter professional sports, although some played amateur basketball, track, swimming, golf, or tennis.[21] Following World War II, the civil rights and women's rights movements began removing political, economic, and social discrimination against blacks and women. By the late 1940's, blacks began participating in professional

11

baseball, football, and basketball. Since that time, Jackie Robinson, Willie Mays, Hank Aaron, Jimmy Brown, O.J. Simpson, Earl Campbell, Bill Russell, Wilt Chamberlain, Kareem Jabbar, and other blacks have excelled in those sports. Professional basketball teams now consist largely of black players, while once segregated colleges and universities actively recruit black football and basketball players. There has been a dramatic increase in the number of women involved in professional and amateur sports. Tennis players Billie Jean King, Chris Evert Lloyd, and Tracy Austin, golfer Nancy Lopez-Melton, basketball players Ann Myers, and Nancy Lieberman, and auto racer Janet Guthrie have achieved success in their respective sports.[22]

Sports, in summary, have played a significant role in American history and mirrored major patterns in American society. Drawing upon lectures, discussion, debates, and guest speakers, I attempt to describe the historical development of and assess the significance of athletics in my sport history course. As I have outlined, there are several reasons why colleges and especially universities should offer courses in American Sports History. Such courses not only provide an interesting, exciting, and innovative way of examining American history, but probably would attract sizeable enrollments in this sports-minded era. History departments confronted with declining enrollments particularly should consider offering such courses.

Footnotes

[1] Some sport history works written before 1960 were John Allen Krout, Annals of American Sport (New Haven, 1929); Herbert Manchester, Four Centuries of Sport in America 1490-1890 (New York, 1931); Robert B. Weaver, Amusements and Sports in American Life (Chicago, 1939); Foster Rhea Dulles, America Learns to Play: A History of Popular Recreation, 1607-1940 (New York, 1940); and John Durant and Otto Bettmann, Pictorial History of American Sports From Colonial Times to the Present (New York, 1952).

[2] John A. Lucas and Ronald A. Smith, Saga of American Sport (Philadelphia, 1978) is the best and most complete history of American sport yet written. Other recent sport histories include John Rickards Betts, America's Sporting Heritage: 1850-1950 (Reading, Mass., 1974) and Wells Twombly, 200 Years of Sport in America: A Pageant of a Nation at Play (New York, 1976). Within the last decade the American Historical Association and the Organization of American Historians, the two largest historical societies, have included sessions on sport history at their annual conventions. The Journal of American History, the second largest American history review, published an essay in 1979 on sport history.

[3] The North American Society for Sport History, with over 275 individual members in 1979, publishes the Journal of Sport History, while the 830 member Society for American Baseball Research publishes the Baseball Research Journal.

[4] For colonial sports, see Lucas and Smith, Saga, pp. 1-54; Dulles, America Learns to Play, pp. 3-83; and Twombly, 200 Years, pp. 18-39. A model colonial study is Jane Carson, Colonial Virginians at Play (Charlottesville, 1965).

[5] The principal works on nineteenth century baseball are Harold Seymour, Baseball: The Early Years (New York, 1960); David Quentin Voigt, American Baseball: From Gentleman's Sport to the Commissioner System (Norman, 1966); and Robert Smith, Illustrated History of Baseball (New York, 1973). For the Doubleday myth, see Robert W. Henderson, Ball, Bat, and Bishop (New York, 1947).

[6] The principal works on nineteenth century intercollegiate football are Parke Hill Davis, Football: The American Intercollegiate Game (New York, 1911); Louis Baker, Football: Facts and Figures (New York, 1945); Alexander M. Weyand, The Saga of American Football (New York, 1955); Allison Danzig, The History of American Football (Englewood Cliffs, 1956); and Ivan N. Kaye, Good Clean Violence: A History of College Football (Philadelphia, 1973). For Camp's role, see Harford Powell, Jr., Walter Camp, the Father of American Football (Boston, 1926).

[7] For these sports, see Bernice Larson Webb, The Basketball Man: James Naismith (Lawrence, Kan., 1973); Nat Fleischer and Sam Andre, A Pictorial History of Boxing (New York, 1959); and John Hervey, Racing in America, 1665-1865, 2 vols. (New York, 1944).

[8] The principal works on twentieth century baseball are Harold Seymour, Baseball: The Golden Age (New York, 1971); David Quentin Voigt, American

Baseball: From the Commissioners to Continental Expansion (Norman, 1970); David Quentin Voigt, America Through Baseball (Chicago, 1976); Frederick Lieb, The Baseball Story (New York, 1950); Lee Allen, The National League Story (New York, 1961); Lee Allen, The American League Story (New York, 1962); Lawrence Ritter and Donald Honig, The Image of Their Greatness: An Illustrated History of Baseball from 1900 to the Present (New York, 1979).

[9]The principal works on twentieth century intercollegiate football are Weyand, Saga of American Football; Danzig, American Football; John Durant and Les Etter, Highlights of College Football (New York, 1970); and Kaye, Good Clean Violence. For professional football, see Howard Roberts, The Story of Pro Football (Chicago, 1954); Robert Smith, Pro Football: The History of the Game and the Great Players (Garden City, 1963); Myron Cope, The Game That Was: An Illustrated Account of the Tumultuous Early Days of Pro Football (New York, 1970); and Mickey Herskowitz, The Golden Age of Pro Football: A Remembrance of Pro Football in the 1950's (New York, 1974).

[10]For twentieth century basketball, see Alexander Weyand, The Cavalcade of Basketball (New York, 1960); Neil Isaacs, All the Moves: A History of College Basketball (Philadelphia, 1975); and Leonard Koppett, 24 Seconds to Shoot (New York, 1968). Will Grimsley, Golf: Its History, People and Events (Englewood Cliffs, 1966) and Herbert Wind, The Story of American Golf (New York, 1956) describe golf history, while Will Grimsley, Tennis: Its History, People, and Events (Englewood Cliffs, 1971) and Parke Cummings, American Tennis: The Story of a Game and Its People (Boston, 1957) recount tennis history. For twentieth century boxers, see Al Tony Gilmore, Bad Nigger! The National Impact of Jack Johnson (Port Washington, 1974); Randy Roberts, Jack Dempsey: The Manassa Mauler (Baton Rouge, 1979); and Anthony Edmonds, Joe Louis (Grand Rapids, 1973). For other athletes, see Richard D. Mandell, The Nazi Olympics (New York, 1971) and Frank Deford, Big Bill Tilden: The Triumphs and the Tragedy (New York, 1976).

[11]Lawrence S. Ritter, The Glory of Their Times (New York, 1966); Robert Creamer, Babe: The Legend Comes to Life (New York, 1974); James A. Michener, Sports in America (New York, 1976).

[12]Besides Michener, Sports in America, some other books providing debate topics include: Robert Boyle, Sport: Mirror of American Life (Boston, 1963); Arnold Beissner, The Madness in Sports (New York, 1967); Jack Scott, The Athletic Revolution (New York, 1971); Paul Weiss, Sport: A Philosophic Inquiry (Carbondale, Ill., 1969); Joseph Durso, The All-American Dollar: The Big Business of Sports (Boston, 1971); Paul Hoch, Rip Off the Big Game (New York, 1972); John McCarthy, (ed.), After the Game (New York, 1972); John Talamini and Robert Page (eds.), Sport and Society (Boston, 1973); J. Robert Evans, Blowing the Whistle on Intercollegiate Sports (Chicago, 1974); and Robert Lipsyte, Sports World: An American Dreamland (New York, 1975).

[13]The guests in American Sport History this year were Colman McCarthy on February 5, 1981 and Will Grimsley on April 14-15, 1981.

[14]Several books stress how sports are a mirror of American society, most notably Boyle, Sport: Mirror of American Life.

[15]For the relationship between socio-economic classes and sports, see Betts, America's Sporting Heritage and Lucas and Smith, Saga.

[16] A model study for the impact of sports on urban history is Dale Somers, The Rise of Sports in New Orleans, 1850-1900 (Baton Rouge, 1972).

[17] Pertinent books include Mike Kelly, Play Ball (Boston, 1888) and John L. Sullivan, Life and Reminiscences of a 19th Century Gladiator (Boston, 1892).

[18] For the impact of technology, see Betts, America's Sporting Heritage.

[19] For economic issues, see Seymour, Baseball 2 vols.; Voigt, American Baseball 2 vols.; Voigt, America Through Baseball; Ralph Andreano, No Joy In Mudville: The Dilemma of Major League Baseball (Cambridge, Mass., 1965); and Durso, All-American Dollar.

[20] For Presidents Harding and Coolidge, see Robert K. Murray, The Harding Era: Warren G. Harding and His Administration (Minneapolis; 1969) and Donald R. McCoy, Calvin Coolidge: The Quiet President (New York, 1967). Grantland Rice, The Tumult and the Shouting (New York, 1954) provides a deft portrait of prominent athletes in the Harding-Coolidge era.

[21] For the problems of the black athlete before World War II, see Robert Peterson, Only the Ball Was White (Englewood Cliffs, 1970); William Heward, Some Are Called Clowns (New York, 1974); and Mandell, Nazi Olympics. Mildred Didrikson Zaharias, This Life I've Led: My Autobiography (New York, 1955) describes how one American woman excelled at sports before World War II. Lucas and Smith, Saga, pp. 342-400 describe problems facing the black and women athletes.

[22] For modern black athlete, see Jackie Robinson, I Never Had It Made (New York, 1972); Edwin B. Henderson, The Black Athlete: Emergence and Arrival (New York, 1970); and Ocania Chalk, Black College Sport (New York, 1976). Other accounts of modern black athlete include Harry Edwards, The Revolt of the Black Athlete (New York, 1969); Jack Olsen, The Black Athlete: A Shameful Story (New York, 1969); and Jack Orr, The Black Athlete (New York, 1969). For accounts of modern women athletes, see Ellen Gerber et al., The American Woman in Sports (Reading, Mass., 1974); Billie Jean King, Billie Jean (New York, 1974); and Grace Lichtenstein, A Long Way, Baby (New York, 1974).

Nancy L. Struna
University of Maryland
24 March 1986

Conceptualizing and Questioning

In Undergraduate Sport History

Teaching is very much like research in at least
one important way. As does the investigator, the instructor
has the responsibility for "making sense" of the material.
"Making sense" means binding behaviors, attitudes, and
beliefs into classes, tying together, drawing conclusions -
putting, in other words, various kinds and difficulty
levels of information into "containers". Depending on the
form and complexity of the information involved, these
"containers" may be descriptive, analytic (or explanatory),
or synthesizing propositions.

In history, any one of these three forms of
"containers" of information differs from generalizations
of knowledge in science. For example, a concept in science,
whether "hard" or "soft" science, is a "transferable
explanatory principle." It is a collapsed summation of
some aspect of reality that can be applied to different
situations regardless of time and space, and it is
therefore predictive. A concept in history, however, is
not transferable and predictive for the simple reason
that history treats the unique, the particular. Historical

17

concepts capture the meaningfulness of the unique, the
particular, in the past of human experience.

These "containers" of historical knowledge help
in each of three primary acts involved in the teaching of
sport history: describing, analyzing, and synthesizing.
Quite probably, one can not fully separate these "acts"
this way; none of the three has a wholly distinguishable
life in the process of teaching. For the sake of developing
the examples, however, this discussion proceeds as if
description can be separated from analysis and both from
synthesis.

Descriptive concepts define or "name" types of
activities and experiences. In terms of both time and
endeavor, they are one-dimensional representations. They
result from the collapsing of discrete bits of information
about a particular segment of time - they generalize the
"what", the historical product or process. Ball games,
for instance, is a descriptive concept. The term desig-
nates a class of action with shared rules, goals, and movement forms. So, too, are the terms puritan, feminism,
urbanization, victorianism, anthropometry, and hero.

Descriptive concepts function in two primary ways
in an undergraduate class. First, because they define
or "name" a part of historical reality via one generalization from the whole, they focus the students' learning
and help to formulate a "sense of," to capture the "essence"
of a mass of details. To describe, for example, the "what

was really happening" in the process of sport form definition and organizational structuring in the mid and late
nineteenth century, I use two concepts - the "quest for
better ways to play" and the "quest for order in the sporting
environment." Presented jointly, these two "quests" contain or bind the mass of detail about rule changes, alter-
ations in styles of play, the connections among various
forms of voluntary organizations (e.g., from local clubs
to regional and national governing bodies), among other
things, evident in baseball, men's and women's college
athletics, urban athletic clubs, the parks and playgrounds,
and so on. Further, these two conceptualized "quests"
(for better ways to play and for order in the sporting
environment) enable one to describe "across" the particular. They enable one to compare and contrast various sport
forms; the behaviors and attitudes of individuals from
Albert Spaulding to William Curtis to Senda Berenson; and
the relationships among owners and players, organizational
constituencies, and sport and other sets of social endeavors.

Descriptive concepts are also helpful when one
wishes to isolate and to highlight change over time,
particularly lengthy periods of time. Again, by encapsu-
lating the "what" - only on this occasion, the "what" has
changed (or did not change) over time - an instructor can
simplify the change without misstating its major characteristics. In talking about contrasts in prominent forms of
sport between the mid eighteenth and nineteenth centuries,

for instance, I use two descriptive concepts: "natural" sport forms, hunting for example, and "artificial" ones such as baseball. These are unevaluative descriptors that embody a variety of characteristics about the sports, the "natural" and the "artificial" ones, and the societies from which they are generalized. The two terms also are generalizations about the same characteristics - location and setting, equipment, actual movements and modes of performance, and time of occurrence - at different points in time. They help students to make sense of the multiple changes that both occurred across time and were a part of what occurred within, about, and as a result of changes in sport forms.

No matter how thoroughly descriptive concepts help students to organize information, the fact remains that there is only so much that these "containers" can convey. But, the limitedness of descriptive concepts may be an asset. Because descriptive concepts only treat the "what," they set up a host of questions, most of which interested and inquiring students will ask. How, for instance, did the change from the prominence of "natural" sport forms to "artificial" ones occur, and why did the transformation take place? Why did the "quest for better ways to play" arise when it did; and did the changes occurring within styles of play affect views of the body as an instrument of progress? How was the ordering process within post-Civil War sporting sub-communities alike and different from that in other social arenas?

To answer these and other questions raised in the process of describing the "what" of sport, one turns to the explanatory, or analytic, conceptualizations. To some extent, to be sure, this is a somewhat misleading term, for even in descriptive concepts some explanation has occurred because of the contexting that occurs as one describes something historical and, relatedly, because one selects and orders characteristics as he or she derives the generalization. But, as used here, the notion of explanatory conceptualization treats the "how" and "why" questions that accompany the description of the "what."

Unfortunately, sport historians have few appropriate explanatory generalizations already shaped to explain either the significance of something or how and why something happened. Some of the material misstates descriptive concepts as explanations. One of these concepts is urbanization, a term that collapses or "contains" discrete changes in social structure and organization but does not provide an explanation of how and why change occurred. So one is very much on his or her own to conceptualize either significance or how and why things happened as they did. For example, in attempting to explain in what way sport was meaningful, as well as why it developed as it did, among the gentry of the early eighteenth century Chesapeake, my starting point is the concept of "cultural performance," drawn from anthropology. The term itself might be used to explain significance at other points in time, as well, but the "act" of "culture in

action" that "cultural performance" signifies will always
be time-specific. In the case of the largest landowners in
the Chesapeake, the "what" of the specific cultural performance
involved the making of a distinctive sporting style -- competitions bounded by a set of "right actions," oriented to
the goal of prowess, and contested in separate events. The
"how" of this development involved the individual and collective choices that the gentlemen made as they extended
social relations at a time of profound social change in the
region. The "why" involved the process of elite formation.
The gentry conceived of sport as useful competitive recreation (both instrumental and representational) at a time when
they needed to develop prowess, to strike a "white alliance"
with common planters, and to establish their legitimacy as
an elite. Their "cultural performance" was a facet of the
shaping of a collective Anglo-American identity and a more
orderly society, as well as the relocation of sport from
work to leisure.

The final step in the "making sense" of the history
of sport takes us to the third form of generalization, the
synthesizing proposition. This pulls together description
and explanation of change, or the lack of it, across time.
These are the most complex notions that "contain" conclusions about what happened, how it happened, and why something
happened across an entire period, across several periods, or
across the whole of American history. Synthetic propositions
or generalizations would answer such broad, "loaded" questions as "what was the colonial sporting experience really

22

all about;" or "what was the relationship, the connection, of this era to the sporting culture of the early nineteenth century;" or "what was it about the late 19th century and the Progressive era that really 'set up' the 'golden age' of the 1920's?" In contrast to the other forms, generalizations that synthesize rarely, if ever, appear as single words or terms, in part at least because they must collapse numerous descriptive and explanatory notions into one final, comprehensive statement of meaningfulness. Consequently, an answer to the question about the colonial period might be something like this: colonials formalized particular forms of sport out of more general one and relocated sport from work and traditional rituals, times, and spaces to an emerging, separate sphere of leisure.

The process of synthesizing also enables, and perhaps even encourages, us to treat the old problem of historical periodization. One does not need to "buy" all of the traditional politics-dependent periods, themselves generalizations of experience. Indeed, the facts and explanations within the sporting experience do not necessarily "fit" the time schemes contoured largely by political and/or military events and trends. In one particular case -- the late colonial period, the era of the "new nation" and the Jacksonian decades of the antebellum years -- what was happening can not be adequately encased in the old periods. To make a long story short, what we might talk about is a formative, defining period of American sport lasting until about 1810. A second period seems to exist from that point until the decade of the Civil War, that is clearly a significant demarker of a change in social behavior. What occurred during the years between about 1810 and the 1860's were various, sometimes isolated and unique attempts to deal with leisure, even to reconcile different perceptions of and social relations within leisure, as a separate sphere of life. Hence, coexisting were Transcendentalists commercialized as well as romanticized recreation, and academy gymnastic programs, among other things. If, however, we throw in gender as a variable, the periodization seems to change. As active agents in the "making of sport" process, women's involvement (white, middling rank women only perhaps) may be both distinguishable from men's and distinctive from at least the 1740's onward, thus marking the beginning of a "new" sub or transitional period that lasted until the 1830's. In either case, either by extending the "colonial" period or by conceiving of a "new" gender-specific period, the synthesizing process has probably produced a more accurate conceptualization of social behavior and its significance.

Now, a course shaped around the three forms of generalizations that this paper has all too briefly suggested causes one to reconceive outcome and evaluation. First, what one emphasizes in terms of outcome, student learning, are generalizations, ideas, and questions. Clearly, a course in which concepts such as the ones described earlier prevail may focus on the "forest" rather than on the "trees." It treats the full range of what we know and what we don't know about sport in the social historical whole. It also limits

24

the amount of particular detail, much of which is entertaining and enlightening but which may not facilitate and
sharpen students' understanding of sport in the past of American society as much as do concepts (at least in the course
of one semester).

Along with this change in outcome comes a change
in what one evaluates. Below are a few exam and project
questions that demonstrate the kinds of questions that a
concept-dependent course might pose.

Project Questions

1. Compare and contrast the histories of thoroughbred racing and
harness racing (trotting) from ca. 1820-1870. Why did one lan-
quish and the other emerge as more popular in the urban setting?
Is the modernization paradigm, as suggested by Adelman (in
Riess), sufficient to explain why the outcomes of these sports
differed; if not, why not?

2. Using football as an example, show how a sport form developed
and changed in relation to specific cultural conditions and human
choices during the 19th and early 20th centures. In the case of
collegiate football, how were the two quests of these years - for
better ways to play and for order in the total sporting environment - realized and related, both to each other and to goals of
the colleges and universities?

3. How did American views and perceptions of the body change over
the course of the 19th century? What was the effect of the emergence of the notion of the body as instrument and symbol, and why
did this appear?

4. Historians of nineteenth century America now believe that no
single, uniform, even "mainstream" sporting culture ever truly
existed during this period. In other words, no longer can this
sporting culture be adequately described and analyzed from the
perspective of "white, middle-class males" who formed the backbone
of organized amateur and professional sport. Although this aspect
of sport history remains important, it needs to be augmented by an
understanding of sporting experiences affected by race, gender,
and status or "class." Select one of these three variables (i.e.,
race, gender, status) and explain (1) when it probably began to
noticeably affect what was happening in American sport, (2) what
the "real" history of the nineteenth century is when this variable
is considered, and (3) why it should be considered and explored
further.

5. Historians have developed two views about the relationship of sport and American society. One is fairly accurately rendered in John R. Betts' essay, "The Technological Revolution and the Rise of Sport" (in Riess). This view suggests that sport essentially "mirrors" society, meaning that the change and "development" of sport both depends upon and reflects the broader course of societal change. In this article, technological change was the independent variable and sport was the dependent variable - and sport underwent changes similar to the rest of society as technology affected them both. On the other hand, the second view, identified in part in Richard Harmond's article, "Progress and Flight. . ." (also in Riess), suggests that the relationship between sport and society is more complex, more interdependent . In the case of the bicycle, Harmond argued that this machine not only was affected by society (including technology) in the late 19th century but also that it affected human views, behaviors, and conditions . Which of the two views is probably most nearly accurate, and why? Has sport been a dependent variable; has it depended on and reflected whatever else occurred in American social history? Or has the sporting culture affected American society, as well as having been affected by it?

6. Describe the primary sources which the historians whose work you have read have used to narrate colonial sport history . About what and whom can these sources tell us little or nothing? What kinds of sources of evidence might historians in the future use to describe and analyze the sport of colonial people about whom we now know little?

Test Questions

1. "Modern" games (especially of the team sport variety) appear to have developed in antebellum cities once which of the following conditions was (were) met?
   A. The body was conceived of as an instrument to be trained.
   B. Time, space, and human movements were separated into patterns of actions distinct from those found in work and other endeavors.
   C. Participants ceased to rely strictly on natural talent once they recognized the advantages for performance found in strategically using the body, time, and space.
   D. All of the above.
   E. None of the above.

2. Considered in the long-term history of the relationships between the body and morality, the health reformers of the 1830's and 1840's were:
   A. The first to view ill health and physical degeneracy as signs of God's disfavor.
   B. Transitional figures between 17th century intellectuals who viewed the body as a housing for the soul and late 19th century intellectuals who argued that character development depended primarily on physical development and learning.
   C. Transitional figures between Enlightenment intellectuals who maintained that God alone was responsible for physical health

26

and late 19th century intellectuals who believed that the body was not significant at all in improving morality.

    D.   The first to view sport participation as the primary means of character development.

3.   Based on what you have heard and read about colonial and nineteenth century sport, which of the following most adequately describes the relationship between changes in sport form/organizations and the broader social life?

    A.   Sport forms and organizations changed most rapidly and significantly during periods of significant and widespread social instability when the interactions between sport and the broader society increased and enabled numerous specific actions and organizations to come out of older and more general ones.

    B.   Sport forms and organizations changed most rapidly at times when clubs of men and women already existed and could incorporate sport as an activity for the members.

    C.   Sport forms and organizations changed gradually and evenly over time as the technology that made sporting changes possible appeared.

    D.   Sport forms and organizations changed least during periods of rapid and widespread changes in society because the people perceived of sport as a means of retaining valuable behaviors and values.

4.   One of the significant effects of the Progressive era "reforms" on sporting organizations was?

    A.   The placement of active players on governing boards so that they could advise owners and coaches.

    B.   Congressional establishment of the Amateur Athletic Union as the umbrella organization responsible for regulating all other amateur sport organizations.

    C.   The transformation of once voluntary organizations (those which people or teams could join) into full-fledged, obligatory bureaucracies (those which people or teams really had to join and/or submit to the decisions of if they wanted to compete.

    D.   The elimination of betting and gambling.

5.   One of the fears that people like Dudley Sargent had about expanding sporting participation for women early in the 20th century was:

    A.   That if women competed in athletic competition they would not want to become mothers and wives; consequently women's involvement in sport really posed a danger to social stability.

    B.   That high level, strenuous competition would, by reducing or ignoring "natural" biological and social role differences among the sexes, change the natural course of human evolution and eventually threaten the ability of the human race to regenerate itself.

    C.   That high level, strenuous gymnastic competition would prepare women to take over industrial jobs from men.

    D.   That women would come to expect to participate against men in sport, a fact which would encourage women to demand equal pay and legal rights.

6. Although Tex Rickard and Grantland Rice had different occupations in the sporting culture of the "golden age", their promotional efforts shared a common theme. This was:
    A. To achieve what Progressive "reforms" had really not achieved: morally upright owners, coaches, and players.
    B. Building the largest facilities for spectator sports in American sport history.
    C. Tying sport to a romanticized image of a heroic past in which national greatness depended on individual achievement.
    D. All of the above.
    E. None of the above.

7. In several ways the sporting culture of the 1920's and 1930's was a bridge or a transition from that of the late 19th century to that of post-World War II America. Which of the following correctly identifies one type of transition stimulated by developments in these two decades?
    A. Sport promoters transformed once elite sports like hockey and football into forms for mass consumption.
    B. National championships emerged as intermediate links between grassroots and international events, and all were controlled by the International Olympic Committee.
    C. Teams like the Pottsville Maroons and individuals like Joe Louis helped to unite several diverse sub-communities into a single-interest community.
    D. Self-governing bodies such as the AAU and the NCAA began to give away their internal regulating powers to Congress.

8. During the 20th century, why did federal courts only gradually change the non-business conception of organized, professional sports rather than rapidly and sweepingly declare that such sports were liable to federal laws?
    A. Court decisions revolve around precedents which are only slowly displaced; and in the case of sport, a 1922 decision had essentially declared baseball as not liable to anti-trust laws.
    B. Courts tend to preserve the status quo unless the evidence overwhelmingly suggests a need for change, and the evidence about the interstate commerce of sport emerged in only a piece-meal fashion.
    C. There were no laws declaring sport as business which the courts could interpret.
    D. All of the above.
    E. None of the above.

Focusing on concepts and generalizations and the

questions that they encourage enables one to shape a differ-

ent course than that for which our current textbooks are

appropriate. The whole process of presenting "containers"

of information about the history of sport has led me at

28

least to a very different position about what it is I am
teaching and why I am teaching it than where I was even a
few years ago. It has also, I believe, made teaching a
great deal of fun! But half of that fun comes from the
challenge inherent in teaching concepts - the challenge
to present sufficient description to make the concepts
meaningful, to help students understand how the concepts
were derived, and to know what questions need to be asked.

SELECTED BIBLIOGRAPHY OF REVIEW ARTICLES AND
PUBLICATIONS ON AMERICAN SPORT HISTORY

compiled by Douglas A. Noverr
Michigan State University

Adelman, Melvin A. "Academicians and American Athletics: A Decade of
Progress," Journal of Sport History, 10 (Spring, 1983), 80-106.

_____. "Academicians and Athletics: Historians' Views of
American Sport," Maryland Historian, 4 (Fall, 1973), 123-34.

_____. "The Role of the Sports Historian," Quest, 12 (Spring,
1969), 61-65.

Carter, John Marshall. "Sport History: Social History or Hack History?,"
North Carolina Journal for the Social Studies, 27. (Winter, 1981),
17-20.

Clark, Mark W. "'New Ground' in the History of Sport," Journal of
Physical Education and Recreation, 50 (April, 1979), 78-79.

Chu, Donald. "The History of Sport," Chapter 4 in Dimensions of Sport
Studies by Donald Chu. New York: John Wiley & Sons, 1982, pp. 64-102.

Dewing, Rolland. "History of American Sports: Academic Featherbedding or
Neglected Area?" The Social Science Journal, 14 (October, 1977),
73-82.

Gutttman, Allen. "Who's on First? or, Books on the History of American
Sports," The Journal of American History, 66 (September, 1979),
348-54.

Harper, William. "Teaching History With a Human Touch," Journal of
Physical Education and Recreation, 52 (April, 1981), 64-66.

Higgs, Robert J. Sports: A Reference Guide. Westport, Connecticut:
Greenwood Press, 1982.

Howell, Maxwell L. "Toward a History of Sport," Canadian Journal of
History of Sport and Physical Education, 1 (May, 1970), 8-16.

Jebsen, Harry Jr. "Integrating Sports History into American History Courses,"
The Social Studies (March-April, 1984), 62-67.

Lucas, John A. "Sport History Through Biography," Quest, 31 (1979),
216-221.

Metcalfe, Alan. "North American Sport History: A Review of North American
Sport Historians and Their Works," in Exercise and Sport Sciences
Review, ed. Jack H. Wilmore. New York: Academic, 1974, pp. 225-238.

Orlard, Michael. "On the Current Status of Sports Fiction," Arete:
The Journal of Sport Literature, 1 (Fall, 1983), 7-20.

Park, Roberta J. "Research and Scholarship in History of Physical Education
and Sport: The Current State of Affairs," Research Quarterly for
Exercise and Sport, 54 (June, 1983), 93-103.

Rader, Benjamin. "Modern Sports: In Search of Interpretations," Journal
of Social History, 13 (Winter, 1979), 307-21.

Remley, Mary L. Sport History in the United States: An Overview.
Bloomington, Indiana: Organization of American Historians, 1983.

Riess, Steven A. "Sport History in the Classroom," AHA Perspectives
(Newsletter of the American Historical Association), 20 (September,
1982), 29-30.

_____. "Sport and the American Dream: A Review Essay," Journal
of Social History, 14 (Winter, 1980), 295-301.

Struna, Nancy L. "Beyond Mapping Experience: The Need for Understanding in
the History of American Sporting Women," Journal of Sport History,
11 (Spring, 1984), 120-133.

Umphlett, Wiley Lee. "The Dynamics of Film on the Aesthetics of the Sport
Film," Arete: The Journal of Sport Literature, 1 (Spring, 1984),
113-21.

Wiggins, David K. "From Plantation to Playing Field: Historical Writings on
the Black Athlete in American Sport," Research Quarterly for
Exercise and Sport, 57 No.2 (June, 1986), 101-16.

_____. "Clio and the Black Athlete in America: Myths, Heroes,
and Realities," Quest, 32 (1980), 217-25.

Winkler, Karen J. "A Lot More than Trading Baseball Cards: Sport History
Gains a New Respectability," The Chronicle of Higher Education
(June 5, 1985), 5, 8.

Zeigler, Earle F. "Introduction to the History of Physical Education and
Sport," Canadian Journal of History of Sport and Physical Education,
1 (May, 1970), 4-7.

SELECTIVE BIBLIOGRAPHY OF COURSE
TEXTS IN SPORTS HISTORY AND STUDIES
compiled by Douglas A. Noverr

Baker, William J. Sports in the Western World. Totowa, New Jersey: Rowman and
    Allanheld, 1982.

Baker, William J. and John M. Carroll, eds. Sports in Modern America. St. Louis: River
    City Publishers, 1981.

Bennett, Bruce L., et. al. Comparative Physical Education and Sport. 2nd edition.
    Philadelphia: Lea & Febiger, 1983.

Bennett, Bruce L. and Deobold H. Van Dalen. A World History of Physical Education:
    Cultural, Philosophical, Comparative. 2nd edition. Englewood Cliffs, New Jersey:
    Prentice-Hall, 1971.

Betts, John R. America's Sporting Heritage: 1850-1950. Reading, Massachusetts:
    Addison-Wesley, 1974.

Boutilier, Mary A. and Lucinda San Giovanni. The Sporting Woman. Champaign, Illinois:
    Human Kinetics Publishers, 1983.

Boyle, Robert H. Sport: Mirror of American Life. Boston: Little Brown, 1963.

Brady, John and James Hall, eds. Sports Literature. New York: McGraw-Hill, 1974.

Cady, Edwin H. The Big Game: College Sports and American Life. Knoxville, Tennessee:
    University of Tennessee Press, 1978.

Calhoun, Donald W. Sports, Culture, and Personality. West Point, New York: Leisure
    Press, 1981.

Cashman, Richard and Michael McKernan, eds. Sport in History: The Making of Modern
    Sporting History. St. Lucia, Australia: University of Queensland Press, 1979.

Chu, Donald, Jeffery O. Seagrave, and Beverly J. Becker, eds. Sport and Higher Education.
    Champaign, Illinois: Human Kinetics Publishers, 1985.

Chu, Donald. Dimensions of Sport Studies. New York: Wiley, 1982.

Coakley, Jay J. Sport in Society: Issues and Controversies. 2nd edition. St. Louis :
    Mosby, 1981.

33

Curry, Timothy and Robert Jiobu. Sports: A Social Perspective. Englewood Cliffs, New Jersey: Prentice-Hall, 1984.

Dodge, Tom, ed. A Literature of Sports. Lexington, Massachusetts: D.C. Heath and Company, 1980.

Dunleavy, Aidan O. and Andrew W. Miracle, eds. Studies in the Sociology of Sport. Fort Worth, Texas: Texas Christian University Press, 1982.

Eitzen, D. Stanley. Sport in Contemporary Society. 2nd edition. New York: St. Martin's Press, 1984.

Eitzen, D. Stanley and George H. Sage. Sociology of American Sport. 2nd edition. Dubuque, Iowa: Wm. C. Brown, 1982.

_____ Sociology of North American Sport. 3rd edition. Dubuque, Iowa: Wm. C. Brown, 1986.

Glader, Eugene. Amateurism and Athletics. West Point, New York: Leisure Press, 1978.

Guttmann, Allen. From Ritual to Record: The Nature of Modern Sports. New York: Columbia University Press, 1979.

Harkness, Don, ed. Sports in American Culture, 1980. Proceedings. (Sport in American Culture Conference, University of South Florida, May 8-9, 1980). Tampa, Florida: American Studies Press, 1980.

Harris, Janet C. and Roberta J. Park, eds. Play, Games and Sports in Cultural Contexts. Champaign, Illinois: Human Kinetics Publishers, Inc., 1983.

Hart, Marie and Susan Birrell. Sport in the Socio-Cultural Process. 3rd edition. Dubuque, Iowa: Wm. C. Brown, 1981.

Higgs, Robert J. and Neil D. Isaacs, eds. The Sporting Spirit: Athletes in Literature and Life. New York: Harcourt Brace Jovanovich, 1977.

Hoberman, John M. Sport and Political Ideology. Austin, Texas: University of Texas Press, 1984.

Hoover, Dwight W. and John T. Koumoulides, eds. Sport and Society. Muncie, Indiana: Ball State University Press, 1983.

Howell, Reet, ed. Her Story: A Historical Anthology of Women in Sports. West Point, New York: Leisure Press, 1982.

Johnson, William, ed. Sport and Physical Education Around the World. Champaign, Illinois: Stipes, 1980.

Lee, A. Mabel. History of Physical Education and Sports in the U.S. New York: John Wiley and Sons, Inc., 1983.

Lipsky, Richard. How We Play the Game: Why Sports Dominate American Life. Boston: Beacon Press, 1981.

Lucas, John A. and Ronald A. Smith. Saga of American Sport. Philadelphia: Lea & Febiger., 1978.

Mandell, Richard D. Sport: A Cultural History. New York: Columbia University Press, 1986.

Markel, Robert. For the Record: Women in Sports. New York: Ballantine, 1985.

Michener, James A. Sports in America. New York: Random House, 1976.

Mrozek, Donald J. Sport and American Mentality, 1880-1910. Knoxville, Tennessee: The University of Tennessee Press, 1983.

Nixon II, Howard L. Sport and the American Dream. West Point, New York: Leisure Press, 1984.

Naverr, Douglas A. and Lawrence E. Ziewacz. The Games They Played: Sports in American History, 1865-1980. Chicago: Nelson-Hall, 1983.

Ogelsby, Carole A., ed. Women and Sport: From Myth to Reality. Philadelphia: Lea & Febiger, 1978.

Oriard, Michael. Dreaming of Heroes: American Sports Fiction, 1868-1980. Chicago: Nelson-Hall, 1982.

Rader, Benjamin. American Sports From the Age of Folk Games to the Age of Spectators. Englewood Cliffs, New Jersey: Prentice-Hall, 1983.

Riess, Steven A., ed. The American Sporting Experience: A Historical Anthology of Sport in America. West Point, New York: Leisure Press, 1983.

Sage, George H., ed. Sport and American Society: Selected Readings. Reading, Massachusetts: Addison-Wesley, 1980.

Simon, Robert L. Sports and Social Values. Englewood Cliffs, New Jersey: Prentice-Hall, 1985.

Snyder, Eldon E. and Elmer M. Spreitzer. Social Aspects of Sport. Englewood Cliffs, New Jersey: Prentice-Hall, 1983.

Spears, Betty M. and Richard A. Swanson. History of Sport and Physical Activity in the United States. Dubuque, Iowa: Wm. C. Brown, 1978.

Spivey, Donald, ed. Sport in America: New Historical Perspectives. Westport, Connecticut: Greenwood Press, 1985.

Theberge, Nancy and Peter Donnelly, eds. Sport and the Sociological Imagination. Fort Worth, Texas: Texas Christian University Press, 1984.

Thomas, Carolyn E. Sport in a Philosophic Context. Philadelphia: Lea & Febiger, 1983.

Twin, Stephanie L., ed. Out of the Bleachers: Writings on Women and Sport. New York: The Feminist Press and McGraw-Hill, 1979.

Vanderwerken, David L. and Spencer K. Wertz, eds. Sport Inside Out: Readings in Literature and Philosophy. Fort Worth, Texas: Texas Christian University Press, 1985.

VanderZwagg, Harold and Tom Sheerhan. Introduction to Sports Studies: From the Classroom to the Ball Park. Dubuque, Iowa: Wm. C. Brown, 1978.

Weiss, Paul. Sport: A Philosophic Inquiry. Carbondale, Illinois: Southern Illinois University Press, 1971.

Ziegler, Earle F. History of Sport and Physical Education to 1900. Champaign, Illinois: Stipes, 1973.

_____ Ethics and Morality in Sport and Physical Education: An Experiential Approach. Champaign, Illinois: Stipes, 1984.

_____, ed. History of Physical Education and Sport. Englewood Cliffs, New Jersey: Prentice-Hall, 1979.

II. ANCIENT SPORTS

SPORT IN THE ANCIENT WORLD

HISTORY 4388—002

COURSE OUTLINE

MF 12:00-1:20 PM; 104 UH

Don Kyle 309 UH; 273-2884

Office Hours: MW 1:30-3:00 or by appointment

Course Description

Sport was as popular and significant in ancient times as it is today. The Greeks saw sport as an essential element distinguishing their culture from that of other peoples, and the spectator sports of Rome formed one of the most characteristic aspects of that civilization. Enduring from early Greece to the late Roman Empire, the Olympic Games remained a major focus of interest. An appreciation of the role of sport in both Greece and Rome thus is fundamental to an understanding of ancient history and the classical foundations of Western Civilization. Furthermore, the sources and issues involved offer excellent materials for the historian's craft. A variety of types of literary and archaeological evidence must be used, and the history of sport is a growing and challenging field in which scholarly controversies abound.

Course Objectives

This course will examine the nature, variety and role of sports in ancient history. How and why was sport an integral part of Greek and Roman life? Issues to be confronted include: the origins and development of sport in Greece and Rome; the Olympic Games; religious and political implications; the nature of events and contests; intellectual and popular attitudes; and sport in art and society. The primary focus will be on athletics in Greece and spectator sports in Rome, but consideration will be given to recreation, physical education and leisure.

The course will include lectures, audio-visual presentations, and class discussions. Students are responsible for readings and discussions, and for an essay on some issue or problem in ancient sport. There will be a term test and a final exam.

Texts

Gardiner, Athletics of the Ancient World (= G)

Robinson, Sources for the History of Greek Athletics (= R)

Young, <u>The Olympic Myth of Greek Amateur Athletics</u>

<u>Requirements and Grading</u>

Class mark...... 10%
Test............ 20%
Essay........... 30% (Due April 1)
Final Exam...... 40% (Sat. May 4, 11:00-1:30 PM)

<u>Outline of Lessons</u>

1. Introduction- Definitions and Sources (G 1-3)

2. Prolegomena- Origin of Sport; Near East (G 4-14)

3. Bronze Age- Crete and Mycenae (AV)

4. Sport in Homer- Patroclus and Phaeacia (G 18-27, R 1-28)

5. Olympia- Origin of the Games; Program and Management (G 28-36, 222-229, R 35-55, 108-112)

6. Olympia- Site and Sights (AV)

7. Gymnastic and Heavy Events (G 128-221)

8. Equestrian and Other Events (R 112-115)

9. Panhellenic and Local Festivals (G 36-44)

10. Sport in Athens (AV)

11. Pindar and Lyric Poetry (G 68-71, R 92-104)

12. Art and Architecture (AV) (G 53-68, 72-82, R 152-155)

TEST

13. Critics and Criticisms: Dissenting Voices (G 99-116, R 90-91, 116-117, 137-139)

14. Young on Olympism (Young, <u>Olympic Myth</u>, Part One)

15. Rewards, Professionalism and Society (G 98-116, Young <u>Olympic Myth</u>, Part Two)

16. Physical Education (G 82-98, R 62-78)

17. Philosophy and Sport (R 123-137)

18. The Other Half- Nudity, Homosexuality and Women (R 109, 163)

19. Hellenistic Age and Etruria (AV) (G 44-52, 119-123)

20. Early Rome and Greek Sport; Virgil (Aeneid V handout) (G 117-119, 123-127, R 164-165)

21. Roman Spectator Sports— Ludi and Munera, "Bread and Circuses" (Juvenal handout)

22. Roman Recreation— Baths and Physical Education (Women handout)

23. Spectacles— Hunts (Martial handout)

24. Spectacles— Gladiators and the Amphitheatre (AV)

25. Circus, Charioteers and Crowds (Ovid handout)

26. Jews and Christians

27. Byzantium

28. Review

For Your Information

1) Late essays (due April 1) may be penalized (10% per week). Very late essays normally will not be accepted.

2) Make-up tests will be given only in unusual or pre-arranged circumstances.

3) Attendance at lectures is highly recommended but not mandatory (after Census day Jan. 28). Last drop date is April 12.

4) Plagiarism— the presentation of the writing and/or particular ideas of another as your own without due credit to the original author— is a serious offence, as are all cases of academic dishonesty. Such actions are neither advisable nor advantageous; cases will be dealt with through official UTA channels.

WELCOME!

SPORT IN THE ANCIENT WORLD - Bibliography

(*On reserve in library)

A) <u>Texts</u>:

* E.N. Gardiner, <u>Athletics of the Ancient World</u>, Chicago: 1978 (1930).

* R.S. Robinson, <u>Sources for the History of Greek Athletics</u>, Chicago: 1979 (1955).

* D. Young, <u>The Olympic Myth of Greek Amateur Athletics</u>, Chicago: 1984.

B) Recommended Readings:

<u>Ancient World</u>, Vol. 7 (1983) (<u>Athletics in Antiquity</u>); Vol. 9 (1984) (<u>Ancient Games and Athletics</u>).

R. Auguet, <u>Cruelty and Civilization: the Roman Games</u>, London: 1972 (1970).

J. P. V. D. Balsdon, <u>Life and Leisure in Ancient Rome</u>, New York: 1969.

Raymond Bloch, "The Origins of the Olympic Games," <u>Scientific American</u>, (August, 1968): 78-87.

Raymond Bloch, "Sports in the Ancient World," <u>Diogenes</u> 94 (1976): 53-77.

A.D. Booth, "Roman Attitudes to Physical Education," <u>Classical News and Views</u> 19 (1975): 27-34.

L. Drees, <u>Olympia: Gods, Artists and Athletes</u>, London: 1968.

M. I. Finley and H. W. Pleket, <u>The Olympic Games: the First Thousand Years</u>, London: 1976.

C. A. Forbes, <u>Greek Physical Education</u>, New York: 1929.

E. N. Gardiner, <u>Greek Athletic Sports and Festivals</u>, London: 1910.

M. Grant, <u>Gladiators</u>, London: 1967.

H. A. Harris, <u>Greek Athletes and Athletics</u>, London: 1971.

H. A. Harris, <u>Sport in Greece and Rome</u>, London: 1972.

<u>Journal of Sport History</u> (1984) (<u>Ancient Athletics and Ancient Society</u>).

H. I. Marrou, <u>A History of Education in Antiquity</u>, London: 1956.

S. G. Miller, <u>Arete, Ancient Writers, Papyri and Inscriptions on the History and Ideals of Greek Athletics and Games</u>, Chicago: 1979.

N. Robertson, "The Ancient Olympics: Sport, Spectacle and Ritual," <u>Classical News and Views</u> 20 (1976): 73-85.

T. B. L. Webster, <u>Everyday Life in Classical Athens</u>, New York: 1969.

Nicolaos Yalouris, ed., <u>The Eternal Olympics</u>, New Rochelle: 1979.

NOTE: For further bibliographical help see the instructor or refer to *Thomas F. Scanlon, <u>Greek and Roman Athletics, A Bibliography</u>, Chicago: 1984.

Dr. Kyle
History 4388-2

SPORT IN THE ANCIENT WORLD - Essay Suggestions

1. Discuss the nature and role of sport in ancient Egypt or Crete.

2. Discuss the various ancient accounts and modern interpretations of the origins of the Olympic Games (include a discussion of Robinson pp. 32-55).

3. Reconstruct the history of sport at Olympia or Athens from primary evidence in Robinson and Miller.

4. How was the victor chosen in the pentathlon?

5. Discuss Theseus and Herakles as gods of athletics.

6. Explain how Sparta experienced both success and failure in athletics and physical education.

7. Examine the relationship between developments in Greek athletics and medicine.

8. Discuss the sporting activities of women in Greek or Roman society.

9. Examine swimming and boating among the Greeks and Romans.

10. Examine athletics and physical education in the works of Plato or Aristotle.

11. Concentrating on ancient evidence, reconstruct the life of a Greek athlete or a Roman gladiator.

12. Using Robinson and Miller, assess the value of inscriptions as evidence for ancient sport.

13. Compare the aims and achievements of Alcibiades and Nero as chariot racers.

14. Compare hunting as presented by Xenophon (On Hunting) and Nemesianus (Cynegetica).

15. Discuss sport in Plutarch (The Rise and Fall of Athens) or Suetonius (The Twelve Caesars).

16. A discussion from primary evidence of the Lusus Troia or the Roman Iuven.

17. Discuss and compare the charioteers or the spectators in the Roman and Byzantine circus.

18. A suitable topic, employing ancient evidence, if approved by the instructor.

SPORT IN ANTIQUITY

Ph. Ed. 442, with James G. Thompson

LECTURES:

1. Introduction
2. The Evidence and Historical Research
3. Minoan-Mycenaean Civilization and Sport
4. Minoan-Mycenaean Continued
5. The Homeric Period and Physical Activity
6. Sparta: Historical Development
7. Sparta: Physical Fitness and Obedience to Authority
8. Sparta: Continued
9. Athens: An Education To All Greece
10. Athens and Physical Education
11. A Third Stage of Education at Athens
12. Review Period
13. Exam
14. Physical Education and Athletics in the Rest of the Greek World
15. Facilities for Greek Athletics
16-22. Olympic Games
23. Quiz
24. Pattee Library
25-27. The Modern Olympic Games
28. Isthmian, Pythian, Nemean Games and Some Local Festivals
29. Athletics vs. Gymnastics in Classical Antiquity
30. The Charge at Marathon: Possible or Impossible?
31. Summary and Conclusions on Ancient Greece
32. Exam
33. Etruscan Civilization
34. Introduction to Rome
35. Roman Attitudes Toward Physical Activity
36-38. The Roman Spectaculars: Circus and Gladitorial Combats
39. Roman Thermae
40. Review
41. Quiz

READINGS

#-4 MINOAN-MYCENAEAN CIVILIZATION:

Evans, Arthur, "On a Minoan Bronze Group of a Galloping Bull and Acrobatic
Figure from Crete." Journal of Hellenic Studies, 41 (1921), pp. 247-259.
Evans, Arthur, "The Toreador Frescoes." Greek Heritage, pp. 81-90.
Kazantzakis, Nikos, "The Bull Rituals at Knossos." Greek Heritage, pp. 95-97.
Platon, Nikolas, "Sir Arthur Evans and the Creto Mycenaean Bull Fights."
Greek Heritage, pp. 91-93.
Ward, Anne, "The Cretan Bull Sports." Antiquity, 42 (1968), pp. 117-122.
Graham, J. Walter, "The Central Court as the Minoan Bull-Ring." American
Journal of Archaeology, 61 (1957), pp. 255-262.

#5 Homer: Iliad and Odyssey. Books 23 and 8.

#6-8 SPARTA: Gerousia and Ecclesia
1. Describe the organization and functions of the Gerousia and the Ecclesia
2. What was the crypteia? H. Michell, Sparta, pp. 135-164.

SPARTA: The Spartiates
1. What were the qualifications for Spartan citizenship?
2. What was the place of women in Spartan life?
3. Describe the social organizations of the Spartans: the syssitia and andreia.
   H. Michell, Sparta, pp. 35-63, 281.
   Chrimes-Atkinson, Ancient Sparta, pp. 231-245.

SPARTA: Perioeci and Helots
1. What was the origin of the perioeci?
2. What was their status in relation to the Spartans?
3. What function and service did they provide for the Spartan state?
4. What was the origin of the helots?
5. What was their relationship to the Spartans?
6. How were the helots treated?
   H. Michell, Sparta, pp. 64-75, 75, 92, 251, 32-33.
   Chrimes-Atkinson, Ancient Sparta, pp. 272-304, 382-383.

SPARTA: Discipline
1. Survey the periods of man's life and his military obligation to the state.
2. What means were used to instill discipline and self-reliance into a Spartan youth?
3. What role did women have in the general education scheme?
4. What were the virtues and defects of the Spartan system?
   H. Michell, Sparta, pp. 165-204.

SPARTA: Harley T. Rutherford," The Public Schools of Sparta." Greece and Rome 3 (1934), pp. 129-139.
   Westington, Mars M., "Nazi Germany and Ancient Sparta." Education 65, pp. 152-164.
   "Lycurgus and Education Among the Spartans," American Journal of Education, 14, 611-624.

#9-10 Jarrett, James L., "The School of Athens," Greek Heritage I (1964), 88-95.
   Bryant, Arthur A., "Boyhood and Youth in the Days of Aristophanes," Harvard Studies in Classical Philology (1907), 73-122.

#11 THE EPHEBIC COLLEGE:
   Lofberg, J. O., "The Date of the Athenian Ephebeia," Classical Philology 20 (Oct. 1925), pp. 330-335.
   Reinmuth, O. W., "The Ephebate and Citizenship in Attica," pp. 2-1-230.
   Taylor, John, "The Athenian Ephebic Oath," Classical Journal, 13 (April 1918), pp. 495-501.

#15 THE FACILITIES FOR GREEK ATHLETICS:
   Forbes, Clarence A., "Expanded Uses of the Greek Gymnasium," Classical Philology 40 (Jan. 1945), pp. 32-42.
   Harris, H. A., "Stadia and Starting Grooves," Greece and Rome 7 (1960), 25-35.

45

#16-22 OLYMPIC GAMES:

Frost, K. T., "Greek Boxing," <u>Journal of Hellenic Studies</u> 26 (1906), 213-225.

Gardiner, E. N., "Wrestling," <u>Journal of Hellenic Studies</u> 25 (1905), 14-31.

_____, "Phayllus and His Record Jump," <u>Journal of Hellenic Studies</u> 24 (1904), 70-79 (2 articles).

_____, "Throwing the Diskos," <u>Journal of Hellenic Studies</u> 27 (1907), 1-35.

_____, "Notes on the Greek Footrace," <u>Journal of Hellenic Studies</u> 23 (1908), 261-291.

_____, "Method of Deciding the Pentathlon," <u>Journal of Hellenic Studies</u> 23 (1903), 54-69.

_____, "The Pankration and Wrestling," <u>Journal of Hellenic Studies</u> 26 (1906), 4-22.

Harris, J. A., "The Method of Deciding Victory in the Pentathlon," <u>Greece and Rome</u> 19 (1972), 60-64.

_____, "Greek Javelin Throwing," <u>Greece and Rome</u> 10 (1963), 26-36.

Paleologos, Cleanthes, "Preparation for the Olympic Games in Ancient Greece," <u>Proceedings of the 10th Session of The International Olympic Academy</u> 1970, 71-82.

#25-27 A MODERN LOOK AT OLYMPIC IDEOLOGY:

Berlioux, Monique, "Organization of the Administration of the Modern Olympic Movement," <u>Proceedings of the 12th Session of The International Olympic Academy</u>, pp. 65-72.

Brisson, Jean F., "How Did Pierre De Coubertin Conceive The Olympic Games: Is This Concept Adapted To The Imperatives Of Modern Sport?" <u>Proceedings of the 12th Session of The International Olympic Academy</u>, pp. 73-90.

Szymiczek, O., "The Olympic Philosophy in Antiquity and Our Time," <u>Proceedings of the 12th Session of The International Olympic Academy</u> 1972, pp. 44-54.

Broneer, Oscar, "The Isthmian Games," <u>Greek Heritage</u>, 42-49.

Ringwood, Irene C., "Local Festivals of Euboea," <u>American Journal of Archaeology</u> 33 (1929), 385-392.

#29 ATHLETIC VS. GYMNASTICS:

"Aristotle and his Educational Views," <u>American Journal of Education</u> 25 (June 1964), pp. 131-146.

Chryssafis, Jean, "Aristotle on Physical Education," <u>JOPHER</u> I (Feb. 1930), pp. 14-17, 46-47.

Ibid., (Jan. 1930), pp. 3-8, 50.

Ibid., (Sept. 1930), pp. 14-16, 54-56.

Chryssafis, Jean, "Plato on Physical Education," <u>Pentathlon</u> 5 (April 1929), 3-9.

Ibid., (May 1929), pp. 6-10.

Gardiner, E., "Athleticism in Greece," <u>School Review</u> X (Sept. 1902), 574-578.

Gilbert, A., "Olympic Decadence," <u>Classical Journal</u>, Vol. 21 (Oct. 1925-June 1926), pp. 587-598.

Manning, C., "Professionalism in Greek Athletics," <u>Classical Weekly</u> XI (Dec. 17, 1917), pp. 74-78.

Thompson, James, "Athletic vs. Gymnastics in Classical Antiquity."

#30 Matthews, Victor, "The Hemerodromoi: Ultra Long Distance Running in Antiquity," <u>Classical World</u> 68 (Nov. 1974), 161-169.

#36 GLADIATORS:

Pearson, John, <u>Arena</u>, pp. 75-89.

Ibid., 93-114; <u>Ibid.</u>, 115-132; Ibid., 145-170.

III. SPORT HISTORY -

COMPREHENSIVE SURVERY

THE UNIVERSITY OF TEXAS AT AUSTIN

DEPARTMENT OF PHYSICAL AND HEALTH EDUCATION

PED 330 - HISTORY OF SPORT AND PHYSICAL ACTIVITY
FALL 1985

MWF 8-9   TTH 12:30-2
   11715   11720

Bellmont 202
Dr. LeCompte
Office: Bellmont 222   Mailbox: Bellmont 222
Office Hrs: To be announced - please see me before or after class for appointments until hours are
            scheduled or if you cannot come at scheduled times.

Phone: 471-1273. This is the Physical Education office. If I am not in when you call, please
              leave a message that you called.

Textbooks: Both required: History of Physical Education & Sport by Zeigler
                             History of Sport & Physical Activity, 2nd Edition
                             1983, by Spears and Swanson

Basis for Grade:
              Tests --80%
              Projects ---10%
              Attendance, discussion, participation, homework -------------10%
              (Students consistently late cannot expect credit for attendance!)

CR/F: Students taking the course CR/F must take all tests and have an overall grade of 60% or
              more to get credit for the course.

Class attendance and preparation for discussion are expected. Excessive absences and unpreparedness
will affect your grade adversely. Extra credit projects will be announced when opportunities arise.
Points earned on projects will be added to the appropriate quiz grades.

Bring the course syllabus outline and textbooks with you to each class for reference, revision, etc.

There are many excellent sport reference books and encyclopedias in the reference rooms of both the
PCL and Academic Center libraries. They have Library of Congress call numbers in the GV group and
are shelved accordingly.

Course Objectives

1. Students will know and understand the origins of sport and sport tradition.

2. Studnets will know the sources and/or causes of contemporary problems, issues and conflicts in
   organized sport.

3. Students will know and understand the development of a relationship between Physical Education
   and Intercollegiate/Interscholastic athletics in the United States.

(OVER)

4. Students will understand both the historic and contemporary relationships between school sports, professional sports and international amateur sports in the United States and in other representative nations, including the USSR, the GDR, and FRG.

5. Students will understand sport in perspective; be knowledgeable about the achievements of the Great Civilizations of hte past and appreciative of the accomplishments and viewpoints of other nations today.

Study Suggestions: Quizzes cover class work, lectures, projects, and presentations, textbook assignments special reading, films, slides, tapes, etc. and bulletin board.

1. Quizzes will be essay, short answer, identificaiton, fill in the blanks, and sometimes multiple choice.

2. Comcepts to be learned: Role of sport in society. Influence of the following on sport and physical activity: Religion, Economics, Government, Militarism, and Education. Similarities and differences among the cultures and time periods studies.

3. Important names, events, concepts, and dates (very few) aree included in the outline which follows.

4. Textbook readings as indicated on the Course Outline.

TENTATIVE QUIZ SCHEDULE

TTH CLASS	MWF CLASS	QUIZ TOPIC	% GRADE
26 Sept.	27 Sept	Part I: Overview, Sport in Antiquity	22.5%
24 Oct.	25 Oct	Part II: Middle Ages, Modern Olympics	22.5%
*13 Dec 2:00 P.M.	*17 Dec 7:00 P.M.	Part III: Sport in America	35%

* This is the regularly scheduled examination period.

Policy on Cheating: Students who violate University rules on scholistic dishonesty are subject to disciplinary penalties, including the possibility of failure in the course and dismissal from The University. Since dishonesty harms the individual, fellow students, and the integrity of The University, policies on scholastic dishonesty will be strictly enforced.

****

PLEASE. . .

Do not bring tape recorders to class.

Be considerate of classmates and teacher - refrain from talking, eating, drinking, smoking, chewing during class.

THANK YOU VERY MUCH!

PED 330: HISTORY OF SPORT AND PHYSICAL ACTIVITY
COURSE OUTLINE - LECOMPTE

(S & S refers to text by Spears & Swanson; Z refers to text by Zeigler)

PART ONE

1. OVER. EW: Sport in the 1980's - S & S, 344-48
   A. The Olympics as a measure of national strength, fitness and sporting skills

      1. Organization, national eligibility, sport federations, International Olympic Committee (IOC) and National Olympic Committee (NOC).
      2. Counting Medals: What does it really mean?

   B. National Sport Systems and Olympic "Success"

      1. Countries to be discussed: USA, Germany-East & West, USSR
         a. Major features of National Sport Systems
         b. Role of Government, Schools, other agencies in sport
         c. How teachers and coaches are trained, certified, etc.
         d. Training, selection and support of Olympic athletes, Olympic trials, etc.

      2. Names and Places to know

         Leipzig, Dinamo Clubs, Spartakiade, GTO

II. Sport in Antiquity Z, 43-52

   A. Primitive Society and Early Civilizations: Z section 1

   B. Greek civilizations: S & S, 317-42; Z, 20-37
      1. Minoan Greeks of Crete and Thera: A, 20-29. Knossos, toreador sports, the first stadium.

      2. Mycenean Greeks: Funeral Games - The first organized sports: S&S, 320-24; events, facilities, competitors, traditions. Names and terms to know: Iliad, Odyssey, Persian Wars, Sir Arthur Evens, Heinrich Schliemann.

51

3. Classical Greek Civilization: 700's B.C. – 146 B.C.
   a. City States: Athens and Sparta; contrasting cultures and their attitudes toward sport and physical education: S & S 324
   b. Organized Athletics: S&S 324-338. Z 29-37

      1. Olympic Games (776 B.C. – 551 A.D.)
      2. Other Crown Festivals: Delphi, Nemea Corinth
      3. Important items to know about Greek festivals:
         Events & Rules   Athletes   Awards
         Facilities   Significance   Rituals & Traditions

C. Roman Empire Z 37-43; S&S 341.

   1. Roman society, government, economy and their impact on sport

   2. Recreational Activities and social life at the thermae

   3. Spectator Sports
      a. Gladiator fights, animal fights and other bloody events at arenas such as the Coliseum
      b. Chariot races, particularly at the Circus Maximus.
      c. Athletes, their social class and life
      d. Spectators, factions, traditions

   4. Greek Sport under Roman and Byzantine Rule S&S 338-342.
      a. Impact of Roman conquest and Christianity
      b. Influence of Nero and Herod Atticus

PED 330 Part Two: Western Europe from the Middle Ages to the Modern Olympics

I. Middle Ages and Renaissance: Z-section 2; S&S 25-41

    A. Christian Church and Church schools

        1. Philosophy of Acesticism

        2. Influence on sport and society

    B. Feudal system: social organization and social classess

        1. Knighthood: training, role in society, influence on sport

        2. Tournaments and amusements of various social classes

    C. The rise of modern sport

        1. Peasant football & Florentine Calcio

        2. Voltiqe: horsemanship, ballet, gymnastics

        3. Golf, tennis, bowling, fencing

II. Catholic and protestant reformations, and the rise of nationalism, Z-75-91.

III. Nineteenth-century nationalism and sport

    A. Gymnastics Systems

        1. German

            a. Gutsmuths and developmental gymnastics, Z-110-22

            b. Fredrich Jahn and the German Turnvereins, Z 109-117

            c. The spread of the Turnvereins and German Gymnastics

        2. Swedish Gymanstics: Ling, and the Royal Central Institute of Gymnastics, Z-109-117.

        3. Czechoslovakia: Miroslav Tyrs and the Czech Sokol, Z 109-117

B. British Empire and the export of team and individual sports,
    Z-126-65.

    1. Victorianism, health, and Muscular Christianity

    2. British public schools and universities: intramurals,
        sportsmanship

    3. Amateurism

IV. The Modern Olympic Games, Z 144-7, S&S 342-54

    A. Pierre de Coubertin-The Olympic Dream and the IOC

    B. The First Modern Olympic Games - Athens, 1896

        1. Facilities, rules, athletes, events, ceremonies

        2. Spiros Louis (also called Spiridon Louis), the first modern
            Olympic hero

        3. Similarities and differences in the Olympics of 1896 and 1984

    C. Evolution of the Olympics through 1912

PED 330 Part Three: Sport and Physical Activity in America
(all page numbers refer to the text by Spears and Swanson,
2nd edition)

I. Recreation and pastimes of the eastern colonies. 46-59, 73-80.

II. Gamblers and promoters and the first professional sports: Boxing
and horseracing. 67-73.

III. Sports of Texas and the southwest. 108, 168, handuot

Corridas and charreadas

Fairs and festivals

Wild West shows and rodeo

IV. Club sports and the amateur ideal 110-118, 157-166

Gentlemen's clubs: yachting, baseball, track and field

Country clubs: tennis, golf, figure skating

Turnvereins and YMCA's 120-1

V. Team Sports - 203-13, 253-76

Town teams and YMCA's

Baseball - the first major professional sport 104-5, 150-3

Football

NCAA 126-32, 179-86, 226-9, 292-7

NFL

Basketball 169-71

VI. Women's Sports: 133-6, 186-91, 230-6, 298-303

VII. Intercollegiate sports and the law

Title IX of the Educational Amendments to the Civil Rights Act of 1964,
enacted 1972. 8, 302-5

IV. PHYSICAL EDUCATION

AND SPORT

UNIVERSITY OF CALIFORNIA   BERKELEY
DEPARTMENT OF PHYSICAL EDUCATION   FALL
PROFESSOR R.J. PARK

PHYSICAL EDUCATION 130

History of Physical Education and Sport

(Survey Course)

Texts and Assigned Readings

Van Dalen, D.B. and Bennett, B.L. A World History of Physical Education: Cultural, Philosophical, Comparative. 2nd. ed. Lea & Febiger, 1971.

Lucas, J.A. and Smith, R.A. Saga of American Sport. Lea & Febiger, 1978.

Rader, B.G. American Sports: From the Age of Folk Games to the Age of Spectators. Prentice Hall, 1983.

Articles will also be assigned from such journals as:

The Journal of Sport History

The Canadian Journal of History of Sport and Physical Education

Research Quarterly for Exercise and Sport

Stadion

Social History

American Quarterly

Reminders and Recommendations to Students:

(1) This course is intended to provide an overview of the history of "sport", physical education, and health in the Western World (ca. 776 B.C. - 1940 A.D.). The period from 1941 to the present will only be touched upon in lectures as it is well-covered in the readings.

(2) The emphasis will be on: Classical Greece; Imperial Rome; Renaissance Humanism and the education of a "gentlemen"; 17th century contributions to educational theory and physiology; 18th century contributions to educational theory and "public" health; the 19th century and the rise of organized sport (both in schools and colleges and in the broader society); 19th century "athleticism" (Britain and the United States); the origins of the modern Olympic Games; 19th century contributions to public health and personal hygiene; the rise of professional physical education; 19th century physical education as it relates to 19th century medicine and physiology; American "sport" before WWI; American women and "sport" 1840-1930; the rise of the playground movement and theories of "developmental play"; recreation; sport and athletics in the "Golden 20's".

(3) Students are reminded that sport, athletics, physical education, concepts of health, etc. do _not_ exist in a vacuum. They derive from and are related to broader social, cultural and/or intellectual concerns.

(4) Students should remember that past societies were not likely to have conceived of things in the same way that we do. To believe that they did is to act ahistorically. Certainly, no American in 1856, for example, would have our comprehension of "a Toyota Truck".

(5) Students should be aware that the instructor will _not_ lecture on every topic covered in the readings. However, examination questions could come from any portion of the readings. Also, the instructor _will_ lecture on several things which are not found in the readings. Examination questions for the mid-term will come from lectures (about 75%) and readings (about 25%). Final examination questions will come from lectures (about 50%) and readings (about 50%).

(6) Students are reminded that the term paper, which is to be _original research_, is a very important part of this course. (A separate handout outlines the requirements of the term paper.) Techniques of historical research are discussed in lectures, and more fully in section meetings.

(7) The term-paper assignment is intended to serve several purposes. Among these are:

(a) To encourage the student to do critical thinking, analyze both sources and concepts, and present her/his own ideas with _clarity_ and _logic_.

(b) To introduce those students who have not yet had the experience to _original research_ using a variety of library and bibliographical techniques, including that of consulting "_primary_" source materials.

(c) To stimulate (hopefully) at least a modicum of enthusiasm for proper historical scholarship.

(d) To permit the student to pursue some aspect of this course in considerable _depth_.

Fall 1983 - Dr. R.J. Park

PHYSICAL EDUCATION 130
STUDY QUESTIONS

1. Discuss the role of Pan-Hellenic and "funeral" games in Ancient Greece.

2. Compare and/or contrast "physical education" and "agonistic athletics" in classical Greece. What were the views of Plato and Aristotle concerning each of these?

3. Discuss the role of the "circus" and the "ampitheater" in Imperial Rome.

4. Describe Roman "physical education" in the period from 100 B.C. to 300 A.D.

5. Discuss "the education of a knight" with special reference to "physical education."

6. What was the Renaissance attitude toward "things of the body" and "things of the mind"? What earlier culture had a considerable impact upon the attitudes of Renaissance thinkers? Give several examples, including ones especially pertinent to physical education.

7. Describe the attitudes of the "English Puritan educational reformers" of the 1600's toward: (a) education; (b) physical education. Have these attitudes been reflected in American education? If so, give several examples.

8. Discuss the scientific and medical discoveries of the 16th, 17th, and 18th centuries which had a major impact upon the development of physiology and public health and, as a consequence, influenced theories of "physical education."

9. Discuss western European and American attitudes toward "women" in the 17th, 18th, and 19th centuries with special reference to: (a) education in general; (b) physical education.

10. Discuss leisure pursuits and recreation in the United States from 1776 to 1865 (Civil War).

11. Discuss ideas and events in the United States between 1820 and 1880 which fostered concern for physical education.

12. Describe the major "philosophies", purposes and programs (including curricula) of American physical education from 1865 to 1915.

13. Discuss the rise of intercollegiate sport in American colleges and universities from 1870 to 1920.

14. What was the "Boston Conference of 1889"? What major topics were discussed at this conference?

15. Describe physical education and athletic sport for American women (including college women) from 1880 to 1920. Comment upon pertinent social, ideological and educational beliefs and events.

16. Describe the extent of opportunities for black sportsmen and athletes in
    the United States from 1865 to 1970. Comment upon pertinent social and
    ideological events.

17. Discuss the changing emphases in physical education curricula in American
    colleges from 1880 to 1930.

18. Choose two of the following "themes" which have influenced attitudes toward
    "physical education" (take physical education in the broad sense) from
    Classical times to the present, and discuss in detail those periods in history
    when each has received particular attention.

    (a) Be sure to relate developments in "physical education" to the general
    social and ideological milieu.
    (b) Support your answer with an adequate number of pertinent facts.
    Themes:

        (1) medical/therapeutic
        (2) military/nationalistic
        (3) all-round harmonious development
        (4) developmental play
        (5) recreation
        (6) athleticism

DEPARTMENT OF PHYSICAL EDUCATION   UNIVERSITY OF CALIFORNIA
FALL 1985   BERKELEY
PROFESSOR R.J. PARK

PHYSICAL EDUCATION 230

History of Sport & Physical Education
(Graduate Seminar)

I.   Within the last decade interest in researching the history of "sport"
(a generic term which has encompassed athletics, physical recreations, certain
aspects of leisure, physical education, and the like) has grown markedly and
has attracted the attention of scholars in departments of physical education,
history, and less so, sociology, anthropology, and literature. The June 7, 1985
<u>Chronicle of Higher Education</u> declared: "Sport History Gains a New Respectability:
Research in the Field Has Become More Sophisticated and Interdisciplinary."
       While much has been done in the last few years, still more remains to be
done. It is hoped that this seminar will contribute to this growing field of
investigation, and the various readings and other activities have been designed
with this objective in mind. While we will look at sport as a social institution,
we will also spend considerable time on a subject which has as yet received far
too little attention: ways in which nineteenth century developments in biology
and nineteenth century evolutionary theories influenced: (1) concepts of the
human body, and its health; (2) the rise of professional physical education;
(3) and contributed to the precipitous rise of interest in institutionalized
sport in the second half of the nineteenth century. The focus will be upon the
period from 1830 to 1920, and on the United States. Some attention will be
given to Britain (especially England) and selected developments in France, Germany, and Scandinavia.

II.   Seminar members will be expected to: (1) be prepared to discuss the
various readings assigned each week; (2) lead one - or a substantial portion of
one - seminar meeting; (3) prepare a written report which will be presented in
summary form during the last two weeks of the course. This report may take
one of two forms: (a) a <u>research paper</u> on a narrowly focused topic, using substantial primary evidence and conforming to the canons of historical scholarship; (2) an integrative <u>essay</u> which draws together a number of studies by
researchers as well as appropriate contemporary sources pertinent to the history
of sport. In general, the scope of the essay will be larger than that of the
research paper, and must include critical analyses of the sources used. The
essay must also conform to the proper canons of scholarship.
       A number of assignments during the early weeks of the semester should help
the student to focus upon her/his paper subject. Additionally, each of the
seminar meetings will include information which will be of value in helping
students to develop a proper historical study.

III.   The course grade will be determined on the basis of the student's performance on: (1) class participation; (2) leading a class discussion; (3)
term project.

IV.   In an effort to achieve the objectives outlined above, the semester's work
has been organized around four broad topics which are interrelated. Cutting
across these is a fifth which deals with how historians go about their tasks.

PHYSICAL EDUCATION 230
History of Sport & Physical Education

IV. (Cont.)

    (1) the historical development of physical education in the United States
(ca. 1830-1920) with particular emphasis upon the organization of
the profession (1885) and its first three decades.

    (2) selected aspects of nineteenth century biology and medicine as these
influenced and drew from the emerging Victorian interest in health,
hygiene, and physical training in the United States and England.

    (3) selected aspects of nineteenth century evolutionary theorizing as
these influenced and drew from American and British concerns about
health, hygiene, physical training, and "race" in the nineteenth
and early twentieth centuries.

    (4) sport as a social institution in the United States (with some consideration
to British, especially English, influences), with particular attention
to school-sport.

    (5) an examination of several of the newer approaches to historical
investigation, with particular attention devoted to how each might
help to explicate the history of sport, physical education, and the
like.

V. Weekly Organization and Readings. (Note that the heavier reading assignments
tend to concentrate in the first two-thirds of the semester.)

August 27: Overview of the History of American Physical Education Up to WW I.
          (Park)

September 3: Bruce L. Bennett and Mabel Lee, "This Is Our Heritage: 75 Years
          of the American Association for Health, Physical Education
          and Recreation," Journal of Health, Physical Education, and
          Recreation, 31:4 (April 1960): 25-85 *; Centennial Issue,
          Research Quarterly for Exercise and Sport (April 1985), all
          pages.

September 10: Ellen W. Gerber, Innovators and Institutions in Physical
             Education (Philadelphia, 1971), 267-396* Physical Education:
             A Full Report of the Papers and Discussions of the Conference
             Held in Boston in November 1899, ed., Isabel C. Barrows
             (Boston: George H. Ellis, 1899), 1-28; 35-51; 57-59; 62-77;
             112-120**. Roberta J. Park, "Research and Scholarship in the
             History of Physical Education and Sport..." Research Quarterly
             for Exercise and Sport, 54:2 (1983): 93-103.

PHYSICAL EDUCATION 230

History of Sport & Physical Education

V.
Weekly Organization and Readings (cont.):

September 17: Donald J. Mrozek, Sport and American Mentality, 1880-1910
(Knoxville, 1983)**; Melvin L. Adelman, "Academicians
and American Athletics: A Decade of Progress," Journal of
Sport History, 10: 1 (1983): 80-106**; William J. Baker,
"The State of British Sport History," ibid., 53-66.**

September 24: Daniel T. Rodgers, The Work Ethic in Industrial America,
1850-1920 (Chicago, 1974), xi-xv; 1-29; 94-152; 182-209**;
John Higham, "The Reorientation of American Culture in the
1890s," in John Highan, ed., Writing American History:
Essays on Modern Scholarship (Bloomington, 1972), 73-102**;
Hal A. Lawson and Alan G. Ingham, "Conflicting Ideologies
Concerning the University and Intercollegiate Athletics:
Harper and Hutchins at Chicago, 1892-1940," Journal of Sport
History, 7:3 (1980): 37-67.**

October 1: Bruce Haley, The Healthy Body and Victorian Culture (Cambridge, MA:
1978), 3-119#; "Physiological Riddles--How We Act," Cornhill,
2 (1862): 21-32**; "Physiological Riddles--Why We Grow," ibid.:
167-174**; Henry R. Harrington, "Charles Kingsley's Fallen
Athlete," Victorian Studies (Fall 1977): 73-86.**

October 8: Haley, Healthy Body, 123-261#; Asa Briggs, Victorian People
(Chicago, 1955), 140-167 ("Thomas Hughes and the Public
Schools")**; Keith P. Sandiford, "Cricket and the Victorian
Society," Journal of Social History (1983): 304-317**;

October 15: John Lesch, Science and Medicine in France: The Beginnings of
Experimental Physiology, 1795-1855 (Cambridge, MA: 1985)#.

October 22: L.S. Jacyna, "Somatic Theories of Mind and the Interests of
Medicine in Britain, 1850-1879," Medical History, 26 (1982):
233-258±; J. William White, "A Physician's View of Exercise and
Athletics," Lippincott's Magazine, 39 (June 1887): 1008-1033**;
James C. Whorton, "Athlete's Heart': The Medical Debate Over
Athleticism, 1870-1920," Journal of Sport History, 9:1 (1982):
30-52.**

October 29: William Coleman, Biology in the Nineteenth Century: Problems of
Form, Function, and Transformation (Cambridge, 1977). All, but
especially pp. 1-34; 92-159; Editorial, Physical Education, 1:5
(July 1982): 1; 76-78; "Physical Education in its Relation
to the Mental and Spiritual Life of Women," ibid.: 79-83;
"Bicycling for Women," ibid.: 83-85.**

PHYSICAL EDUCATION 230

History of Physical Education & Sport

V. Weekly Organization and Readings (cont.)

November 5: John C. Greene, Science. Ideology. and World View: Essays in the History of Evolutionary Ideas (Berkeley, 1981). All, but especially, pp. ix-x; 1-94; 128-157; Edward Mussey Hartwell, "On Physical Training," Report of the Commissioner of Education for the Year 1904. vol. 1 (Washington: Government Printing Office, 1905), 721-757.

November 12: R. J. Park. Sport, Gender. and Society in a Transatlantic Victorian Perspective,' British Journal of Sports History, 2:1 (1985): 5-28**; Lyman B. Sperry, Confidential Talks With Young Women (Chicago, 1894), 11-14; 80-119; 144-161;** Charles Woodhull Eaton, Things A Young Man Should Know.... (Des Moines. 1884). Table of Contents, 125-137; 171-177;193-195; 221-223.**

November 19: Open

November 26: Reports on Papers (Presentations limited to 12 minutes--at 10 minutes presenter will be notified that 2 minutes remain; followed by 5 minutes of discussion)

December 3: Reports continue

Final typed drafts of papers due: DECEMBER 6, 1985

#= Hearst Gymnasium Library only

** = Hearst Gymnasium and Graduate Humanities Service

*** = Hearst Gymnasium, Doe Library, Tolman Library

± = Hearst Gymnasium, Graduate Humanities, Biology Library

PH. ED. 140--HISTORY AND ORIENTATION TO PHYSICAL EDUCATION

James G. Thompson, Instructor--Fall Semester 1985

TEXT: Smith, Ronald. History of Physical Education and Sport (Penn State Series No. A, 1972).

REQUIRED READINGS: See Listing

LECTURES:

1.	Introduction
2.	Ancient Civilizations: Background for Games and Sports
3.	Ancient Greece: Ancient in Time Only
4-5.	Early Greece and Homeric Times
6-7.	Ancient Greece Continued
8-11.	Olympic Games and Pan Hellenic Festivals
12.	Etruscan Civilizations: Background for Sports and Games
13.	Ancient Rome
14-16.	Roman Ludi
17.	Review Period
18.	Exam
19.	Sports and Games in Medieval Times
20.	The Renaissance and its Effect on Physical Education
21-22.	Nationalism and the Rise of German and Swedish Gymnastics
23-24.	Early American Sports and Games
25.	The Place of Physical Activity in Mid-19th Century America
26-27.	Early U.S. Physical Education Programs
28.	Rise of Organized Sport in America
29-30.	Growth of College Athletics
31.	Review Period
32.	Exam
33.	Physical Education, Gymnastics and the Battle of the Systems
34-36.	The New Physical Education
37.	Urbanization, Industrialization and the Playground Movement
38.	Effects of World War I Upon Physical Education
39.	World War II, Korean War and Physical Education
40.	Women in Sport
41.	History of Dance
42.	Film: Two Ball Games
43.	Student Teaching Option
44.	Exercise and Sports Science Option
45.	Review

READINGS:

Ancient Sports

1. Smith text, Homer, "The Funeral and the Games," pp. 1-13.
2. Smith text, Forbes, "Athenian Physical Education in the Fifth Century, B.C.," pp. 14-23.
3. Smith text, Harris, "The Spread of Greek Athletics," pp. 33-36.
4. Smith text, Harris, "Women in Greek Athletics," pp. 47-52.
5. Lawther Reading Room, Smiley, "Olympic and Greek Athletics," Art and Archaeology.
6. Lawther Reading Room, Thompson, "Athletics vs. Gymnastics in Classical Antiquity," Canadian Journal of Sport History.
7. Lawther Reading Room, Thompson, "Logos PROTREPTIKOS: Building Pride in the Profession," Canadian Journal of Sport History.
8. Lawther Reading Room, Thompson, "Ancient Sparta: Two Phases of Cultural and Athletic Development," Canadian Journal of Sport History.
9. Lawther Reading Room, Thompson, "The Ancient Olympic Games and Historical Errors," The Gamut.
10. Smith text, Umminger, "To Make a Roman Holiday," pp. 53-58.

Medieval Sports

1. Rice text, Chapters IV, V.
2. Smith text, Durant, "Chivalry," pp. 59-62.
3. Smith text, Umminger, "The Parfit Knights," pp. 63-69.
4. Smith text, Dunning, "Football in Its Early Stages," pp. 79-80.

Early Modern Period

1. Rice text, Chapter VI, VII, IIX, pp. 70-78, 87-89.
2. Smith text, Milton "Of Education," pp. 81-82.
3. Smith text, Locke, "Some Thoughts Concerning Education," pp. 83-88.
4. Smith text, Rousseau, "Emile," pp. 89-90.

Early American Period

1. Smith text, Dulles, "In Detestation of Idleness," pp. 91-105.
2. Smith text, "The New England Primer," pp. 109-110.
3. Smith text, Dulles, "The Frontier," pp. 111-122.

U.S. to Mid-Nineteenth Century

1. Rice text, pp. 147-156.
2. Smith text, Beecher, "Home Exercises," pp. 123-128.
3. Smith text, Lewis, "The New Gymnastics," pp. 129-144.
4. Smith text, Lucas, "Thomas Wentworth Higginson Early Apostle of Health and Fitness," pp. 145-153.

Rise of Organized Sport and College Athletics

1. Smith text, Betts, "The Technological Revolution and the Rise of Sport," pp. 154-176.
2. Smith text, Young, "College Athletic Sports," pp. 185-192.
3. Smith text, Naismith, "Basket Ball," pp. 193-203.
4. Smith text, Giddens, "The Scramble for College Athletics," pp. 221-227.
5. Keating Monography, "Sportsmanship as a Moral Category," _Ethics_, LXXV (October 1964), pp. 25-35.

Late 19th and Early 20th Century Physical Education

1. Rice text, pp. 175-182, 199-215, 230-233.
2. Smith text, Hitchcock, "Athletics in American Colleges," pp. 228-230.
3. Smith text, Sargent, "Physical Education in Colleges," pp. 231-234.
4. Smith text, Spencer, "Physical Education," pp. 239-241.
5. Smith text, Hetherington, "Fundamental Education," pp. 256-262.
6. Smith text, Hammett, "Influence of Athletics Upon Physical Education in American Colleges," pp. 271-273.

World War I to the Present

1. Rice text, pp. 283-293.
2. Smith text, pp. 278-279.
3. Smith text, Kennedy, "The Soft American," pp. 286-289.
4. Smith text, Levitt, "Reconstruction in Physical Education," pp. 290-293.
5. Smith text, Gilbert, "Drugs in Sport," pp. 294-304.
6. Smith text, Alley, "Physical Education in the Year 2000," pp. 305-313.

PCs13/12

Faculty of Part-Time and Continuing Education
The University of Western Ontario
PE 261b (A Survey History of Physical Education and Sport)
Intersession (commencing May 28, 1979)
London, Thames Hall, Room 200
Time: 7:00 p.m.
Instructor: Prof. E. F. Zeigler

A Survey History of Physical Education and Sport (P.E. 261b)

A survey world history of sport and physical activity from the
earliest recorded period down to the present; the sport, dance, and
exercise patterns of men and women in the various world cultures;
an analysis of the persistent historical problems (both social
forces and professional concerns) in the field in the Western
world primarily.

Antirequisite: Former P. E. 260

Half course; class will meet for twelve (12) two and one-half
(2½) hour periods (divided into sessions) each night from Mon.
through Thursday.

Course Content:

This course is designed to assist the undergraduate student to
develop a comprehensive overview of sport, dance, exercise, and
related physical activity in the world. It is hoped that the student
will develop an understanding and appreciation of the historical
foundations of the field (and to a lesser degree the field of health
and safety education and the field of recreation and leisure studies).
Lectures and relevant discussion will revolve around the persistent
historical problems of the field.

Schedule of Classes:

Each evening there will be three sessions of 50 mins.; 35 mins.;
and 50 mins., respectively (with a coffee break at the end of the
second session). Session #1 will be a lecture by the instructor;
Session #2 will be a discussion period based on the required reading
and questions related to the lectures; and Session #3 will take the
form of an historical slide presentation with appropriate comments.

The lectures will revolve around the following pivotal social
forces and professional concerns--the persistent historical problems--
presented sequentially:

1. Values and Norms Related to Physical Education and Sport

2. The Influence of Politics (type of political state)
3. The Influence of Nationalism
4. The Influence of Economics
5. The Influence of Religion
6. The Influence of Ecology (human's use of environment)
7. Curriculum (what has it included?)
8. Methods of Instruction (how has the curriculum been taught?)
9. Professional Preparation (differing overall patterns)
10. The Concept of 'The Healthy Body' Throughout History
11. Women in Sport and Physical Education (their evolving role)
12. Dance in Culture and Physical Education (its evolving role)
13. The Use of Leisure (primarily sport and physical activity as viewed in historical perspective)
14. Amateurism and Professionalism in Sport (an evolving concept)
15. The Role of Management in Sport and Physical Education (thought, theory, and practice)
16. The Concept of 'Progress' (viewed historically both within society generally and related to sport and physical education specifically)

<u>Recommended Readings</u> (basically from course texts)

<u>Note</u>: This is a three-week course that counts as a half course. Yet it doesn't meet for the same number of hours as the term course held during the year. Usually there has been a considerable amount of reading, and there will be quite a bit of reading during this time too (but not as much and it should be carried out in a certain way). All together, therefore, you will be expected to read more than six hundred pages, but you will not be expected to remember minutia (except as something is held up for class inspection and discussion).

The specific reading assignments are given below on a day-by-day basis below. They are taken from the following two <u>course texts</u>:

<u>A History of Sport and Physical Education to 1900</u> (Selected Topics). Champaign, Ill.: Stipes Publishing Company, 1973. (<u>red</u> cover)

<u>History of Physical Education and Sport</u>. Englewood Cliffs, N.J.: Prentice-Hall, Inc., 1979.

(Both volumes were edited, with selected essays written also, by E. F. Zeigler.)

<u>Reading Assignments</u>:

First Day--(1973 red text)--Prologue and Chapters 1-5
Second Day--Chapters 6-11

Third Day--Chapters 12-17
Fourth Day--Chapters 18-22
Fifth Day--Chapters 23-27
Sixth Day--Chapter 28 and Epilogue
Seventh Day--Preface & Section One   (1979 white covered text)
Eighth Day--Section Two
Ninth Day--Section Three
Tenth Day--Section Four
Eleventh Day--Section Five
Twelfth Day--catch up and prepare for final)

Important Note: It is very important that you attend all twelve
evenings of classes. If you must miss a class, please let the
instructor know in advance. If this is not possible, make certain
that you check with the instructor and learn exactly what was
covered during that evening.

Evaluation:

Students will be expected to read the two course text systematically and in order. There will be a thirty-minute quiz of
a matching nature on the fourth, eighth, and twelfth evenings.
Then there will be a final examination (as discussed in class)
scheduled by the Registrar's Office during the first few days of
the week immediately following completion of the course. The
final examination typically includes matching and essay questions.

Weighting of quizzes and final examination, etc.

Quizzes--each counts 20% of total grade (total of 60%)

Final Exam--30% of total grade   (These percentages can
                                        be debated and changed by
Instructor evaluation--10% of total grade strong majority
       (class participation, etc.)   opinion)

Note: The instructor has been developing a retrieval system of
historical references and abstracts over the years. This may be used
when his outer office is open. Also, the instructor maintains
regular office hours and welcomes the opportunity to discuss course
progress and problems. For this time period, he will be available
Monday through Thursday from 3:30 to 5:00 p.m.; if these times are
out of the question, please make an appointment. Please do take
the opportunity to get acquainted.

Winter Term, 1980
Time: 3 hours
Instructor: E.F. Zeigler

PHYSICAL EDUCATION 261b
Survey History of Sport and Physical Education

See Page 4 also for further instructions

FINAL EXAMINATION

Instructions: Match the number of the word, term or phrase from the
right hand column with the appropriate answer in the left hand column.
Each correct answer counts one (1) point out of a total of fifty (50)
points for this half of the examination.

( ) Johann Friedrich Guts Muths

( ) Germany and France

( ) Dr. Thomas Arnold

( ) France

( ) Gaulhofer, Austria

( ) Jake Gaudaur and Ned Hanlan

( ) Little organized, purposive
     instruction in games and
     physical education

( ) Influenced inclusion of physical
     education in curricula elsewhere

( ) Women's status was high

( ) Pestalozzi, Guts Muths, Gaulhofer,
     Streicher and Laban

( ) Friedrich Ludwig Jahn

( ) Pehr Henrik Ling

( ) Started in England

( ) Origin of ideas for physical
     training in the Renaissance

( ) View that Greeks were not
     paragons of amateurism

1. Ancient Greece

2. Aretē

3. Harold A. Harris

4. Development of all-sided man in court

5. That "The Church" was against the
    idea of all exercise and Physical
    training

6. Sharply criticized athletics of the
    time

7. Roman credited with Mens sana in
    corpore sano (sound mind, etc.)

8. Fitness; character; arts

9. Largely responsible for original
    mind-body dualism

10. Ancient Greek athletic festivals

11. Homer's Odyssey

12. Mesoamerica

13. Wrestling

14. Bull-vaulting artifact

15. Turnverein Movement

( ) Vittorino da Feltre

( ) Made a plea for natural education in Emile

( ) "Ever faster, higher, stronger"

( ) Condemned the extreme violence that had crept into U.S. football

( ) Amateurism; development of health & character; international sport contributing to peace

( ) World leader historically in sport and games

( ) Strong influence on physical training in U.S. in 19th century

( ) Years from 1880 to 1890 in the U.S.

( ) Urged viewing the curriculum as child-centered

( ) A large philanthropic donation designed to help Canadian physical education

( ) The award for the Canadian inter-collegiate football championship before 1925

( ) Jahn, Ling, Nachtegall and socialist nations

( ) Juvenal

( ) Knightly arts

( ) Plato

( ) Isthmian; Pythean

( ) Conducted a crusade toward improve-ment of women's health and Phys.Ed.

( ) All-round excellence & all-round activity

( ) Xenophanes

( ) An indigeneous native sport in Canada

16. "Battle of the Systems" (foreign ones!)

17. John Dewey

18. Emerging nationalism in Europe

19. In primitive societies

20. A number of educational theorists in Renaissance Italy

21. Early Crete

22. England

23. Early German "scientific" physical educator

24. Natural movement; worked with Margarete Streicher

25. Both employed physical activity for nationalistic purposes

26. Famous Headmaster of Rugby School in early 19th century

27. Has been somewhat slow historically to develop physical education scien-tifically

28. Father of German gymnastics; started on the Hasenheide

29. Important figure in Swedish physical education history

30. The idea of "movement education"

31. Strathcona Trust

32. The Grey Cup

33. Canadian rowing champions

34. Lacrosse

35. Canada

36. President Theodore Roosevelt of the U.S.A.

37. Catharine Beecher

( ) Includes a famous archery contest

( ) Highly organized competitive ball games

( ) Advanced sport in ancient world

( ) Reflected a sporting tradition from three different cultures

( ) Famous Aegean Island fresco

( ) "Great Protestant Legend"

( ) Off-duty British soldiers

( ) Canadian football developed from it

( ) Czechoslovakian system of gymnastic exercises

( ) Sharply curtailed sporting activities on the Sabbath

( ) "The most important religious building in Canada"--stated Wm. Kilbourn

( ) Ethical values relating to global level; ecological concern; presently utopian

( ) Beauty, harmony, excellence, development of mind and body and other individual virtues (Glassford)

( ) "A sound mind in a sound body is a short but full description of a Happy State in this World"-- the tabula rasa theory

( ) Had a direct relationship to physical training development

38. Blue Laws in one of the 50 states

39. Toronto's gardens where "King Harold" rules

40. The Olympic motto

41. The philosophy of Olympism

42. Spread certain sporting activities to various parts of the world

43. Rugby

44. Anthropocentric ethic

45. Egocentric ethic

46. Biocentric ethic

47. Ethnocentric ethic

48. Jean Jacques Rousseau

49. John Locke

50. Sokol (Falcon)

<u>Further Instructions</u>: Please check at this time to make certain that your name and i.d. no. are on <u>each</u> <u>sheet</u> upon which you write.

Divide the total amount of time available carefully. For example, the matching should take you no more than 50 minutes to 1 hour; thus leave approximately 30 minutes each for the two essay questions.

You are to write answers to question #1 and <u>either</u> #2 <u>or</u> #3 of the following three questions. You will find it helpful if you <u>try</u> to outline each answer as best possible <u>before</u> you finally write it out. Further, do not hesitate to use diagrams and/or to outline your answer in detail with short descriptive phrases (if you feel that such an approach can serve your purpose best). Each answer will count 25 points.

<u>Do write as legibly as possible; avoid crowding of lines</u>.

1. a) List as many of the different purposes that physical activity in sport, dance, play and exercise have served.
    b) Using a diagrammatic outline place the various societies and countries that we have included in the readings in chronological order as best you can on the left side of several pages.
    c) Now   opposite the society (or country) on the page indicate the purposes (aims or objectives) that were best served by developmental physical activity in sport, dance, play and exercise in each society. <u>Limit</u> <u>yourself</u> by giving <u>no</u> <u>more</u> <u>than</u> three (3) of the most important purposes in that particular society.

2. a) Name the six persistent problems that were listed as social forces or influences.
    b) Now describe the persistent problem (social force) relating to our use <u>historically</u> of our physical environment; tell what the situation is today in the world; finally, discuss some of the implications for education and then for sport and physical education.
    c) Finally, what did we explain as the <u>final</u> persistent problem identified as <u>both</u> a social influence <u>and</u> also a professional concern. Discuss it briefly from both a historical standpoint and also at present.

3. a) Name the <u>nine</u> professional concerns presented in the last chapter that were discussed in class.
    b) Discuss one of them that relates more to what goes on in <u>the educational</u> <u>system</u> specifically; do this <u>historically</u> from the standpoint of society generally, education, and sport and physical activity.
    c) Discuss another one of them that relates more directly to <u>society in general</u>; review this historically as well from the standpoint of society, education, and sport and physical activity specifically.

THE UNIVERSITY OF WESTERN ONTARIO
FACULTY OF PHYSICAL EDUCATION

Quiz #4 (March 21, 1980)
Physical Education 261b

Survey History of Physical
Education and Sport

Instructions: Match the number of the word, term or phrase from the right hand
column with the appropriate answer in the left hand column. (3
points for each)

( ) A civilization was named after
this famous legendary king

( ) Beehive Tomb; Clytemnestra;
Schliemann

( ) Pursuit; chance; strategy;dexter-
ity; vertigo; imitation; enigma

( ) Defeat of the Saxon kingdoms at
Hastings

( ) Reconciling medieval relig'ous
belief with material world and
developing secular interests

( ) Developed a synthesis between
natural and supernatural theology
for The Church

( ) Status of women was evidently
higher than in most early civilizations

( ) A question-and-answer technique
that encouraged men to think for
themselves

( ) Important for Persians (Herodotus)

( ) Fertile Crescent

( ) An ancient civilization that has
somehow survived

( ) Major and minor Crusades

( ) Characterized by independent city
states well into Modern Period

( ) Powerful, supportive creatures
who took up arms when necessary

( ) Strong Reformation figure who
liked wrestling

( ) Other than required physical
labour, climate tended to negate
sports & games (as did religion)

1. "To ride, to use the bow, and to speak
the truth"

2. Sumeria--one of the earliest civilizations

3. Egypt

4. Lasted about 150 years and were against
the Turks

5. What is now known as Italy

6. Ancient India

7. 1066; William the Conqueror

8. Forerunners of Renaissance universities in Western world

9. Western European countries

10. Minoan

11. Usually given credit for discovery of
old manuscripts about the Classical
Age

12. Renaissance humanists

13. Francis Bacon

14. Erasmus

15. Mycenae

16. Characteristics of games of early
civilizations

17. St. Thomas Aquinas

18. Ancient Crete

19. Socrates

20. Hellenic Civilization

21. Part of the advanced curriculum of the
Seven Free Arts

77

( ) Monastic & cathedral schools

( ) Their ideas about education spread slowly elsewhere to the north

( ) It was brought to a halt when Roman Civilization fell

( ) Jousting, falconing, swimming, horsemanship and boxing

( ) Restored a balance to the educational curriculum

( ) Francesco Petrarca (Petrarch)

( ) A great humanist but showed no great enthusiasm for the Greek ideal in physical culture

( ) Able to adapt to "alien inheritances" and provided more opportunities for people to get involved

( ) Important figure in early development of scientific thought; also, argued consistently for inclusion of physical training in curriculum

22. Specific recommendations of Renaissance humanists about place of physical training

23. Visigoth women

24. Martin L. (the monk)

25. Underlying major problem of period of feudalism

Instructions: Answer one of the following two questions on app. one page. Try to write as clearly as possible. Do not hesitate to outline if you wish. (Counts 25 points)

1. Define religion in the Western world narrowly and broadly. Discuss its development historically insofar as its social importance and not forgetting its relationship to education. Lastly, discuss its relationship to sport, dance, play and exercise from a historical standpoint, as well as for health and recreation.

2. Define ecology. Discuss it as a persistent problem historically. What does it indicate insofar as our pattern of education today is concerned? Specifically, what implications does it have for sport and exercise, as well as for health and recreation?

Test #5 (April 9, 1980)   Survey History of Physical
Physical Education 261b   Education and Sport

Note: This test is optional. You may simply walk out right now, and use it with
the others to study for the final examination. Or you may take it and see
how you score on it. This paper may then be picked up from Wednesday afternoon on, April 16--typically between 2:15 and 4:00 p.m. I will record your
score and--if you don't want to use it--you must tell me personally.

Instructions: Match the number of the word, term or phrase from the right hand
column with the appropriate answer in the left hand column.

( ) Toronto's Maple Leaf Gardens

( ) Recommended "a quiet death and
      seemly burial" (Harold Harris)

( ) A very rapid transition from
      asceticism to athleticism

( ) More than 100 nations from 5
      continents take part

( ) "the Cradle of Canadian Sport"

( ) A radical departure from the
      ancient Games

( ) Only individual sport competitions
      were held then

( ) Five rings of blue, yellow, black,
      green and red

( ) Philosophy of Olympism

( ) Sport progress in the last 3 or
      4 decades was phenomenal

( ) Spread sport in various parts
      of the world

( ) The sport of rugby

( ) Egocentric ethic

( ) Biocentric ethic

( ) Ontario did formerly but now a
      number of countries require it

( ) Johann Guts Muths

( ) Sokol (Falcons)

1. "Brutality and foul play should
    receive the same summary punishment
    given to a man who cheats at cards"

2. Sharply curtailed sporting activities
    on the Sabbath

3. Jahn, Ling, Nachtegall and socialist
    nations

4. Reflected a sporting tradition from
    three different cultures

5. Donald Smith's $500,000 donation
    called the Strathcona Trust

6. Toronto, McGill and Queen's played
    for it before 1925

7. Conducted a 19th century crusade
    toward improvement in health and
    physical well-being of women

8. Typified by a shift away from energy
    sources of a human and/or animal nat-
    ure to that based on non-living mech-
    anisms

9. Boston Conference "in the Interest of
    Physical Training"

10. Ned Hanlan & Jake Gaudaur

11. "A Sound Mind in a Sound Body is a
    short but full Description of a Happy
    State in this World"--tabula rasa

12. The "Big Train"--hockey, football, etc.

13. "The most important religious building
    in Canada"--Jake Kilbourn

14. Was never declared Canada's national
    sport

( ) Disciples of Jahn who emigrated to the US in the early 1800s

( ) Per Henrik Ling

( ) Anthropocentric ethic

( ) Laid the foundation for belief that natural laws control the world

( ) John Locke

( ) The political organization of European nations had long been based on it

( ) The Industrial Revolution

( ) Agricultural Revolution became a significant force in this century

( ) Benjamin Franklin stated this ethic of early New England

( ) A myth about the origin of baseball (now discredited)

( ) In 1882 the great John L. Sullivan lost to James J. Corbett

( ) President Theodore Roosevelt

( ) Pennsylvania Blue Laws

( ) Ethnocentric Ethic

( ) Canadian sport & games

( ) Influenced Canadian physical education considerably

( ) The Grey Cup

( ) Catharine Beecher

( ) Leaders among women (Hemenway and Homans)

( ) Rowing champions

( ) Lionel Conacher

( ) Lacrosse

( ) Jean Jacques Rousseau

15. Beauty, harmony, excellence and development of mind and body (and other individual virtues)

16. Czechoslovakian system of gymnastic exercises

17. Ethical values relating to global level; ecological concern; presently utopian

18. Amateurism; development of health and character; international sport contributing to peace; and sport an integral part of culture

19. Pestalozzi, Guts Muths, Gaulhofer, Streicher, Laban

20. Made a strong plea for natural, progressive education in Emile

21. The Royal Central Gymnastics Institute (Sweden)

22. The "Grandfather of physical education"; concerned with students' developmental records; wrote a famous exercise book

23. Off-duty British soldiers

24. Canadian and American football more akin to it than soccer

25. Boxing

26. That Abner Doubleday invented it

27. "America's recreation is business"

28. For the modern Olympic Games

29. The modern Western church

30. 18th century

31. World Cup (soccer)

32. The modern Winter Olympic Games

33. The ancient Olympic Games

34. Dynastic Monarchy

35. Galileo, Copernicus, Kepler and Newton

36. The 19th century

80

37. Montreal

38. Beck, Lieber and Follen

39. The Olympic flag

40. Pre-military training at secondary
    school level

BE CERTAIN YOUR NAME IS ON EACH SHEET! Each matching question counts 2½ points.

Please note the following:

1. Class will not meet on Friday, April 11.

2. In place of this class, two voluntary sessions will be held in Room 101, Thames
   Hall, Tuesday and Wednesday, April 29 & 30 at 4:30 p.m.--just prior to final
   exam on May 1.

3. Grades for this test will be available on Wednesday, April 16, 2:15 p.m. in
   Room 132a, Somerville House (and typically thereafter during regular office
   hours from 2:15 - 3:30 p.m.)

4. I must know from you "IN PERSON" or "IN WRITING" whether you wish me to use
   Test #5 score in determining your class average!!

Physical Education 402
(History of Physical Education and Sport)

Catalogue Description of Course:

An analysis of the research literature related to the historical foundations of physical education and sport; lectures and discussion of such persistent historical problems as the influence of economics, politics and nationalism, curriculum and methods
of instruction, professional preparation, the concept of health, dance, the use of
leisure, amateur and professional sport, and the concept of progress; the use of slides
and film strips to supplement background knowledge about the great civilizations of
the past.

Further Discussion of Objectives:

Our primary concern in this course is to help graduate students in physical education
and related fields to develop an understanding and appreciation of the historical
foundations of physical education and sport and, to a lesser degree, of health education and recreation education.

Another specific objective will be to provide interested students with some competency
and background in the use of certain research techniques of historical method. It
should be emphasized, however, that appropriate background study in history and history
of education would typically be necessary prior to undertaking a significant project
in this area of interest.

Class Organization:

Class lectures, discussions, the viewing of audio-visual materials, and critiques of
completed research will be the typical pattern of course organization. Students are
invited to make recommendations and offer opinions regarding the teaching-learning
process employed. Sessions will be devoted to organizational problems, historical
method, background and related information, and lectures covering the persistent historical problems and other studies.

Assignments and Projects:

Students will be expected to read widely from the text and the many books and sources
on the reserve shelf in the Physical Education Library, as well as from Microcard
Publications and Doctoral Dissertation Abstracts (and available microfilms). Some of
the basic historical material will of necessity have to be obtained from the Education
Library and the historical collection.

Students will be asked to critique, after reading and preparing abstracts of, completed
research. Abstracts should be available for distribution one week in advance of class
presentation and discussion. The actual class presentation itself should be discussed in advance with the instructor to insure that it will be the best possible
type of critical evaluation.

Students will be asked to prepare a term paper based on original research on some
phase of one of the persistent historical problems (or some other persistent historical
problem, the selection of which is defensible).

Depending on the outcome of a class vote, the final examination will be either of the
standard type or of a take-home variety.

Primarily for their own future use, students will be asked to contribute to the development of an historical time scale relating to physical education and sport.

Textbooks:

Zeigler, Earle F. <u>Problems in the History and Philosophy of Physical Education and Sport</u>. Englewood Cliffs, N.J.: Prentice-Hall, 1968.

Zeigler, Earle F. (Editor). <u>A History of Physical Education and Sport: Selected Readings</u>. Pacific Palisades, California: Goodyear Publishing Company, 1971. (<u>In press</u>)

Supplementary Textbook

Zeigler, Earle F., Howell, Maxwell L., and Trekell, Marianna. <u>Research in the History, Philosophy, and Comparative Aspects of Physical Education and Sport: Techniques and Bibliographies</u>. Champaign, Ill.: Stipes Publishing Company, 1971. (<u>In press</u>)

TENTATIVE SCHEDULE OF CLASSES

Note: Each week the class runs from 8:30 - 11:00 a.m. The first and third sessions each week are 50 minutes long. The inbetween session is typically thirty minutes long (20 minutes for critique, and 10 minutes for discussion). There are 10-minute breaks at the end of the first and second sessions.

Week 1

    Session 1 - Introduction and Discussion of Course Outline
            2 - Historical Method of Research
            3 - Status of Research in Phys. Ed. and Sport (Historical)

Week 2

    Session 4 - Introduction to Philosophy of History
            5 - Development of Historical Research Prospectus for Course
                  Term Paper
            6 - Development of Historical Time Scale for HPER

Week 3

    Session 7 - Historical Foundations (Social and Educational)
            8 - Historical Study Critique
            9 - Values in Physical, Health, and Recreation Education (Problem 1)

Week 4

    Session 10 - Historical Foundations
            11 - Historical Study Critique
            12 - The Influence of Politics (Problem 2)

Week 5

    Session 13 - Historical Foundations
            14 - Historical Study Critique
            15 - The Influence of Nationalism (Problem 3)

Session 43 - The Concept of Progress (15)
44 - (If time permits an additional persistent problem will be discussed, but only if all critiques have been completed.)
45 - Summary Statement and Course Evaluation

Some Due Dates:

1) Abstracts - by December 15 or to class one week before class presentation
2) Term Paper - next to last class
3) Final examination - either at scheduled time or by last class (depending upon class vote).

READING LIST

PE 402 - History of Physical Education and Sport

Week 1

1. Good and Scates, Methods of Research, pp. 170-254.
2. AAHPER, Research Methods Applied to HPER, pp. 465-481.
3. Zeigler, Problems in the History of, etc., Chapter I.
4. Cantor and Werthman, A History of Popular Culture, read Sources, Contents, and Introduction.

Week 2

1. Nevins, The Gateway to History, pp. 13-63.
2. Aron, Introduction to the Philosophy of History, pp. 15-44.
3. Van Dalen et al., A World History of Physical Education, pp. 5-94.
4. Howell, "An Historical Survey of the Role of Sports in Society," read Acknowledgements, Abstract, Table of Contents, List of Figures, Chapter 1, and examine generally.

Week 3 - (Values)

1. Hammond's World Atlas (see historical atlas in back of book).
2. Also, for further study, Muir's New School Atlas of Universal History, Barnes & Noble, 1961.
2. Van Loon, The Arts, pp. 3-154.
4. Woody, Life and Education, etc., Preface, Introduction, and look over generally.
4. Zeigler, Course Text, pp. 19-50.
5. Brubacher, A History of the Problems, etc., pp. 1-22.

Week 4 - (Politics)

1. Handlin et al., Harvard Guide to American History (New York: Atheneum, 1967), look over Parts 1 and 2 -- and be aware of the remainder.
2. Marrou, A History of Education in Antiquity, read Introduction, look over Part I, and read pp. 165-186.
3. Brubacher, A History of the Problems of Education, pp. 23-52, and look over generally (including Preface).
4. Zeigler, Course Text, pp. 52-55.

Week 5 - (Nationalism)

1. Muller, <u>The Uses of the Past</u>, Preface, Chapters 2 & 3 (pp. 33-75), and look
   over generally.
2. Brubacher, <u>A History of</u>, etc., pp. 53-75.
3. Zeigler, Course Text, pp. 56-59.
   (Check, if possible, Reisner, <u>Nationalism and Educ. Since 1789</u>, Chaps. 1 & 18)

Week 6 - (Economics)

1. Robinson, <u>Sources for the History of Greek Athletics</u>, Preface and look over
   generally.
2. Brubacher, <u>A History of the</u>, etc., pp. 76-97.
3. Zeigler, Course Text, pp. 60-65.

Week 7 - (Religion)

1. Brubacher, <u>A History of</u>, etc., Chapter 11, pp. 303-337.
2. Zeigler, Course Text, pp. 66-75.
3. Ballou, Ralph B., <u>An Analysis of the Writings of Selected Church Fathers</u>, etc.,
   read summary and conclusions chapter.
4. Zeigler, <u>An Introduction to the Philosophy of Religion</u> (Stipes), 27 p.

Week 8 - (Professional Preparation)

1. Brubacher, <u>A History of</u>, etc., pp. 465-506
2. Please familiarize yourself with the 1962 publication of AAHPER entitled <u>Professional
   in HEPERE</u>, and also the 1967 AAHPER publication <u>Graduate Education in HEPERESE&D</u>.
3. Zeigler, "A History of Professional Preparation for Physical Education in the United
   States, 1861-1948," look over generally if you are especially interested in this
   subject.

Week 9 - (Methods of Instruction)

1. Brubacher, <u>A History of</u>, etc., pp. 167-241.
2. Zeigler, Course Text, pp. 76-82.
3. Van Dalen et al., <u>A World History of</u>, etc., check "methods of physical education"
   in Index, etc.

Week 10 - (Administration)

1. Brubacher, A History of, etc., pp. 540-580.
2. Zeigler, Course Text, pp. 83-89.
3. Gross, Bertram, <u>The Managing of Organization</u> (Vol. 1), Chapter 5 (pp. 91-118),
   and look over generally.

Week 11 - (The Concept of Health)

1. Woody, <u>Life and Education</u>, etc., pp. Chapters 13 & 24.
2. Sigerist, <u>Landmarks in the History of Hygiene</u>, look over generally.
3. Zeigler, Course Text, pp. 90-94.

Week 12 - (The Use of Leisure)

1. Brubacher, <u>A History of</u>, etc., pp. 78, 82-84, 92, 93.
2. Zeigler, Course Text, pp. 95-101.

3. Woody, "Leisure in the Light of History," in <u>Recreation In the Age of Automation</u>.
   Philadelphia: <u>The Annals</u> of the American Academy of Political and Social Science,
   1957, pp. 4-11, and look over generally.

<u>Week 13</u> - (The Amateur, Semi-Professional, and Professional)

1. Savage, <u>American College Athletics</u>, Preface, and Chapter 2.
2. Flath, "A History of Relations between the NCAA and the AAU," available as a
   thesis and also as a paperback book, look over generally.
3. Zeigler, Course Text, pp. 102-116.

<u>Week 14</u> - (Dance in Physical Education and Recreation)

1. Ashton, Dudley, "Contributions of Dance to Physical Education," (Part I),
   <u>JOHPER</u>, 26, No. 9 (December, 1955). (See also Part II in <u>JOHPER</u> of April, 1956)
2. Zeigler, <u>Philosophical Foundations</u>, etc., pp. 57-58 and 268-271.
3. Zeigler, "A Brief History of Dance," unpublished paper.

<u>Week 15</u> - (The Concept of Progress)

1. A. A. Ekirch, <u>The Idea of Progress in America</u> (Columbia University Press,
   New York, 1944) in Chapter 7 gives a limited treatment to progress in education.
2. Zeigler, Course Text, pp. 117-124.
3. Brubacher, <u>A History of the Problems</u>, etc., pp. 581-611.

<u>Note</u>: If extra time is available, two additional persistent historical problems will
   be discussed: (1) Physical Education and Sport for Girls and Women (Problem
   #10); and (2) Man's Use of His Environment (Ecology) (Problem # 6).

<u>Selected References</u>:

1. Abernathy, Thomas D. "An Analysis of Master's and Doctoral Studies Related to
   the History of Physical Education Completed in the United States Between 1930
   and 1967," Master's thesis, University of Illinois, Urbana, 1970, 109 p.

2. Adelman, Melvin L. "An Assessment of Sports History Theses in the United States,
   1931-1967," Master's thesis, University of Illinois, Urbana, 1970, 230 p.

3. Ainsworth, Dorothy S., "The History of Physical Education in Colleges for Women,"
   Ph.D. dissertation, Columbia University, 1930.

4. Alexander, Carter, and Burke, A.J., <u>How to Locate Educational Information and Data</u>.
   New York: Bureau of Publications, Teachers College, Columbia University, Third
   Edition, 1950. 439 p. (See later edition, if available)

5. American Assoc. for Health, Physical Education, and Recreation. <u>Research Methods
   Applied to Health, Physical Education, and Recreation</u>. Washington, D.C.:
   A.A.H.P.E. & R., Revised Edition, 1959. 535 p.

6. Aron, Raymond. <u>Introduction to the Philosophy of History</u>. Boston: Beacon Press,
   1961, 351 p.

7. Avery, Catherine B. (Ed.). <u>Classical Handbook</u>. New York: Appleton-Century-Crofts,
   Inc., 1962. 1162 p.

8. Ballou, Ralph B., "An Analysis of the Writings of Selected Church Fathers to A.D. 394 to Reveal Attitudes Regarding Physical Activity." Ph.D. dissertation. University of Oregon. 1965.

9. Barney, Robert K. Turmoil and Triumph (A Narrative History of Intercollegiate Athletics at the University of New Mexico). Albuquerque, New Mexico: San Ignacio Press, 1969. 340 p.

10. Barrows, I. C. Physical Training. Boston: Press of George H. Ellis, 1899. 135 p.

11. Bennett, Bruce L., "The Life of Dudley Allen Sargent, M.D., and His Contributions to Physical Education." Ph.D. dissertation. The University of Michigan, 1947.

12. _____, "Religion and Physical Education." A paper presented at the Cincinnati Convention of the AAHPER, April 10, 1962.

13. Brailsford, Dennis. Sport and Society: Elizabeth to Anne. London: Routledge & Kegan Paul, 1969. 279 p.

14. Brickman, W. W. Guide to Research in Educational History. New York: New York University Bookstore, 1949. 220 p.

15. Bronson, Alice O., "Clark W. Hetherington: Scientist and Philosopher." Ph.D. dissertation, University of Utah, 1955.

16. Brubacher, J.S. A History of the Problems of Education. New York: McGraw-Hill Book Company, 1947. 688 p.

17. Bury, J. B. The Idea of Progress. New York: Dover Publications, Inc., 1955.

18. Butts, R. F. A Cultural History of Education. New York: McGraw-Hill Book Co., 1947, 726 p.

19. Caldwell, Stratton Franklin, "Conceptions of Physical Education in Twentieth Century America: Rosalind Cassidy." Ph.D. dissertation, University of Southern California, 1966.

20. Cantor, Norman F. and Werthman, Michael S. (eds.). The History of Popular Culture. New York: The Macmillan Company, 1968. 788 p.

21. Cozens, F. W., and F. S. Stumpf. Sports in American Life. Chicago: The University of Chicago Press, 1953.

22. Dauer, Victor P., "The Amateur Code in American College Athletics." Ph.D. dissertation. The University of Michigan, 1949.

23. Devambez, Pierre. Greek Sculpture. New York: Tudor Publishing Company, Revised Edition, 1965. 168 p.

24. Doell, C. E. and Fitzgerald, G. B. A Brief History of Parks and Recreation in the United States. Chicago: TheAthletic Institute, 1954. 129 p.

25. Dulles, F. R. America Learns to Play: A History of Popular Recreation, 1607-1940. New York: Appleton-Century Company, 1940.

26. Durant, Will. Our Oriental Heritage. New York: Simon and Schuster, 1954. 1049 p.

27. _____. The Life of Greece. New York: Simon and Schuster, 1939. 754 p.

28. _____. Caesar and Christ. New York: Simon andSchuster, 1944, 751 p.

29. _____. The Age of Faith. New York: Simon and Schuster, 1950. 1196 p.

30. _____. The Renaissance. New York: Simon and Schuster, 1953. 776 p.

31. _____. The Reformation. New York: Simon and Schuster, 1957. 1025 p.

32. Durant, Will and Ariel. The Age of Reason Begins. New York: Simon and Schuster, 1961. 729 p.

33. _____. The Age of Louis XIV. New York: Simon and Schuster, 1963. 802 p.

34. _____. The Age of Voltaire. New York: Simon and Schuster, 1965. 898 p.

35. _____. Rousseau and Revolution. New York: Simon and Schuster, 1967. 1091 p.

36. Durant, Will. The Lessons of History. New York: Simon and Schuster, 1968

37. Ekirch, A. A. The Idea of Progress in America. New York: Columbia University Press, 1944.

38. Evans, A. The Palace of Minos at Knossos. London: The Macmillan Company, Five volumes, 1921-1936.

39. Eyler, Marvin H., "Origins of Some Modern Sports." Ph.D. dissertation, University of Illinois, 1956.

40. Flath, A. W. A History of Relations between the National Collegiate Athletic Association and the Amateur Athletic Union of the United States, (1905-1963). Champaign, Ill.: Stipes Publishing Company, 1964. (Includes a Foreword by Earle F. Zeigler entitled "Amateurism, Semiprofessionalism, and Professionalism in Sport—A Persistent Educational Problem").

41. Freeman, Kenneth J. Schools of Hellas. London: Macmillan and Company, Third Edition, 1922. 299 p.

42. Good, C. V., and Scates, D. E. Methods of Research. New York: Appleton-Century-Crofts, Inc., 1954. 920 p.

43. Gross, Bertram M. The Managing of Organizations. 2 vols. New York: Crowell-Collier Publishing Co., 1964.

44. Hackensmith, C. W. History of Physical Education. New York: Harper & Row, Publishers, 1966.

45. Hambly, W. D. Tribal Dancing and Social Development. London: Witherby, 1926.

46. Hammond's World Atlas. New York: C. S. Hammond & Company, 1954. 312 p. and appendices.

47. Harris, H. A. Greek Athletes and Athletics. London: Hutchinson & Co., 1964.

48. Hartwell, E.M. Physical Training. Washington: Government Printing Office, 1899. pp. 487-589.

49. Hawkes, Jacquetta, and Woolley, Leonard. History of Mankind (Vol. I - Prehistory and the Beginnings of Civilization). New York: Harper and Row, Publishers, 1963.

50. Hayes, Carlton J. Nationalism: A Religion. New York: The Macmillan Company, 1961.

51. Howell, Maxwell L. "An Historical Survey of the Role of Sport in Society, with Particular Reference to Canada Since 1700," Doctor of Physical Education Thesis, University of Stellenbosch, South Africa, 1969. 570 p.

52. Howell, Nancy and Howell, Maxwell L. Sports and Games in Canadian Life: 1700 to the Present. Toronto: Macmillan of Canada, 1969. 378 p.

53. Johnson, Elmer L., "A History of Physical Education in the Young Men's Christian Association." Ed.D. dissertation, University of Southern California, 1954.

54. Leonard, F. E., and Affleck, G. B. The History of Physical Education. Philadelphia: Lea & Febiger, Third Edition, 1947. 480 p.

55. Leonard, F. E. Pioneers of Modern Physical Training. New York: Association Press, Second Edition, 1915. 159 p.

56. Levi, Mario A. Political Power in the Ancient World. New York: The New American Library, Inc., English translation, 1965.

57. Lindsay, Peter L., "Literary Evidence of Physical Education Among the Ancient Romans." M.A. Thesis, The University of Alberta, 1967.

58. Marrou, H. I. A History of Education in Antiquity. Translated by George Lamb. New York: The New American Library of World Literature, Inc., 1964.

59. McDonald, Margaret Anne, "A Study of Ancient Greek Physical Education with Emphasis Upon the Dance, the Women, and the Professional." M. Ed. Thesis, Woman's College, University of North Carolina, 1962.

60. McIntosh, P. C. et al. History of Physical Education. London: Routledge & Kegan Paul, 1957. 218 p.

61. McNeill, William H. The Rise of the West. Chicago: The University of Chicago Press, 1963. 829 p.

62. Means, R. K. A History of Health Education in the United States. Philadelphia: Lea & Febiger, 1962. 412 p.

63. Metzner, Henry. A Brief History of the American Turnerbund. Pittsburgh: National Executive Committee of the American Turnerbund, Revised Edition, 1924, 56 p.

64. Mingazzini, Paolino. Greek Pottery Painting. London: Paul Hamlyn, 1969, 157 p.

65. Morison, Samuel Eliot. The Oxford History of the American People. New York: Oxford University Press, 1965, 1150 p.

66. Morton, Henry W. Soviet Sport. New York: Collier Books, 1963, 221 p.

67. Muller, Herbert J. The Uses of the Past. New York: The New American Library of World Literature, Inc., 1954, 384 p. (Published originally by the Oxford University Press, Inc. in England - 1952).

68. _____. *Freedom in the Ancient World*. New York: Harper & Row, Publishers, 1961, 360 p.

69. _____. *Freedom in the Western World*. New York: Harper & Row, Publishers, 1963, 428 p.

70. _____. *Religion and Freedom in the Modern World*. Chicago: The University of Chicago Press, 1963, 129 p.

71. _____. *Freedom in the Modern World*. New York: Harper & Row, Publishers, 1966.

72. Neumeyer, Martin H., and Neumeyer, Esther S. *Leisure and Recreation*. New York: The Ronald Press Company, Third Edition, 1958, 473 p.

73. Nevins, Allan. *The Gateway to History*. Garden City, N.Y.: Doubleday & Company, Inc., 1962, 440 p.

74. Palmer, Denise, "Sport and Games in the Art of Early Civilizations." M. A. Thesis, The University of Alberta, 1967.

75. Pareti, Luigi (assisted by Paolo Brezzi and Luciano Petech). *History of Mankind* (Vol. II - *The Ancient World*). New York: Harper & Row, Publishers, 1965, 1048 p.

76. Rajagopalan, K. *A Brief History of Physical Education in India*. Delhi: Army Publishers, 1963, 199 p.

77. Rice, E. A., Hutchinson, J. L., and Lee, Mabel. *A Brief History of Physical Education*. New York: The Ronald Press Company, Fourth Edition, 1958, 430 p.

78. Reisner, Edward H. *Nationalism and Education Since 1789*. New York: The Macmillan Company, 1922. 575 p.

79. Robinson, Rachel S. *Sources for the History of Greek Athletics*. Cincinnati, Ohio 45220: Published by the Author, 439 Ludlow Ave., Revised Edition, 1955, 289 p.

80. Sachs, Curt. *World History of the Dance*. New York: W. W. Norton & Company, Inc., 1937.

81.. Sage, George H. *Sport and American Society: Selected Readings*. Reading, Mass.: Addison-Wesley Publishing Company, 1970.

82. Sapora, A. V., and Mitchell, E. D. *The Theory of Play and Recreation*. New York: The Ronald Press Company, Third Edition, 1961, 558 p.

83. Savage, Howard J. *American College Athletics*. (Bulletin #23). New York: The Carnegie Foundation for the Advancement of Teaching, 1929. 383 p.

84. Schwendener, Norma. *A History of Physical Education in the United States*. New York: A. S. Barnes & Co., 1942, 237 p.

85. Setton, Kenneth M. "A New Look at Medieval Europe," National Geographic, Vol. 122, No. 6, (December, 1962). 798-859 p.

86. Sigerist, Henry E. *Landmarks in the History of Hygiene*. London: Oxford University Press, 1956, 78 p.

87. Toynbee, Arnold J. (Abridgement of Vols. I-VI by D. C. Somervell), _A Study of History_. New York and London: Oxford University Press, 1947.

88. Trekell, Marianna, "Gertrude Evelyn Moulton, M.D.: Her Life and Professional Career in Health and Physical Education." Ph.D. dissertation, Ohio State University, 1963.

89. Ulrich, Celeste, "Historical Bibliography, Part I," _JOHPER_, Vol. 31, No. 4 (April, 1960), 100-01.

90. _____, "Historical Bibliography, Part II," _JOHPER_, Vol. 31, No. 5 (May-June 1960), 45-6.

91. Van Dalen, D. B., Mitchell, E. D., and Bennett, B. L. _A World History of Physical Education_. New York: Prentice-Hall, Inc., 1953, 640 p.

92. Van Loon, H. W. _The Arts_. New York: Simon and Schuster, 1937, 677 p. Englewood Cliffs, N. J.: Prentice-Hall, Inc., 1953, 640 p.

93. Ware, Caroline F., K. M. Panikkar, and J. M. Romein. _History of Mankind_ (Vol. VI, _The Twentieth Century_). New York: Harper & Row, 1966.

94. Weaver, R. B. _Amusements and Sports in American Life._ Chicago: University of Chicago Press, 1939.

95. Welch, J. E., "Edward Hitchcock, M. D., Founder of Physical Education in the College Curriculum." Ed.D. dissertation, George Peabody College for Teachers, 1962.

96. Weston, Arthur. _The Making of American Physical Education_. New York: Appleton-Century-Crofts, 1962, 319 p.

97. Woodward, W. H. _Vittorino da Feltre and Other Humanist Educators_. Cambridge: Cambridge University Press, 1905, 261 p.

98. Woody, Thomas. _Life and Education in Early Societies_. New York: The Macmillan Company, 1949, 825 p.

99. Woolley, Leonard. _History Unearthed_. London: Ernest Benn Limited, 1963.

100. Zeigler, Earle F. _Persistent Problems in the History and Philosophy of Physical Education and Sport_. Englewood Cliffs, New Jersey: Prentice-Hall, Inc., 1968.

101. _____. (edited, with introductory and selected essays). _A History of Physical Education and Sport: Selected Readings_. Pacific Palisades, California: Goodyear Publishing Company, 1971. (in press)

102. Zeigler, Earle F., Howell, Maxwell L., and Trekell, Marianna. _Research in the History, Philosophy, and Comparative Aspects of Physical Education and Sport: Techniques and Bibliographies_. Champaign, Ill.: Stipes Publishing Company, 1971.

SELECTED HISTORICAL THESES ON PHYSICAL EDUCATION AND SPORT
(Related to Persistent Historical Problems Identified
by E. F. Zeigler)

1. Values

Edmonson, Cornelia, "A Continuum of Thought on the Value of Health, Physical
Education and Recreation from the Time of John Locke through the Twentieth
Century." Ph.D. dissertation, University of Washington, 1968.

Ervin, Janet R., "Education of the Physical versus Education through the Physical from 1607 - 1964." Ph.D. dissertation, University of California, 1965.

Felshin, Janet R., "Changing Conceptions of the Purpose in Physical Education
in the United States from 1880 to 1930." Ph.D. dissertation, University
of California, Los Angeles, 1958.

Gerber, Ellen W., "Three Interpretations of the Role of Physical Education,
1930-1960: Charles Harold McCloy, Jay Bryan Nash, and Jesse Feiring
Williams." Ph.D. dissertation, University of Southern California, 1966.

Hess, Ford A., "American Objectives of Physical Education from 1900 - 1957
Assessed in Light of Certain Historical Events." Ed.D. dissertation,
New York University, 1959.

Lynn, Minnie L., "Major Emphases of Physical Education in the United States."
Ph.D. dissertation, University of Pittsburgh, 1944.

Sherman, Atara P., "Theoretical Foundations of Physical Education in the
United States: 1886 - 1930." Ph.D. dissertation, University of Southern
California, 1965.

2. Politics

Hill, Phyllis J., "A Cultural History of Frontier Sport in Illinois, 1673-1820."
Ph.D. dissertation, University of Illinois, Urbana, 1966.

3. Nationalism

Drew, A Gwendolyn, "A Historical Study of the Concern of the Federal Government
for the Physical Fitness of Non-age Youth with Reference to the Schools, 1790 -
1941." Ph.D. dissertation, University of Pittsburgh, 1941.

Nash, Willard L., "A Study of the Stated Aims and Purposes of the Departments
of Military Science and Tactics and of Physical Education in Land-Grant
Colleges of the United States." Ph.D. dissertation, Columbia University,
1934.

Fuoss, Donald E., "An Analysis of the Incidents in the Olympic Games from 1924 -
1948 with Reference to the Contribution of the Games to International Goodwill
and Understanding." Ed.D. dissertation, Teachers College, Columbia University,
1951.

4. Economics

Hill, Phyllis J., "A Cultural History of Frontier Sport in Illinois, 1673 - 1820." Ph.D. dissertation, University of Illinois, Urbana, 1966.

Williams, Samuel A., "The Growth of Physical Education in the State Teachers Colleges of New York in Relation to Certain Socio-Economic Factors." Ph.D. dissertation, New York University, 1950.

5. Religion

Ballou, Ralph B., "An Analysis of the Writings of Selected Church Fathers to A.D. 394 to Reveal Attitudes Regarding Physical Activity." Ph.D. dissertation, University of Oregon, 1965.

Hill, Phyllis J. (see above under Economics)

Simri, Uriel, "The Religious and Magical Funtctions of Ball Games in Various Cultures." Ed.D. dissertation, University of West Virginia, 1966. (see Swanson at end of list)
6. Ecology (Man's Use of His Environment)

Ditton, Robert B., "Recreation and Water Resources: A Critical Analysis of Selected Literature." Ph.D. dissertation, University of Illinois, 1969.

Carls, E. Glenn, "The Role of Outdoor Recreation: An Ecological Approach." Unpublished paper, Dept. of Recreation and Park Administration, University of Illinois, Spring, 1970.

7. Professional Preparation

Gilcoyne, Katherine, "The Professional Preparation of Women for Physical Education in the First Half of the Twentieth Century." Ed.D. dissertation, Teachers College, Columbia University, 1958.

Pierro, Armstead A., "A History of Professional Preparation for Physical Education in Selected Negro Colleges and Universities, 1924 - 1958." Ph.D. dissertation, The University of Michigan, 1962.

Zeigler, Earle F., "A History of Professional Preparation for Physical Education in the United States, 1861 - 1948." Ph.D. dissertation, Yale University, 1951.

8. Methods of Instruction

Arasteh, Abdolreza, "Foundations of Modern Educational Methods." Louisiana State, 1953.

Wollitz, Norman E., "An Inquiry into Current Trends in Modern Educational Practice. Columbia. 1960

Note: These studies, and especially their related literature chapters, should have implications and information for this topic as it applies to physical education and sport.

9. Administration (Management)

Note: Administration and/or management has not been treated historically, but related literature chapters in recent studies give some background on this subject as a persistent problem.

Paton, Garth A., "An Analysis of Administrative Theory in Selected Graduate Administration Courses in Physical Education," Ph.D. dissertation, University of Illinois, Urbana, 1970.

Spaeth, Marcia J.,"An Analysis of Administrative Research in Physical Education and Athletics in Relation to a Research Paradigm." Ph.D. dissertation, University of Illinois, Urbana, 1967.

10. The Concept of Health

Casey, Leslie R., "A Topical Analysis of College Hygiene Textbooks, 1922 to 1951." Ed.D. dissertation, Teachers College, Columbia University, 1956.

Piper, David L., "Historical Study of the Concepts Underlying Health Education (Ancient Times to 1800). Ph.D. dissertation, Yale University, 1948.

11. The Use of Leisure

Holliman, Jennie, "American Sports (1785-1835)." Ph.D. dissertation, Columbia University, 1931.

McGrath, Thomas S., "Sport and Outdoor Amusements in America from 1865 to 1875." M.A. thesis, Teachers College, Columbia University, 1932.

Woody, Thomas, "Leisure in the Light of History." In Recreation in the Age of Motivation, September , 1957 issue (Vol. 313) of The Annals (Thorsten Sellin, ed.), Philadelphia, Penna.
    (see Swanson at end of list)

12. Amateurism, Semi-Professionalism, and Professionalism

Boycheff, Kooman, "Intercollegiate Athletics and Physical Education at the University of Chicago, 1892-1952." Ph.D. dissertation, The University of Michigan, 1954.

Dauer, Victor, "The Amateur Code for American Athletics." The University of Michigan, 1949.

Fall, Charles R., "An Examination of the Amateur Code in the United States." Ed.D. dissertation, Teachers College, Columbia University, 1949.

Flath, Arnold W. "A History of the Relationship Between the National Collegiate Athletic Association and the Amateur Athletic Union of the United States (1905-1963)." Ph.D. dissertation, The University of Michigan, 1963.

Korsgaard, Robert, "A History of the Amateur Athletic Union of the United States." Ed.D. dissertation, Teachers College, Columbia University, 1952.

Davenport, Joanna, "The History and Interpretation of Amateurism in the United States Lawn Tennis Association." Ph.D. dissertation, The Ohio State University, 1966.

13. Dance in Physical Education and Recreation

Ashton, Dudley, "An Ethnologic Approach to Regional Dance." Ph.D. dissertation,
State University of Iowa, 1951.

Fortenberry, Helen, "An Investigation of the Types and Forms of Dance Existing
from 476 to 1500." Master of Education thesis, Woman's College, University of
North Carolina, 1955.

Weber, Thomas E., "An Historical Analysis of the Place of Dance in Undergraduate
Men's Professional Physical Education in the United States." Master's thesis,
University of Illinois, Urbana, 1965.
        (see O'Brien at end of list)

14. Physical Education and Sport for Women

Greene, Margaret D., "The Growth of Physical Education for Women in the United
States in the Early Nineteenth Century." Ph.D. dissertation, University of
California, Los Angeles, 1950.

Trekell, Marianna, "The Effect of Cultural Changes on the Sports Activities
of American Women, 1860-1953." Master's thesis, The Ohio State University,
1953.

Watts, Doris P. "Changing Conception of Competitive Sports for Girls and Women
in the United States from 1880-1960." Ph.D. dissertation, University of
California, Los Angeles, 1960.

Zeigler, Earle F. "A Brief History of Physical Education and Sport for
Women." Unpublished paper, 1967.

15. The Concept of Progress

Note: No theses or dissertations on this topic have been written in this
field (?).

Bury, J. B. The Idea of Progress. New York: Dover Publications, Inc., 1955.

Brubacher, John S. A History of the Problems of Education (2nd Edition).
New York: McGraw-Hill Book Company, 1966. (See Chapter 19, p. 581 et ff.)

Commager, Henry Steele, "A Quarter Century - Its Advances," Look, 25, No.
10(June 6, 1961), 80-91.

Curti, Merle. The Growth of American Thought. New York: Harper & Row,
Publishers, 1943.

Simpson, George G. The Meaning of Evolution. New Haven and London: Yale
University Press, 1949.

(List under Religion and Use of Leisure: Swanson, Richard A., "American
Protestantism and Play." Ph.D. dissertation, The Ohio State University, 1967.

(List under Dance in PE and Rec.: O'Brien, Dorothy A., "Theoretical Foundations
of Dance in American Higher Education, 1885-1932." Ph.D. dissertation, Univ.
of Southern California, 1966.)

College of Physical Education   Name: _____
PE 402 - History of Physical Education
            and Sport   Grade: _____

Time: Two Hours

Instructions: Eliminate any <u>two</u> of the questions that you wish. Allow yourself
approximately twenty minutes for each of the <u>six</u> questions that you answer. Outline some of your answers, if you feel that you can cover more information that way.
Don't feel that you have to do this, however. Make every effort to answer succinctly
and yet as completely as possible in the time that you have.

1. Discuss historical method as fully as possible within the time limit allotted.

2. Make an assessment of the various histories of physical education.

3. Which of the reserve shelf books which you read impressed you most? Please
    elaborate on your reasons for selecting this book.

4. a) Name, and describe briefly, as many of the persistent historical problems as
        you can that were listed in the course outline.

    b) Can you suggest any others that might be included?

5. Select one persistent historic l problem (other than the one you prepared as a
    term paper) and outline it broadly throughout hi. tory.

6. Discuss what you felt were the strengths and weaknesses of the doctoral disserta-
    tion which you reported on in the class. Give the title and the name of the
    name of the author.

7. List some key dates throughout history - especially those which were important
    for the history of physical education. Identify each very briefly.

8. Trace the evolution of physical education in the United States in fairly broad
    outline.

EFZ:cms/7/28/64/50

FINAL EXAMINATION

Graduate Department of Physical Education   Name: _____
PE 402 - History of Physical Education
   and Sport   Grade: _____

<u>Note</u>: This examination would normally take about <u>three</u> hours to complete, unless a decision is made that it will be administered as a take-home final examination.

1. In the former case, eliminate any <u>two</u> of the questions that you wish. Allow yourself approximately thirty minutes for each of the <u>six</u> questions that you answer. Outline some of your answers, if you feel that you can cover more information that way. Make every effort to answer succinctly and yet as completely as possible in the time available.

2. In the latter case, all <u>eight</u> questions should be answered, and the time involved in the answering of the questions should presumably not take much more time than the three hours mentioned above <u>and</u> the time that would normally be spent in preparation for such an examination. In any case, do not write more than the equivalent of two single-spaced pages in answering each question.

I. Historians seem to like to classify their efforts as scientific in nature. How can they make such a claim?

II. There are a number of books in the English language that may be classified as histories of physical education. Evaluate each of them briefly.

III. Of all of the books on the reserve shelf, select the one which impressed you most. Please elaborate on your reasons for selecting this particular book.

IV. Summarize <u>each</u> of the persistent historical problems in <u>one</u> paragraph.

Would you delete any of these from the list, or would you add any others? If so, please substantiate your opinion.

V. Select one persistent problem that interested you most and outline a broad history of this particular problem throughout history.

VI. Give the title and name of the author of the historical study that you abstracted. Discuss its strengths and weaknesses.

VII. List, and identify briefly, key dates throughout history which were important for the history of physical education.

VIII. Trace the evolution of physical education in the United States in fairly broad outline.

V. AMERICAN SPORT HISTORY

Summer 1985   Professor Beezley
737-2483   HA 108   1pm daily

Reading:
John Lucas and Ronald Smith, Saga of American Sport
Bill Beezley, The Wolfpack...Intercollegiate Athletics at NCSU (from Kinko's)
Don Mrozek, Sport and American Mentality, 1880-1910
Jules Tygiel, Jackie Robinson and His Legacy
William H. Beezley, Locker Rumors: The Folklore of Football (Nelson-Hall)

assignments:
For the first hour examination: June 3
Lucas and Smith, chapters 1-14 (pp. 3-249)
Beezley, Wolfpack, section one 'pp. 1-60.

For the second hour examination: June 13
Lucas and Smith, chapters 15-18 (pp. 250-328)
Beezley, Wolfpack, section two pp. 61-144.
Mrozek, Sport and American Mentality, 1880-1910 (entire book)

For the third hour examination: June 26
Lucas and Smith, chapters 19-23 (pp. 329-423)
Beezley, section three pp. 145-332.
Jules Tygiel, Jackie Robinson and His Legacy (entire book)
Beezley, Locker Rumors (entire book)

Writing:
Each student is required to write five 3-5 typewritten papers (handwritten
papers are acceptable if they are 750-1,250 words in length, written on every other
line). These papers are due on May 27, June 3, 10, 17, and 24. In order the
topics of the papers are: a sport autobiography; sport in Raleigh as reported
in the News & Observer; interview with a successful athlete; book review;
and sport in Raleigh as reported in the News & Observer.   Specifics about
these papers will be announced in class. The papers based on the News and Observer
will require the student to report on sport during the month and year assigned by
the instructor.

course grades:
each exam and essay have a value of 100 points. Grades will be determined by
the traditional percentages: 90% and above equals an A (that is, 720 or more
points); 80-89% (or 640 to 719 points) equals a B; 70-79% (560 to 639 points)
a C; 60 to 69% (480 to 559 points) a D, fewer than 480 points, no credit.

Because no one can make a perfect grade (40 points) on an essay question on the
examinations or on the written work (100 points), there are a few points that
are impossible for the student to make. There are following opportunities for
bonus points. HAWAIIAN SHIRT DAY. Hawaiian shirt day will be scheduled by the
student Hawaiian shirt day coordinator. Each class member who wears a Hawaiian
shirt to class on that day will receive 3 bonus points. Field trips: The
class will make at least one field trip to see the Durham Bulls play baseball.
Students will receive bonus points for attending the game. A second field trip
may be made (depending on the interests of the class) to a pro wrestling entertainment. Again bonus points will be given.

Big Casino. Each student has the option to join the Big Casino or may be placed in it. A student will have the chance to gamble on the Big Casino on the fifth absence (class attendance begins on May 23; there are no excused absences), failing to submit a paper on or before the beginning of class on the day it is due (no late papers are accepted) or failing to take an examination (no make-ups are permitted). The big casino relieves the student of all class requirements; the student gambles his or her course grade on a three-hour comprehensive final test. The big casino exam consists of two hour-long essay questions and 100 short answer (that is, fill-in-the-blank) questions based on the reading and lectures.

To confine ourselves to the modern world, if we
compare the horse races in London, the bull fights
in Madrid, the spectacles of former days in Paris,
the gondola races in Venice, the animal baiting
in Vienna and the gay, attractive life of the
Corso at Rome, it cannot be difficult to differen-
tiate subtly between the tastes of these several
peoples.

Friedrich Schiller, Letters on the Aesthetic
    Education of Man   (1795)

Sport is a great clue to national character, and
especially to the American character, it is an
important part of our existence and has had a
far-reaching effect upon our clothes, customs,
and culture. Despite its impact, few conscious
efforts have been made by historians or sociologists to assess sport and our attitudes toward
it. As a nation we have accepted sport. One
wonders whether the American people are quite
aware of what has taken place. Nobody had asked
why this thing has become such a tremendous factor
in our lives or summed up the end results for
good or bad.

John R. Tunis

History 34:322 or Physical Education 30:322　　　　　　　　　　　Spring, 1986
American Sports History　　　　　　　　　　　　　　　　　　　　　Porter

　　　　This course is an introductory survey of the basic themes and issues in
American Sports history. It will examine the development of American Sport since
the Colonial Era and assess the historical impact of athletics on American
society and culture. Classes consist of lectures, discussion, and debates. You
will be expected to do all the readings.

Required Texts:

Benjamin Rader, American Sports: From the Age of Folk Games to the Age of
　　　　Spectators
James Michener, Sports in America
William Baker and John Carroll, eds., Sports in Modern America

Course Schedule　　　　Topics　　　　　　　Reading Assignments

Jan. 15-Feb. 7　　　　Sport to 1850　　　　Michener, all; Rader, Ch. 1-2
Feb. 10-Mar. 5　　　　Sport, 1850-1920　　Rader, Ch. 3-8; Baker, Ch. 1-4
Mar. 7-May 3　　　　　Sport since 1920　　Rader, Ch. 9-18; Baker, Ch. 5-13

Examinations:　　Wednesday, March 5, 1986
　　　　　　　　　Tuesday, May 6, 1986 (1-3)

Grading: Each examination will count 33 percent of the total grade and will
consist primarily of essays stressing lectures, discussion, and reading material.
Examinations will be taken in Blue Books, available from the Bookstore. No
make-up examination will be given unless you have a college-approved excuse
and notify me prior to the examination. The remaining 33 percent of the total
grade will be based on discussion, debate, and a paper.

Debate and Paper: There will be several sessions for classroom debates on pertinent issues in American Sports history. You will be responsible for helping
lead one such debate on a particular issue. You will be expected to do considerable library research prior to class so that you will be well prepared to debate
the topic. You also will be expected to summarize your presentation in a five
to ten page documented typewritten paper due one period before the date of the
debate. The dates and specific topics of the debates will be announced early
in the semester.

Extra Credit: You may write an optional five to ten page paper on some pertinent
topic in American Sports history. Papers should be documented and include
description and analysis. Please consult me about topic selection and proper
procedures. No paper will be accepted after Monday, April 28, 1986.

Office Hours:　9:30-10:15 Monday, Wednesday, Friday, or by appointment
Location:　　　Room 110B Penn Hall
Office Phone:　Extension 263
Home Phone:　　673-7609

American Sport History Debate Schedule

<u>Monday, March 24</u> – NCAA Division I college football and basketball players should be paid for their athletic services.

Participants: Bryon Ewing, Mike Han, Dan Reed, Eric Seskis

<u>Monday, March 31</u> – "Redshirting" should be prohibited in NCAA Division I college football and basketball.

Participants: Bill Gernan, Terry Hendershott, Dan Just, Mike Winters

<u>Monday, April 7</u> – Drug testing should be made mandatory for all professional athletes.

Participants: Adrian Banks, Jeff McNulty, Pat Milks, Joe Sales

<u>Monday, April 14</u> – Freshmen should be barred from participation in NCAA Division I varsity college football competition.

Participants: Bill Amuso, Roy Moorman, Bobby Peak, Joey Townsell

<u>Monday, April 21</u> – There should be a playoff to determine the NCAA Division I national college football champion.

Participants: Tom Arter, Tom Lee, Joseph Marin, David Van Ersvelde

<u>Monday, April 28</u> – Academic admission requirements should be upgraded for NCAA Division I college athletes.

Participants: Chuck Brooks, Scott Farrington, Bill Hardy, Marty Polka, Bob Snow

HISTORY OF SPORT IN AMERICA
P.E. 441 with Ronald A. Smith
M.W.F. 11:15-12:05 Fall 1984

Basic Course Outline

Lecture-Discussion No.
1. Sport and Social History: Introduction and Orientation
2. Sport in America in the 1980s
3. The English Background for American Sport
4. Sports and Games of the American Indians
5. The Puritans: A Radical Approach to Life and Sport
6. Sport in Puritan New England
7. The Sporting Virginia Colonists
8. Quakers, Blue Laws, and Colonial Pennsylvania Sport
9. Colonial Sport at the Time of the Revolution
10. American Sports: Revolution to the Mid-1800s
11. Industrial and Urban America: Keys to Organized Sport
12. New York City: Leader of American Sport
    Mid-Term
13. Baseball: The Great American Game—The National Pastime
14. The Rise of Professional Baseball
15. Two Nations—Two Myths: William Webb Ellis and Abner Doubleday
16. Education and the Growth of College Sport
17. Intercollegiate Athletics: From Student to Faculty Control
18. Crew: The First Intercollegiate Sport
19. Winning and a Theory of Competitive Sport in America
20. Football: Soccer, to Rugby, to Number One College Sport
21. The Development of the NCAA and the Football Controversy
22. Aspects of Intercollegiate Football
23. The "Nouveau Riche" and 19th Century Sport
24. The Concept of Amateurism in American Sport
25. The AAU-NCAA Conflict: Amateur Sport's Battleground
26. Laissez Faire Mentality and Sport
    Mid-Term
27. The Place of Blacks in Sport in Jim Crow America
28. Boxing and Blacks: Symbolic of American Society
29. Desegregation or Integration: Blacks and Post-World War II Sport
30. Women in Sport: Spooning, Hitting, and Wheeling
31. Competitive vs. Non-Competitive Sport for Women
32. Colleges and Schools as Leaders of Non-Competitive Sport for Women
33. The Women's Movement, Title IX, and the Growth of Sport for Women
34. Sport in the Roaring Twenties
35. The Olympics as the Pinnacle of Non-professional Sport
36. The Berlin Olympics of 1936: Politics in Sport
37. Sport During the Depression and the Impact of World War II
38. The Dynamics of Television on Commercialized Sport
39. Labor Unions and Collective Bargaining in Professional Sports
40. The Pro-College Monopoly: Transfer Rule, Draft, and Option Clause
41. Violence in Sport: Legal Noise or Substance?
42. International Sport Since World War II
43. Sport as an Aesthetic Experience
    Final

P.E. 441 ASSIGNED READINGS AND CRITICAL ORAL REVIEW

Required_Readings

There are about 30 required readings in P.E. 441 in addition to a
text. You are to read the appropriate material before the class
period in which it is to be discussed. Wehn reading the articles,
you should take short notes on the following:
---the author's theme or major contention,
---criticism of the article, both positive and negative, and
---questions which you have regarding the article, or comments on
   the article.
It is suggested that each article be recorded on a 5 x 8 card so that
when the class discusses the article you can take out your card to
review the article. Part of your educational experience in this
class should be the interaction_with_others concerning material you
have read_collectively.

Critical_Reviews

1. Each student will have the opportunity to critically review one of
   the required readings. This will be a verbal review in class of
   5 minutes or less.
2. It is to be a critical_review,_not_a_summary of the article. (It
   is assumed that everyone will have read the article prior to
   your review.
3. The presentation should be limited to 4 or 5 minutes (practice
   helps).
4. Some of the things you should be concerned about are:
   1) Who is the author? (See if you can find out. Pattee Reference
      Room might be helpful. Start with the Biography_and_Geneology
      Master_Index. [Ask at the main desk.] See also, for instance,
      the Social Science and Humanities Citation Index; Directory of
      American Scholars [Vol. I History; Vol. II English; Vol. IV
      philosophy-Religion-Law]; Who's Who; Who Was Who; Dictionary
      of American Biography; and Current Biography.)
   2) What is the author's major_emphasis, thesis, or contention?
   3) Does the author prove his point?
   4) Does the article shed_light on the history of sport or on the
      present sport scene?
   5) Has the author used facts or opinions? Is the article biased?
   6) Has the article evinced or revealed any new_thoughts on your
      part or has it reinforced any of your ideas?
   7) Is the article worthy?
5. Your review can include anything else you believe is worthy or
   which might stimulate discussion.
6. It is important to include your own personal experience.
7. Remember, this is NOT A SUMMARY of the article, it is a CRITICAL
   REVIEW. You do some THINKING ON YOUR OWN which will add meaning
   to the article or to sport.

P.E. 441 READINGS

The Modern Scene

1. Keating, James W., "Winning in Sport and Athletics," Thought, XXXVII (Summer 1963), 201-210.
2. Sullivan, Robert, "The Legacy of These Games," Sports Illustrated, LXI (20 August 1984), 96-99.
3. Deford, Frank, "Cheer, Cheer, Cheer for the Home Team," Sports Illustrated, LXI (13 August 1984), 38-41.
4. Alfano, Peter, "The Tug-of-War. . ." New York Times, 27 March 1983), Sec. S, pp. 1, 9.
5. Reid, Ron, "This Stones Left None Unturned," Sports Illustrated, L (2 April 1979), 22-23.
6. "Pride in Being Part of the Team," Sports Illustrated, LIV (23 February 1981), 79.
7. Thurow, Lester, "Where's America's Old Team Spirit?" New York Times, 26 July 1981, Sec. 3, p. 3.

Colonial Era

1. Lucas and Smith, Saga of American Sport, 1978, pp. 3-54.
2. King James I, "Book of Sports," 1618, 4 p.
3. Mather, Increase, "An Arrow Against Profane and Promiscuous Dancing," in Perry Miller, The Puritans. NY: Harper & Row, 1963, pp. 411-413.
4. Breen, T. H. "Horses and Gentlemen: The Cultural Significane of Gambling Among the Gentry of Virginia," William and Mary Quarterly, XXXIV (April 1977), 239-257.

American Revolution to the Civil War

1. Lucas and Smith, Saga of American Sport, 1978, pp. 55-121.
2. Jable, J. Thomas, "Aspects of Moral Reform in Nineteenth Century Pennsylvania," Pennsylvania Magazine of History and Biography, CII (July 1978), 344-363.
3. Miles, Edwin A., "President Adams' Billiard Table," The New England Quarterly, XLV (March 1972), 31-43.
4. Dulles, Foster Rhea, "The Frontier," A History of Recreation: America Learns to Play, 2nd ed., NY: Appleton-Century-Crofts, 1965, pp.67-83.
5. MacLeod, Duncan, "Racing to War: Antebellum Match Races Between the North and the South," Southern Exposure, VII (Fall 1979), pp. 7-10.

Rise of Organized Sport Including College Athletics

1. Lucas and Smith, Saga of American Sport, 1978, pp. 125-249.
2. Lucas, John A., "Pedestrianism and the Struggle for the Sir John Astley Belt," Research Quarterly, XXXIX (October 1968), pp. 587-593.
3. Mathews, Joseph, "The First Harv 1-Oxford Boat Race," New England Quarterly, XXXIII (March 196 74-82.
4. Bourget, Paul, "American Pleasur ," Outre-Mer: Impressions of America. NY: Charles Scribner's Sons, 1895, pp. 326-333.
5. Rader, Benjamin G., "The Impact of Sports on the Social Elites," in William J. Baker and John M. Carroll (eds.), Sports in Modern America. St. Louis: River City, 1981, pp. 17-26.
6. Deford, Frank, "Homecoming: Princeton 1957-1962," Sports Illustrated, LI (22 October 1979), pp. 96-98.
7. Jones, Richard W., "Are Pro Football's Roots in Pittsburgh?" Pittsburgh Press, 9 November 1980, p. 3.

Twentieth Century Sport

1. Lucas and Smith, Saga of American Sprt, 1978, pp. 250-413.
2. Epernay, Mark, "Allston Wheat's Crusade," Harper's Magazine, CCXXVI (May 1963), pp. 53-57.
3. Kennedy, Robert F., "A Bold Proposal for American Sport," Sports Illustrated, XXI (27 July 1964), pp. 12-15.
4. Roberts, Randy, "Boxing and Reform," in William J. Baker and John M. Carroll (eds.), Sports and Modern America. St. Louis: River City, 1981, pp. 27-38.
5. Roberts, Randy, "Prologue: Scars," and "Love and Hate," in his Papa Jack: Jack Johnson and the Era of White Hopes. New York: Free Press, 1983. pp. xi-xiii and 155-168.
6. Edwards, Harry, "Educating Black Athletes," Atlantic Monthly, CCLII (August 1983), 31-36.
7. Twin, Stephanie L., "Introduction," Out of the Bleachers: Writings on Women and Sport. Old Westbury, NY: The Feminist Press, 1979, pp. xv-xli.
8. Brooks, Christine, "The Day They All Fell!" Scholastic Coach, L (December 1980), pp. 59-60, 84.
9. Davenport, Jody, "Eleonora Sears," in Reet Howell (ed.), Her Story in Sport. West Point, NY: Leisure Press, 1982, pp. 266-272.
10. Emery, Lynne, "First Intercollegiate Contest for Women," in Reet Howell (ed.), Her Story in Sport. West Point, NY: Leisure Press, 1982), pp. 417-423.
11. Kruger, Arnd, "'Fair Play for American Athletes' A Study of Anti-Semitism," Canadian Journal of History of Sport and Physical Education, IX (May 1978), pp. 43-57.
12. Guttmann, Allen, "The Games Must Go On: On the Origins of Avery Brundage's Life-Credo," Stadion, V, 2 (1979), pp. 253-262.
13. Santayana, George, "Philosophy on the Bleachers," Harvard Monthly, XVIII (July 1894), 181-190.

Written Critique (Due Wednesday, August 29, 1984)

Each member of class is responsible to write a 3 page critique of the first 7 articles, "The Modern Scene" of the assigned readings. The critique should be typed double-spaced and consist of the following:

1. No cover page, but at the top of the first page should be a title, P.E. 441, date, and your name.
2. Following a 4 line break, write 7 paragraphs giving an overview of each of the 7 articles. (Make each paragraph a concise, generalizing one.)
3. This will be followed by finding 2 themes which run through a majority of the articles and writing a paragraph on each. In your paragraphs discuss the theme and how each of the authors approached the theme.
4. Using the 6th and 7th articles, write a paragraph relating any two other articles to the theme of the 6th and 7th articles.
5. Complete your 3 page paper with a paragraph on which of the seven articles was most meaningful and why it gave meaning to you.

HISTORY OF SPORT IN AMERICAN SOCIETY

TERM PAPER

> I think that the purpose of higher education is to establish the right habit of thinking, by which I mean thinking that holds its conclusions open to revision and is ready to consider any new evidence that is apparently reliable. That habit I believe is better acquired by a wide acquaintance with history, letters, and the arts than by specialized but limited disciplines. The main thing is what will be the student's temper of approach to his problem when he gets through. (Judge Learned Hand)

An important part of this course will consist of an independent historical research project on some aspect of the history of American sport. You will be expected to choose a subject which can be researched in depth. To be successful a small aspect of some sport, movement, personality, or controversy should be chosen as your focus. You are to:

1) Select an event of your choice (see next page for examples),
2) Compile a list of primary sources (first hand accounts) of the event,
3) Obtain at least two secondary sources (second hand accounts such as history books) on the general subject of your research,
4) Take notes on your primary sources and compare with your secondary sources,
5) Digest your material,
6) Write an historical narrative (story) based on your research from seven to twelve pages in length,
   --In your own words tell the reader what happened,
   --Show the significance of the event,
   --Tie the event into the larger picture of sport and society,
7) Write in a scholarly manner,
   --Write in past tense primarily,
   --Show evidence of using primary sources,
   --Use quotes if appropriate, but with discrimination (quotes of more than three lines should be single spaced and indented),
   --Use statements which you can substantiate,
   --Footnote all statements which are not commonly known,
   --Footnote consecutively (1,2,3, etc.) throughout the paper and collect them on a separate page(s) at the end of the narrative,
   --Develop paragraphs from topic sentences,
   --Have smooth transitions between paragraphs,
   --Include a bibliography of primary and secondary sources in alphabetical order on a separate page at the end of the paper,
8) Type the paper, being sure to double space and paginate,
9) Include no cover page; on the first page include at the top:
   --Title of your paper,
   --Your name,
   --P.E. 441,
   --The date,
   --Follow this with your narrative,
10) Turn in your paper in duplicate (xerox or carbon) to your instruction on Monday, November 26th.

This paper, in short, should consist of:
1) Selecting an appropriate topic,
2) Finding relevant evidence (See Information Retrieval on next page),
3) Taking notes on it,
4) Evaluating your evidence, and
5) Arranging it into a true and meaningful pattern.

PRIMARY SOURCES AND INFORMATION RETRIEVAL

It is likely that the primary sources for your research will be found in contemporary newspapers and periodicals, though some may be found in such sources
as autobiographies, memoirs, reminiscences, and diaries. Some indices for
newspapers (generally found in Pattee microform room) and periodicals (generally found in Pattee reference room) are as follows:

Periodicals	Newspapers
Readers Guide to Periodical Literature (1900-present)	New York Times Index (1851-present)
Nineteenth Century Readers Guide (1890-1899)	New York Tribune Index (1876-1909)
	Christian Science Monitor Index (1960-present)
Poole's Index to Periodical Literature (1802-1906)	Wall Street Journal Index (1955-present)
	Washington Post Index (1971-present)
Education Index (1929-present)	Atlantic Constitution Index (1971-present)
International Index (1907-1965)	Chicago Tribune Index (1972-present)
Social Science and Humanities Index (1965-present)	Los Angeles Times Index (1972-present)
	New Orleans Times-Picayune Index (1972-present)
Biography Index (1946-present)	Index to Black Newspapers (1977-present)
	Philadelphia Inquirer Index (1978-present)
	London Times Index (1786-present)
	Virginia Gazette Index (1736-1780)
	New York Times Name Index (1851-1974)

Some useful Sources include:
1.) List of newspapers on microfilm in Microform Room of Pattee
2.) Spirit of the Times (1831-1903) on microfilm in Microform Room of Pattee
3.) The Sporting News (1886-1946) on microfilm in Microform Room of Pattee
4.) Outing Magazine (1888-1923) in stacks at Pattee
5.) Harper's Weekly (1857-1916) in stacks at Pattee
6.) Frank Leslie's Illustrated (1858-1904) in stacks at Pattee
7.) Sports Illustrated (1954-present) in stacks at Pattee
8.) Journal of Sport History (1974-present) in stacks at Pattee and Lawther
   Reading Room
9.) New York Clipper (1868-1903) on microfilm in Microform Room of Pattee

FOOTNOTES

Purpose: Footnotes are used to give information about the materials on which
the paper is based; to explain and amplify statements made in the text; and to
protect the writer against the charge of plagiarism and improper use of materials.
References should be given for all important statements of fact requiring proof,
and for any inference or interpretation borrowed from another writer. Footnotes should be numbered consecutively for the entire paper. The index number
should be written above the line at the end of the passage to which it refers.
The footnote citations may be gathered at the end of the paper (endnotes)
rather than at the bottom of the page.

Citation: The first time a work is cited in a footnote, complete bibliographical
information should be given as follows:
1.) The author's, editor's, or compiler's name, in normal order (first name,
   middle initial, and surname),
2.) The exact title. Titles of books, pamphlets, periodicals, and newspapers
   are underlined; titles of articles within periodicals or books are enclosed
   in quotation marks, and precede the periodical or book in which they are found,
3.) The place and date of publication in parentheses (preceded, where appli-
   cable, by the number of volumes if more than one, the series title and series
   volume number, and the number of the edition). See examples below.
4.) The page reference.

Examples of Complete Citations; Books, Periodicals, and Newspapers

[1]John A. Lucas and Ronald A. Smith, _Saga of American Sport_ (Philadelphia: Lea & Febiger, 1978), 211.

[2]James G. Thompson, "Solon on Athletics," _Journal of Sport History_, V (Spring 1978), 23.

[3]"Shall Intercollegiate Football Be Abolished," _Literary Digest_, LXXXVII (October 10, 1925), 68-78. (This form is used if the author is unknown).

[4]_New York Times_, January 23, 1909, p. 12.

Shortened form of Citation

Subsequent references to the same work need include only (1) the surname of the author, (2) a shortened form of the title, and (3) page references, thus:

[5]Lucas and Smith, _Saga of American Sport_, 127.

If a footnote is immediately followed on the same page by another note citing the same work, the Latin abbreviation "Ibid." (for ibidem, "in the same place") may be substituted for author and title, thus:

[6]Lucas and Smith, _Saga of American Sport_, 205

[7]Ibid., 303 (that is, Lucas and Smith, _Saga of American Sport_, 303)

BIBLIOGRAPHY

The bibliography should list all books, pamphlets, articles, newspapers, and documents used in the preparation of the paper. Arrangement should be alphabetical by author, editor, or title (newspapers and works published anonymously). You may wish to annotate your bibliography by describing in a sentence or two the scope or value of the work to your article. In a bibliography, where each entry stands by itself, periods rather than commas are used as punctuation; the second and succeeding lines are indented five spaced under the first; thus:

Atwell, Robert H. "Some Reflections on Collegiate Athletics," _Educational Record_, LX (Fall, 1979), 367-373.

Bennett, Patricia. "The History and Objectives of the National Section for Girls and Women's Sports," Ed.D. dissertation, Mills College, 1956. (Do not underline a thesis or dissertation title).

Chase, Stuart. "Play," _Whither Mankind_, Charles A. Beard, ed. New York: Longsman Green and Co., 1928, pp. 332-353.

Krout, John A. "Some Reflections on the Rise of American Sport," Association of History Teachers of Middle States and Maryland _Proceedings_, XXVI (1929), 84-93.

Lucas, John. "Early Olympic Antagonists: Pierre de Coubertin Versus James E. Sullivan," _Stadion_, III (1977), 258-272.

New York Times. January-June, 1890.

Philadelphia Inquirer. April 13, 1936, p. 1.

Smith, Ronald A. "The Paul Robeson--Jackie Robinson Saga and a Political Collission," _Journal of Sport History_, VI (Summer 1979), 5-27.

ELEMENTS OF STYLE

a. _Words_. A good dictionary or thesaurus will aid you in phrasing the exact meaning you wish to convey and in finding synonyms for overworked expressions. A fresh direction of approach to your line of thought may help you to eliminate cliches; and a walk about the room or a stroll around the block is sometimes the best way of finding the precise expression that fits your thought. If you must break a word at the end of a line, follow proper syllabification-- taking particular care in the case of proper names. Never leave a single letter from a word standing alone.

b. _Sentences_. Short, simple, declarative sentences that are predominantly in the active voice--but sufficiently varied to avoid monotony--should be the workhorses of your narration. Use adjectives sparingly, adverbs scarecely less so, and only when you are confident that they will stimulate rather than becloud the reader's imagination. Narration (a story which relates events) takes precedence over description, and both over prolonged commentary. You can normally gain in clarity by bringing as closely together as possible adjectives and the nouns which they describe, adverbs and the verbs they modify, and qualifying phrases or clauses and the things to which they relate. An occasional balanced sentence can, where appropriate, provide a touch of classical dignity, or an inverted one lead the way to a climax. Standard rules of punctuation serve, through habituated usage, as directional signs that help the reader to follow the nuances of your meaning. Often, however, you must exercise a choice as to whether a comma, dash, semicolon, or a period--each of them able to check the eye of the reader as an inflection of the voice or a pause does for the ear--best serves your purpose at any given point. The skilled and experienced writer can make his own exceptions to the rules. There is a military adage that "a good general does not place his army with its back to a river, unless he is of a mind to do so." The significant word here is "mind", indicating that there should be a good reason for an action contrary to accepted practice. But the beginner should be wary of incautious experimentation.

c. _Paragraphs_. In opening a paragraph, a topic sentence should serve as a bridge from the preceding paragraph--sometimes by echoing a key word or concept--and should announce the essence of what is to follow. The rest of the paragraph should then prove the thesis of the opening statement. The concluding sentence should be a summary or comment that serves as an approach to the next bridge. Occasionally it may offer a flourish or peroration on the rising note to drive home an idea. The opening and closing chapters of a book, together with the first and last paragraphs of each of the other chapters and the topic and concluding sentences of each of the other paragraphs--all in their proper sequence--should ideally, state the essence of the book in intelligible form. Use properly documented quotations where they will be most apt. Exercise the strictest economy of expression that will suffice to convey your full meaning. It is axiomatic that the more thoroughly you have mastered your subject, the more succinctly you can express it. Figures of speech and flecks of color can tone up a narrative; but immoderate indulgence arouses a distaste comparable to that of a banquet consisting entirely of pastries. Revision and rewriting consist largely of excision and condensation while, at the same time, bringing out the deeper meanings and larger implications of your subject. When you doubt the need for any word, phrase, or paragraph, eliminate it.

(From Wood Gray, and others, _Historian's Handbook_ [Boston, Houghton Miffling Co., 1964], pp. 85-86).

EXAMPLES OF SPORT RESEARCH TOPICS

1. Tom Molineux, American black champion boxer, fights Tom Cribb for the English championship in 1810 and 1811.
2. The great, May 1823, North-South horse race between Eclipse and Sir Henry at the Union Course on Long Island.
3. Early long distant foot races (pedestrianism) at the Union Course on Long Island in 1835.
4. Long distant races at Union Course on Long Island in 1844 and 1845.
5. The epic North-South, Fashion-Peytona horse race of May 1845 at Union Course.
6. The yacht of John Stevens, the "America", beats the English and the America's Cup is established in August 1851.
7. The Heenan-Sayers boxing match of April 1860 as seen by the English and Americans.
8. The attitudes of Americans when the crew from Harvard was defeated in the first international college crew race by Oxford in August 1869.
9. The Harvard University baseball team tours the country for a 44-10 record and nearly defeats the Cincinnati Red Stockings, July-August 1870.
10. The Cincinnati Red Stockings long win streak is ended by the Brooklyn Atlantics in June 1870.
11. The development of college track and field in colleges during the Intercollegiate Regattas at Saratoga, New York, 1873, 1874, and 1875.
12. Baseball is started at Penn State under Monty War in 1875.
13. The withdrawal of Yale and Harvard from the Intercollegiate Regatta at Saratoga causes the decline of national crew competition in 1875 and 1876.
14. Yale and Princeton play in the first national Thanksgiving Day football championship in 1876.
15. Americans and English view the outcomes of the Sir John Astley pedestrian matches in 1878 and 1879.
16. Canadian Champion sculler, Ned Hanlan, and American Charles Courtney are involved in a controversial rowing series, 1878-1880.
17. The place of athletics at Penn State in the 1880's.
18. The Player's League lasts one year in major league baseball, 1890.
19. The place of athletics at Penn State in the 1890's.
20. John L. Sullivan fights James J. Corbett for the heavyweight championship boxing match in New Orleans in September 1892.
21. Americans and English view the outcome of the first international track meet in New York in September 1895.
22. Bob Fitzsimmons and James J. Corbett fight for the heavyweight championship in Carson City, Nevada, 1897.
23. Major Taylor, black bicycle champion, races his greatest race against Jimmie Michaels at Manhattan Beach track in the summer of 1898.
24. Star baseball player Napoleon Lajoie of the Philadelphia Athletics is the center of the Pennsylvania Supreme Court battle over player contracts in 1901 and 1902.
25. The American League challenges the National League in the first modern World Series (1903).
26. May Sutton changes women's tennis by winning the U.S. title in May of 1904 and soon becomes the first Wimbledon Champion from America.
27. President Charles W. Eliot of Harvard takes on President Teddy Roosevelt on ethics in athletics: The rowing controversy of June 1908.
28. President Teddy Roosevelt entertains the Olympic Heroes from the London Olympics of 1908 in his home at Sagamore Hill, August-September 1908.
29. The disputed marathon race of Italy's Dorando Pietri in the July 1908, London Olympics leads to a rematch with Olympic winner, John Hayes in NYC, November 1908.

30. Greatest players of their times: Honus Wagner (Pittsburgh) competes against Ty Cobb (Detroit) in the 1909 World Series.
31. Race riots follow the Jack Johnson-Jim Jeffries "Great White Hope" boxing match in July of 1910.
32. Francis Ouimet of the U.S. defeats Harry Vardon in the U.S. Open and startles England, Summer 1913.
33. Jess Willard becomes the fulfilled "Great White Hope" when he defeats heavyweight champion, Jack Johnson, April 1915.
34. The U.S. dominates the Inter-Allied Games concluding American participation in World War I in Paris, France, June-July 1919.
35. Babe Ruth is traded from Boston to New York and sets the home run record in his first year with the Yankees, 1919.
36. Jack Dempsey becomes champion by defeating Jess Willard, Summer 1919.
37. The Black Sox World Series Scandal of 1919 breaks, September 1920.
38. The most important Supreme Court case in professional sport: Federal League Club of Baltimore v. National League, 295U.S.200 in 1922.
39. Track star Charlie Paddock participates in a Paris, France meet of collegians which leads to an NCAA-AAU conflict in May 1923.
40. Penn State goes to the 1923 Rose Bowl after a 6-3 season, Fall 1922.
41. Red Grange goes pro before graduation, Nov-Dec 1925 as does Hershel Walker, March 1983.
42. Helen Wills of the U.S. is beaten by Suzanne Lenglen of France in a show down tennis match in France, April 1926.
43. Gene Tunney beats Jack Dempsey in the famous long count boxing match of September 1927 after he defeats Dempsey a year earlier in Philadelphia.
44. Track star and Olympian, Charlie Paddock, fights his case of professionalism in July 1928.
45. Ray Conger, later Penn State professor, beats the great Paavo Nurmi at the Millrose Games in Madison Square Gardens, February 1929.
46. Women physical educators attempt to ban American women's participation in the Amsterdam Olympics of 1928 and the Los Angeles Olympics of 1932.
47. Controversy surrounds Babe Didrickson at the 1932 Olympics including the denial of a Gold medal in the high jump, August 1932.
48. Women physical educators inugurate play days to take the place of competitive athletics for women in the 1920's and early 1930's.
49. Babe Didrikson wins six gold medals and breaks four world records in a pre-Olympic, AAU meet in Evanston, Illinois, July 1932.
50. Jesse Owens sets or equals four world records in one track meet in May 1935 and continues to dominate track during the 1936 Berlin Olympics.
51. Blackman Joe Louis in racist America beats Nazi Max Schmelling from racist Germany in the first round boxing championship of June 1938.
52. Baseball's Hall of Fame opens in Cooperstown, New York, site of the fictitious origin of baseball, June 1939.
53. The first women's intercollegiate golf tourney creates great controversy among women physical educators when it was played at Ohio State University, Spring 1941.
54. The Daily Worker (Communist Newspaper in America) campaigns actively for the desegregation of major league baseball during World War II, starting in Spring 1942.
55. Babe Didrikson Zaharias, Patty Berg, and others begin the Ladies Professional Golf Association, 1949.
56. Drake University reacts to its black quarterback, Johnny Bright, being victimized by racial hatred in a game with Oklahoma A&M, October 1951.
57. A scandal breaks in football and basketball at William & Mary College, 1951.

58. The Soviets enter their first Olympics, Summer 1952.
59. Althea Gibson, the first Negro to play tennis in the U.S. Nationals at Forest Hills in May 1954.
60. Georgia Tech challenges Pittsburgh's playing of a black fullback in the Sugar Bowl, December-January, 1955-56.
61. Pro football stars, Paul Hornung and Alex Karras, are involved in gambling controversy, April 1963.
62. Joe Namath becomes a New York Jet for $400,000, helping the AFL, January 1965.
63. Pro football's NFL and AFL merge, June 1966.
64. Black athletes attempt to boycott the 1968 Mexico City Olympics, October 1968,
65. The Curt Flood v. Bowie Kuhn case, 407U.S.258, 32 L Ed. 2d 728 92 S. Ct. (1972), reaffirms the Reserve Clause in Major League baseball.
66. Title IX is announced in 1972 and creates controversy in its first years.
67. Billie Jean King wipes out Bobby Riggs in the "Battle of the Sexes", September 1973.
68. Pele joins the New York Cosmos soccer team, Summer 1975.
69. Andy Messersmith-David McNally Arbitration Case creates baseball free agents, Dec. 1975
70. Mackey v. NFL, 407 F. Supp. 1000 (D. Minn. 1975) attacks "Rozelle Rule"

THE ABOVE ARE EXAMPLES. IF YOU HAVE A SPORT, AN INCIDENT, OR AN ERA WHICH YOU WOULD RATHER CHOOSE FOR A PAPER, PLEASE SEE YOUR INSTRUCTOR TO DISCUSS THAT POSSIBILITY.

HISTORY OF ATHLETICS IN HIGHER EDUCATION
Spring 1985
with Ronald A. Smith

Lecture — Group Discussion — Readings

1. INTRODUCTION: SPORT IN HIGHER EDUCATION

2. THE CONSTANCY OF PROBLEMS IN INTERCOLLEGIATE ATHLETICS
    1) Randall Savage, "Academics vs. Athletics," MACON [Georgia]
       TELEGRAPH AND NEWS, 9 Spetember 1984, pp. 1A, 6A-7A.
    2) Joseph Durso, "Sports Recruiting: A College Crisis," NEW
       YORK TIMES, 10 March 1974, p. 1, 52, and 15 March 1974, p. 24C.
    3) Clarence Deming, "The Money Power in College Athletics," OUTLOOK,
       LXXX (1 July 1905), 569-572.
    4) Charles W. Eliot, "College Sports," JOURNAL OF EDUCATION, LXVII
       21 May 1908), 572.
    5) E. L. Godkin, "The Athletic Craze," NATION, (7 December 1893),
       422-423.

3. THE ENGLISH BACKGROUND
    1) John S. Brubacher and Willis Rudy, "Beginnings: English
       Influences," in HIGHER EDUCATION IN TRANSITION (New York:
       Harper & Row, 1958), pp. 3-5.
    2) "The Rowing Match Between the Oxonians and the Cantabs," THE
       SPORTING MAGAZINE, XXIV (July 1829), 249-252.
    3) Gordon Ross, "The First Six Races: 1829-1842," THE BOAT RACE:
       THE STORY OF THE FIRST HUNDRED RACES BETWEEN OXFORD AND
       CAMBRIDGE (London: Hodder & Stoughton, 1954), pp. 33-38.

4. THE COLLEGIATE WAY
    1) John S. Brubacher and Willis Rudy, "Early Student Life," in
       HIGHER EDUCATION IN TRANSITION (New York: Harper & Row, 1958),
       pp. 39-56.
    2) James Axtell, "The Collegiate Way," in his THE SCHOOL UPON A HILL:
       EDUCATION AND SOCIETY IN COLONIAL NEW ENGLAND (New Haven, CT:
       Yale University Press, 1974), pp. 201-244.
    3) Frederick Rudolph, "Legacy of the Revolution," THE AMERICAN
       COLLEGE AND UNIVERSITY: A HISTORY (New York: Vintage Books,
       1962), pp. 39-43.

5. EARLY AMERICAN COLLEGE CUSTOMS
    1) "The Ancient Customs of Harvard College, Anno 1734-5," THE
       AMERICAN COLLEGE, I (December 1909), 224-225.
    2) "Early Laws of the (Brown) College," in Walter C. Bronson, THE
       HISTORY OF BROWN UNIVERSITY, 1764-1914 (Providence, RI:
       Brown University, 1914), pp. 508-519.

6. PATTEE LIBRARY RESEARCH

7. COLLEGE SPORT AS RITUAL AND SENSE OF COMMUNITY
    1) John Sibley, "The Burial of Football, 1860," HARVARD GRADUATES'
       MAGAZINE, XV (March 1907), 537-538.
    2) Parke H. Davis, "The Beginnings of Football at Harvard," HARVARD
       ALUMNI BULETIN, XVIII (15 December 1915), 213-219.
    3) Malcolm Townsend, "A Cane Rush," in Norman W. Bingham, Jr., THE
       BOOK OF ATHLETICS AND OUT-OF-DOOR SPORTS (Boston: Lothrop
       Publishing Co., 1895), pp. 225-237.

8. AMERICAN IDEOLOGY AND THE COLLEGE EXTRACURRICULUM
   1) Ronald A. Smith, "Sport, the Extracurriculum, and the Idea of
      Freedom," 1985 typed manuscript.

9. PATTEE LIBRARY RESEARCH

10. CREW: THE FIRST INTERCOLLEGIATE SPORT
    1) James Whiton, "The First Harvard-Yale Regatta (1852)," OUTLOOK,
       LXVIII (June 1901), 286-289.
    2) Charles F. Livermore, "The First Harvard-Yale Race," HARVARD
       GRADUATES' MAGAZINE, II (December 1893), 226-227.

11. COMMERCIALIZING AND FINANCING COLLEGE CREW
    1) FIRST REGATTA OF THE NATIONAL COLLEGE ROWING ASSOCIATION, 21
       JULY 1871 (Amherst, MA: Henry M. McCloud, 1872), pp. 3-25.
    2) Douglas K. Fidler, "The First Big Upset: American Culture and
       the Regatta of 1871," NEW ENGLAND QUARTERLY, L (March 1877),
       68-82.

12. COLLEGE BASEBALL AND THE NATIONAL PASTIME
    1) Frederick Rudolph, "The First College Baseball Game," HOLIDAY,
       XXV (May 1959), 191, 197.
    2) "College Beginnings: First Intercollegiate Ball Game," THE
       AMERICAN COLLEGE, I (December 1909), 221-224.
    3) Henry Chadwick, "Baseball in the Colleges," OUTING, XII (August
       1888), 407-410.
    4) Henry S. Pritchett, "The Evolution of College Base-Ball,"
       SCRIBNER'S MAGAZINE, XLVII (April 1910), 501-505.

13. FOOTBALL: HOW IT CAME TO DOMINATE
    1) "Football Fifty Years Ago," NEW YORK TIMES, 26 Febrary 1901, p.10.
    2) "The Foot-Ball Match" and "Princeton vs. Rutgers," THE [Rutgers]
       TARGUM, November 1869, p. 5.
       NJ: Rutgers University, 1972), pp. 3-23.
    3) John A. Lucas and Ronald A. Smith, "Football: The Dominating
       College Sport," in SAGA OF AMERICAN SPORT (Philadelphia:
       Lea & Febiger, 1978), pp. 229-249.
    4) David Riesman and Reuel Denney, "Football in America: A Study
       in Culture Diffusion," AMERICAN QUARTERLY, III (1951), 309-319.

14. FOOTBALL AS A RATIONALIZED SPORT
    1) Richard H. Davis, " A Day with the Yale Team," HARPER'S WEEKLY,
       XXXVII (18 November 1893), 1110.
    2) David Westby and Alan Sack, "The Commercialization and Functional
       Rationalization of College Football," JOURNAL OF HIGHER
       EDUCATION, XLVII (November-December 1976), 625-647.

15. FOOTBALL: BRUTALITY OR MASCULINITY
    1) Eugene L. Richards, "Intercollegiate Athletics," NEW ENGLANDER,
       XLV (December 1886), 1048-1050.

16. FOOTBALL AND NATIONAL SUPERIORITY
    1) Charles F. Thwing, "Foot-Ball: A Game of Hearts," INDEPENDENT,
       (3 November 1898), 1260-1261.
    2) Henry Cabot Lodge, "Commencement--The Alumni Dinner Speach,"
       HARVARD GRADUATES' MAGAZINE, V (1896), 66-68.

17. BIG THREE CONCERNS ABOUT INTERCOLLEGIATE ATHLETICS
    1) C. A. Young, "College Athletic Sports," FORUM, II (October
       1886), 142-152.
    2) Eugene L. Richards, "College Athletics," POPULAR SCIENCE
       MONTHLY, XXIV (February 1884), 446-453 and (March 1884),
       587-597.
    3) Harvard Overseers Athletic Abuses Report (1888), pp. 1-10.

18. EXCELLENCE VS. PARTICIPATION: THE CHARLES ELIOT PARADOX

19. FACULTY CONCERNS OVER INTERCOLLEGIATE ATHLETIC CONTROL
    1) Eugene L. Richards, "Intercollegiate Athletics and Faculty
       Control," OUTING XXVI (July 1895), 325-328.
    2) George W. Kirchway, "The Problem of Athletic Control," COLUMBIA
       UNIVERISTY QUARTERLY, V (December 1902), 15-23.
    3) "Control of Athletics," COLUMBIA UNIVERSITY QUARTERLY, V (June
       1903), 316-319.

20. PRE-NCAA ATTEMPTS AT FACULTY INTER-INSTITUTIONAL CONTROL
    1) John A. Lucas and Ronald A. Smith, "College Athletics: From
       Student Control to Faculty Control," SAGA OF AMERICAN SPORT
       (Philadelphia: Lea & Febiger, 1978), pp. 210-228.

21. ATHLETIC TRAINING AND PROFESSIONAL COACHING
    1) Caspar Whitney, "The College Athlete Indoors," HARPER'S WEEKLY,
       XXXVI (26 March 1892), 306.

22. THE PRO COACH AND THE PROFESSIONALIZATION OF COLLEGE SPORT
    1) "Professional Coaching," HARVARD GRADUATES' MAGAZINE, XII
       (September 1903), 32-34.
    2) Allen L. Sack, "Yale 29-Harvard 4: Professionalization of
       College Football," QUEST, XIX (Winter 1973), 24-34.

23. THE PROFESSIONAL-AMATEUR ISSUE: SUMMER BASEBALL
    1) James W. Keating, "The Heart of the Problem of Amateur
       Athletics," JOURNAL OF GENERAL EDUCATION, XVI (January
       1965), 261-272.
    2) "(The 1898 Brown) Report on Intercollegiate Sports," pp. 5-14.

24. THE RISE OF BASKETBALL
    1) M. Whitcomb Hess, "The Man Who Invented Basketball," AMERICAN
       SCHOLAR, XVIII (January 1949), 87-89.

25. BASKETBALL: THE WOMEN'S DOMINATING SPORT
    1) Ronald A. Smith, "Senda Berenson," DICTIONARY OF AMERICAN
       BIOGRAPHY (New York: Charles Scribner's Sons, 1978), pp. 51-52.
    2) Elizabeth F. Read, "Basket-Ball at Smith College," OUTLOOK,
       LIV (26 September 1896), 557-558.
    3) "College Girls and Basket-Ball," HARPER'S WEEKLY, XLVI (22
       February 1902), 234-235.

26. THE 1905 FOOTBALL CRISIS
    1) Endicott Peabody, "Report of the Headmaster at Groton School,"
       13 December 1905.
    2) F. S. Bangs, "Columbia Athletic Committee, letter to President
       N. M. Butler, Columbia, 28 October 1905.
    3) President N. M. Butler, Columbia, letter to F. S. Bangs, 3

November 1905.

History of Athletics in Higher Education (4)

27. HARVARD'S INVOLVEMENT IN THE CREATION OF THE NCAA
    1) "From a Graduate's Window," HARVARD GRADUATES' MAGAZINE, XIV
       (December 1905), 216-223.
    2) "National Intercollege Football Conference Rules Committee,"
       ca. 1 January 1906.

28. THE WILLIAM T. REID, JR. CHRONICLE
    1) "H.U.F.B.A. NOTES -- W. T. Reid, Jr. 1905"

29. THE 1909-10 CRISIS--BEGINNINGS OF DEMISE OF THE BIG THREE
    1) John S. Watterson, III "The Football Crisis of 1909-10: The
       Response of the Eastern 'Big Three,'" JOURNAL OF SPORT
       HISTORY, VIII (Spring 1981), 33-49.

30. COMMERCIAL GROWTH OF COLLEGE SPORT IN THE 1920s
    1) Grantland Rice, "The Four Horsemen (1924)," in Herbert Warren
       Wind (ed.), THE REALM OF SPORT (New York: Simon and
       Schuster, 1966), pp. 312-315.
    2) Upton Sinclair, "Killers of Thought: Shall We Abolish Football?"
       THE FORUM, LXXVI (December 1926), 838-843.

31. WOMEN'S SPORT: ANOTHER MODEL
    1) Mabel Lee, "The Case For and Against Intercollegiate Athletics
       for Women and the Situation as It Stands Today," MIND AND
       BODY, XXX (November 1923), 245-256.
    2) Mabel Lee, "The Case For and Against Intercollegiate Athletics
       for Women and the Situation Since 1923 (Summary and
       Conclusion)," RESEARCH QUARTERLY, II (1931), 122-127.

32. THE LOGIC OF THE WOMEN'S MODEL AND A DEFECTOR
    1) Ina E. Gittings, "Why Cramp Competition?" JOURNAL OF HEALTH AND
       PHYSICAL EDUCATION, II (January 1931), 10-12, 54.

33. THE CARNEGIE REPORT ON AMERICAN COLLEGE ATHLETICS
    1) Henry S. Prichett, "The Influence of Organized Alumni on American
       Colleges," The Carnegie Foundation for the Advancement of
       Teaching, SIXTH ANNUAL REPORT (1911), pp. 115-119.
    2) Howard J. Savage, et al., AMERICAN COLLEGE ATHLETICS (New York:
       The Carnegie Foundation for the Advancement of Teaching, 1929),
       pp. v-xxii, 100-103, 188-189, 265.

34. THE UNIVERSITY OF CHICAGO ANOMALY
    1) Hal A. Lawson and Alan G. Ingham, "Conflicting Ideologies
       Concerning the University and Intercollegiate Athletics:
       Harper and Hutchins at Chicago, 1892-1940," JOURNAL OF SPORT
       HISTORY, VII (Winter 1980), 37-67.

35. FAILURE OF THE NCAA SANITY CODE: ATHLETIC SCHOLARSHIPS AND RECRUITING
    1) "Report of the Constitutional Compliance Committee," NCAA
       YEARBOOK (1950), pp. 196-201.

36. THE 1951 SCANDALS AND THE RISE OF NCAA ENFORCEMENT

37. ECONOMICS, T.V., AND THE COMMERCIALISM OF BIG-TIME COLLEGE ATHLETICS
    1) James V. Koch, "A Troubled Cartel: The NCAA," LAW AND
       CONTEMPORARY PROBLEMS, XXXVIII (Winter-Spring 1973), 135-150.

38. WOMEN'S INTERCOLLEGIATE SPORT DEVELOPMENT
    1) Marguerite A. Clifton, "The Future of Intercollegiate Sports for Women," THE PHYSICAL EDUCATOR, XXIII (December 1966),

       158-162.
    2) Angela Lumpkin, "Let's Set the Record Straight," JOURNAL OF PHYSICAL EDUCATION AND RECREATION, (March 1977), 40, 42, 44.

39. THE AIAW BIRTH, LIFE, AND DEATH
    1) Joan Hult, Attainment of AIAW's Educational Goals," AAHPERD Convention (1979), 2 p.
    2) Bonnie Slatton, "A.I.A.W.: The Greening of American Athletics," in James Frey (ed.), THE GOVERNANCE OF INTERCOLLEGIATE ATHLETICS (West Point, NY: Leisure Press, 1982), pp. 144-154.
    3) Ann Uhlir, "Political Victim: The Dream That Was the AIAW," NEW YORK TIMES, 11 July 1982.
    4) Betty Spears, "The Transformation of Women's Collegiate Sports," NATIONAL FORUM, LXII (Winter 1982), 24-25.

40. THE COLLEGE COACH AS STAR VS C.A.R.E.
    1) "Ad Hoc Committee on Varsity Athletics Report," Penn State University, 11 July 1978, 7p.
    2) "ACE Policy Statement," EDUCATIONAL RECORD, LX (Fall 1979), 345=350.
    3) Allen Sack, "Cui Bono? Contradictions in College Sports and Athletes' Rights," in James Frey (ed.), THE GOVERNANCE OF INTERCOLLEGIATE ATHLETICS (West Point, NY: Leisure Press, 1982), pp. 80-90.
    4) Center for Athletes' Rights and Education, "Athletes' Bill of Rights," (1982), 1 p.
    5) Joe Paterno, "Opinion: A College Coach Tells Why Recruiting Abuses Happen," in John Brady and James Hall (eds.), SPORTS LITERATURE (New York: McGraw-Hill, 1975), pp. 260-263.

PHED 293

HISTORY OF SPORT IN AMERICA

Nancy L. Struna
Office, PERH 2355; Phone, x-6663

Course Focus:

This course in social history introduces students to sport in
its historical American settings. Its direction is chronological,
from colonial to contemporary; and it emphasizes facts, concepts,
and interpretations which help one to understand how and why sport
developed as it did within American culture. The intent of this
course is to help students to understand the *particulars* of sport
(i. e., the forms of and attitudes toward sport) as these affected
or were affected by American society in the past.

Course Objectives:

While investigating the development of sport within the
context of American society, each student will:

1. Examine the forms of and attitudes toward sport which were
evident among various generations of Americans in the context of
conceptions of and attitudes toward other endeavors (e. g., work,
religion, and health.
2. Analyze the interactions between sport and other
institutions and social movements in American society.
3. Identify stages of development among various sport
organizations and the manner in which these stages affected and
were affected by developments in other aspects of the culture.
4. Analyze the motives and accomplishments of individuals and
groups which affected or were affected by sport.
5. Synthesize facts and concepts over time in order to begin
to understand the natures of sport and of history.

Required Reading:

1. Rader, Benjamin G. *American Sports. From the Age of Folk
Games to the Age of Spectators*. Englewood Cliffs, NJ:
Prentice-Hall Co., 1983.

2. Riess, Steven. *The American Sporting Experience: A
Historical Anthology*. West Point, NY: Leisure Press, 1984.

3. Selected journal articles and book chapters in a packet available at Kinko's Copies:

Wiggins, David. "Sport and Popular Pastimes: Shadow of the Slavequarter." (1980).

Struna, Nancy L. "The North-South Races: American Thoroughbred Racing in Transition, 1823-1850." (1981).

Kirsch, George B. "American Cricket: Players and Clubs Before the Civil War." (1984).

Fielding, Lawrence. "War and Trifles: Sport in the Shadow of Civil War Army Life." (1977).

Gelber, Steven M. "'Their Hands Are All Out Playing': Business and Amateur Baseball, 1845-1917." (1984).

Voigt, David. "The Boston Red Stockings: The Birth of Major League Baseball." (1970).

LeCompte, Mary Lou. "The Hispanic Influence on the History of Rodeo, 1823-1922." (1985).

Rosenzweig, Roy. "The Struggle Over Recreational Space: The Development of Parks and Playgrounds." (1984).

Uminowicz, Glenn. "Sport in a Middle-Class Utopia: Asbury Park, New Jersey, 1871-1895." (1984).

Whorton, James C. "Philosophy in the Gymnasium." (1982).

Mrozek, Donald. "From Swooning Damsel" to Sportswoman -- The Role of Women as a Constituency in Sport." (1983).

Gudelunas, William and Couch, Stephen. "The Stolen Championship of the Pottsville Maroons: A Case Study in the Emergence of Modern Professional Football." (1982).

Capeci, Dominic J. and Wilkerson, Martha. "Multifarious Hero: Joe Louis, American Society and Race Relations During World Crisis, 1935-1945." (1983).

Tygiel, Jules. "Oh, They Were A Pair," and "The Unwritten Law of the South." (1983).

Kunen, James. "Merrily, Merrily, Merrily, Merrily. . .." (1969)

Lecture/Readings Schedule:

Sept. 3 -- Introduction and Overview

Sept. 5 -- The British Sporting Culture on the Eve of Colonization
    Read: Riess, pp. 12-14

Sept. 10-12 -- The Anglo-American Colonial Sporting Culture
    Read: Rader, pp. 1-22; Riess, pp. 15-54.

Sept. 17 -- The Antebellum Sporting Culture, 1810-1860
    Read: Rader, pp. 24-44; Wiggins

Sept. 19 -- Enlivening the Physical: Antebellum Views of the Body
    Read: Riess, pp. 58-90

Sept. 24 -- Arrangement and Promotion of Sport, 1820-1860
    Read: Riess, pp. 91-134; Struna; Kirsch

Sept. 26 -- The Post-Civil War Sporting Culture
     Read: Fielding; Riess, pp. 138-163

Oct. 1-3 -- The New World of Amateur Athletics
     Read: Rader, 46-86; Riess, pp. 164-167, 239-254; Gelber

Oct. 8 -- Institution Building: The Case of Baseball, 1869-1892
     Read: Rader, pp. 108-122; Voigt

Oct. 10 -- The Sporting Experiences of "Other" Late 19th
               Century Americans
     Read: Rader, pp. 87-106; LeCompte

Oct. 15 -- Urban Recreation, Parks, and Resorts
     Read: Rosenzweig; Uminowicz; Riess, pp. 190-208

Oct. 17 -- Review: The Making of American Sport, I

Oct. 22 -- Midterm Exam

Oct. 24-29 The Emerging Sporting Ideology: Blending
               Recreation, Reform, and Renewal
     Read: Rader, pp. 146-169; Whorton

Oct. 31 -- The Ideology and "Developments": Women,
               Children, and "Non-native" Americans
     Read: Riess, pp. 214-238, 255-264; Mrozek

Nov. 5 -- The Ideology and "Reforms": Booze,
               Brutality, and the "Black Brute"
     Read: Rader, pp. 104-105, 134-144; Riess, 168-189, 306-315

Nov. 7 -- Utopia vs Reality: Professional Baseball in
               the Progressive Era
     Read: Rader, pp. 123-134; Riess, pp. 264-305

Nov. 12 -- Sport of the "Modern" Age, 1920-1970's
     Read: Rader, pp. 171-240, 301-322, 357-360

Nov. 14 -- The Massification of American Sport, 1920's-1930's
     Read: Riess, pp. 316-324; Gudelunas/Couch

Nov. 19 -- Owens, Louis, and Robinson: The Specter of Race
     Read: Riess, pp. 365-370; Tygiel; Capeci/Wilkerson

Nov. 21 -- Televison and Professional Sport
     Read: Rader, pp. 242-299

Nov. 26 -- Rumblings in SportsWorld: The Athletic Revolution
     Read: Rader, pp. 324-344; Kunen

Dec. 3-5 -- Contemporary Issues From the Perspective of the
               Century: Gender, Control, Money, Performance Aids
     Read: Rader, pp. 345-356; Riess, pp. 371-397

Dec. 10 -- Conclusions and Questions: Molding the Past and
the Present

Dec. 12 -- Review: The Making of American Sport, II

Dec. 19 -- Final Exam, 4:00 - 6:00

Course Requirements:

1. Critical reading, questioning, and thought about the material
are expected. This comment applies as well to material in the
readings which will not always be directly reviewed in lectures.

2. Exams -- There are two exams in this course, a midterm and a
final. Each covers material from both lectures and readings, even
if the latter have not been cited in class. The exams include
questions about concrete facts, concepts, and interpretations.
Rather than primarily testing your ability to memorize and
regurgitate the material, the questions test your *understanding* of
the material and your ability to work with it in your minds. The
midterm is worth 65 points and the final is worth 75 points (the
latter will include several comprehensive questions).

· 3. Project -- Each student will select from and complete one of
the following semester projects (worth 75 points). *Each student
must inform us in writing of his/her choice by September 26.* By
October 24 each student selecting projects A and C must turn in a
precise statement of the intent and directions of the project *and*
a list of sources being used. *Failure to meet either of these
deadlines will result in the loss of 10 points (10 for each
deadline) from the possible total of 75.* Projects A, B, and C are
due on December 3. Project D is due December 5. *No* projects will
be accepted *after those dates.*

A. Read 4-6 books (primary research-based as opposed to
opinion or pictorial histories) on a topic or a period in American
sport history and prepare a 6-10 page (typed) *critical review* of
the contents, organization and theme development, and sources.

B. Abstract (on 5 X 8 note cards) twenty-five research-based
history articles written about sport in American history. Include
the following in your abstracts:
a) complete citation, b) synopsis of author's
description/argument,
c) evaluation of sources and argument development, and
d) paragraph relating content of article to the course and
questions you may raise upon reading and considering both the
article and lecture material.
Develop a 6-10 page (typed) paper summarizing the contents and
relating it to lecture material. *Special Note:* This project is
limited to 40 people because of library resource limitations and
articles assigned as class reading can not be included.

125

C.   Research through _primary_ _sources_ (first-hand accounts and evidence) a question which you have about some aspect of sport in American history.   Use secondary sources (i. e., historical journal articles and books) _only_ as background information which helps you to formulate the question you wish to pursue.   Prepare a 6-10 page (typed) paper presenting your narrative and analysis. Footnotes or endnotes are required.

D.   Answer a series of questions to be handed out later.   The answers will require a thorough knowledge of lecture material and assigned readings.   This project will require analysis and synthesis of the material and will probably result in more writing than the other projects.

Grading:

Total points = 215
Scale: 90-100% of 215 = A; 80-89 % = B; etc.

PHED 293
History of Sport in America

Questions for Project D

Of the following twenty-one questions, divided among five
sections, you will answer fifteen.   Each answer is worth five
points (total = 75). Answers should contain "hard" evidence from
readings and lecture. Avoid value judgments (good, better,
worse, etc.), and write in standard English with your answers and
arguments logically organized and developed. Make sure you
proofread and type the final draft of your work.

I.   Write on 1 of the following 3:

1.   Discuss (1) the British sporting culture as it existed just
prior to and during the initial colonization of the North
American mainland (ca. 1607-1640's) and (2) the forms of sport,
the attitudes about sport, and the issues or conflicts involving
sport which Englishmen and women brought to the settlements which
became Massachusetts, Virginia, and Maryland.

2.   How and why did Anglo-American colonials come to conceive of
sport as "useful competitive recreation?" What cultural
expressions, especially in the eighteenth century, did this
conception permit?

3.   Describe the primary sources which the historians whose work
you have read have used to narrate colonial sport history. About
what and whom can these sources tell us little or nothing? What
kinds of sources of evidence might historians in the future use
to describe and analyze the sport of colonial people about whom
we now know little?

II.   Write on 2 of the following 3:

4.   Compare and contrast the histories of thoroughbred and
harness racing (trotting) from 1820-1870. Why did one languish
and the other emerge as more popular in the urban setting? Is
the *modernization* paradigm, as suggested by Adelman (in Riess),
sufficient to explain *why* the outcomes of these sports differed;
if not, why not?

5.   Summarize the nature and role of sport among antebellum
southern plantation slaves. Was the material in the Wiggins
article presented from the perspective of the black slave or the
white master (or white historian)? If the perspective was that
of the latter, what might the author have ignored or missed about
sport in the black slave experience?

6. Discuss the evolution of team sport ball games during the colonial and antebellum years. Consider, especially, how and why a game like "modern" baseball did not appear before 1845, as well as what conditions and decisions finally did affect the emergence of this sport type.

III. Write on 5 of the following 6:

7. What were the economic, social, and moral bases for amateurism as it appeared and existed in the United States in the latter half of the 19th century? Given several factors -- cultural heterogeneity, the American stress on ideals (especially freedom, democracy, talent-based achievement), and the tradition of sport as useful competitive recreation -- was the sporting culture in this period really an appropriate environment for the rooting of "pure" amateurism? If yes, how so; if not, why not?

8. Using football as an example, show how a sport form developed and changed in relation to specific cultural conditions and human choices during the 19th and early 20th centuries. In the case of collegiate football, how were the two quests of these years -- for better ways to play and for order in the total sporting environment -- realized *and* related, both to each other *and* to goals of the colleges and universities?

9. How did American views and perceptions of the body change over the course of the 19th century? What was the effect of the emergence of the notion of the body as instrument and symbol, and why did this appear?

10. Compare (and contrast) the Higginson and Camp articles (in Riess). In what respects were the ideas and beliefs of Higginson, a proponent of Muscular Christianity, and of Camp, a believer of a "genteel" amateurism, both similar and different? What factors help to explain their positions?

11. Historians of nineteenth century America now believe that no single, uniform, even "mainstream" sporting culture ever truly existed during this period.   In other words, no longer can this sporting culture be adequately described and analyzed from the perspective of "white, middle class males" who formed the backbone of organized amateur and professional sport. Although this aspect of sport history remains important, it needs to be augmented by an understanding of sporting experiences affected by race, gender, and status or "class." Select one of these three variables (i. e., race, gender, status) and explain (1) when it *probably* began to noticeably affect what was happening in American sport, (2) what the "real" history of the nineteenth century is when this variable is considered, and (3) why it should be considered and explored further.

12. How and why did "other" sporting "developments" -- such as rodeo, the urban parks and recreation movement, and boxing among blacks and the Irish -- take root and flourish? In what ways were these alike *and* different from primarily urban, white, middle and upper class sports like baseball and football? What distinctive cultural expressions or performances did participants (and perhaps spectators) incorporate?

IV. Write on 4 of the following 5:

13. What was the "ideology" of sport? Of what did it consist, why did it appear when it did, and what implications did it have, both for the short term when it appeared and over the long term in the twentieth century?

14. How and why did baseball, especially the professional version, develop into "America's national game" during the late nineteenth and early twentieth centuries? What happened within the following to affect that change: the organizational structure, the on-field and off-field behaviors of players and management, the way in which the baseball establishment dealt with problems and issues, and the relations with businessmen, the press, and politicos? Was the "reality" which you have just described alike or different from what the sporting public expected baseball to do and be (its idealized form); in either case (or both), in what ways and why?

15. In what ways and why were the sporting experiences of men and women similar and dissimilar during the late nineteenth and early twentieth centuries? Did they interact, or intersect, at any points; if so, why; if not, why not?

16. How and why was the sporting culture of the 1920's and 1930's a period of transition and transformation, one essentially connecting the nineteenth century "past" with the 1980's "present"? Consider, especially, what happened to relations between sport teams and communities, to heroes and heroines, to the media and promotion, to participation and spectatorship, and to the involvement of institutions such as the federal government.

17. Compare (and contrast) the careers and societal perceptions of Jack Johnson, Joe Louis, and Jackie Robinson. In what ways and why were they similar and dissimilar? Consider the nature of the career and the impact that each had on American society in light of American race relations at the time when each was a public figure.

V.   Write on 3 of the following 4:

18.   What was the "athletic revolution" -- its origin, context, major actions and figures? Was it actually a phenomenon brought on by discontented athletes of the 1960's, or was it a "stage" in a longer existing development? Was it "revolutionary"?

19.   Historians have developed two views about the relationship of sport and American society. One is fairly accurately rendered in John R. Betts' essay, "The Technological Revolution and the Rise of Sport" (in Riess). This view suggests that sport essentially "mirrors" society, meaning that the change and "development" of sport both depends upon and reflects the broader course of societal change. In this article, technological change was the independent variable and sport was the dependent variable -- and sport underwent changes similar to the rest of society as technology affected them both. On the other hand, the second view, identified in part in Richard Harmond's article, "Progress and Flight. . ." (also in Riess), suggests that the relationship between sport and society is more complex, more interdependent. In the case of the bicycle, Harmond argued that this machine not only was affected by society (including technology) in the late 19th century but also that it affected human views, behaviors, and conditions. Which of the two views is *probably* most nearly accurate, *and* why? Has sport been a dependent variable; has it depended on and reflected whatever else occurred in American social history? Or has the sporting culture affected American society, as well as having been affected by it?

20.   Devise your own periodization for the history of sport in the United States; explain and provide evidence for your framework. How do your periods relate, or not relate, to other features and factors in American social history?

21.   Identify one clearly stated, researchable question about some aspect of the history of American sport which you would be interesting in exploring. Clarify what leads you to ask this question (including how you derived it from readings and lectures), what meaningful information about both sport and society the answer might provide, and the kinds of primary source evidence you would ideally use to answer it.

A. Course Format
1. Textbooks: Voigt, <u>American Baseball</u>, Vol. 2; <u>American Baseball</u>, Vol. 3 (paper);
    <u>America Through Baseball</u>.
    *These are required reading and are available at the bookstore.
2. Supplementary Sources:
    <u>Macmillan Encyclopedia of Baseball</u> (1979) is on reserve at library desk.
    Other sources that are useful include TSN, SI, BD, etc. Albright Library
    has some 50 books on baseball in 796.357 section. Reading Library has more
    under same listing. I can help with others, especially a list for book
    reviews.
3. Student Grade:
    Overall grade is based on two tests (Jan. 16, Jan. 30) and the student
    presentation (oral or written). Test 1 (Jan. 16) will cover AB Vol. 2 and
    pertinent chapters in <u>Am. Thru Baseball</u>; Test 2 covers AB Vol. 3 plus
    <u>AM. T. BB</u>. Test questions are based on texts, lectures, films, speakers
    and other class materials such as slides and oral presentations.
    a. <u>Attendance</u>—this is very important; more than 2 unexcused absences counts
        against one's grade. Absences for speakers must be excused. Medical reasons
        constitute excused absences, but must be supported. <u>Seating chart is to be
        used</u>. On the positive side, complete attendance is counted <u>as a plus</u>.
    b. <u>Presentations</u>—Can be done orally or as a written paper. By <u>Mon. Jan. 7</u> I
        should receive from each student a written declaration of just what you plan
        to do. Use sheet at bottom of page two of this syllabus.
4. Course Overview:
    We begin with the history of the major league game and move to the game's
    impact on American society and culture (using <u>America Thru Baseball</u>). Readings,
    slides, films, and four speakers are arranged to supplement lectures.

B. Course Outline
1. Week of Jan. 4 (two days)
    —Course integration. History of the major league games begins. Essays in
    <u>Am. T. BB</u>. 19th century baseball; film "Glory of Their Times" shown Fri. Jan. 4.
2. Week of Jan. 11.
    —19th Century through 1920. Read essays in <u>Am. T. BB</u>. (applicable), and
    AmBaseball, II.
    —Slides; films "Sun is Always Shining . . . ," Babe Ruth (Jan. 11).
3. Week of Jan. 18.
    —History of game from 1920s through WWII. Finish <u>Am Baseball II</u>; also
    <u>Am. T. BB</u>. (applicable)
    —Slides; films "50 Yrs. of Baseball Memories;" "Ump in Baseball"
    —Speakers, Gene Benson of Black Major Leagues; Kit Crissey on Japanese Ball.
    Jan. 15.
    —Test 1 on Jan. 16.
4. Week of Jan. 25.
    —History covering Postwar Era into Expansion Eras.
    —Special day set aside for oral presentations.
    —Films "Clemente;" 1983 World Series; "Batty World of Baseball"
    —Speakers: *
5. Week of Jan. 30.
    —History of majors completed to date.
    —Test 2. Covers Vol. 3 and appropriate stuff in lectures and Am. T. Baseball.

*Additional speakers include Jim Honochick (with film clips) and Kevine Kerrane on
scouting. As of this completion of syllabus, dates not yet firmed.

C. Student Presentations
1. Written Version.
   --Each student is required to write a paper of eight pages in length. It is to be based on three sources (minimal) and footnoted. The paper should: 1. Cover a topic of interest in baseball; 2. Fit into the mainstream of baseball history and the larger framework of American culture; 3. Have a paragraph which justifies its importance; 4. Be well written. Judgment is based on these four categories.

   --Suggested topics.
   1. Book reviews--I will make a list of good ones and include a format.
   2. Issues in baseball--race, unionism, sexism, game's impact on Am. life, outside influences on baseball (war, depression, rival sports, salaries, media, fans, etc.)
   3. Changing character of fans--use a book on crowd behavior. Consider varieties of fans--ballpark fans, collectors, TV fans, Trivia nuts, statistical nuts, etc.
   4. Changing major league game--owners and players, Scouts, Umps, Officials, etc.
   5. Subcults of major league baseball--minors, Negro majors, College game, women's majors, softball, etc.--little league, etc.
   6. Literary baseball--novels etc. Writers like Roth, Malamud, Coover, etc. Films and baseball (like Natural) etc.

2. Oral Version.
   --This choice could be an easier way of dealing with the assignment. To minimize stage fright a day will be set aside (week of Jan. 25) to do all of these. The advantage is that topics proved by students get shared by all.
   You may use any of the above. Length of these presentations should not exceed 15 minutes. Be open to questions and encourage them at end of presentation. Collections of bb memorabilia may be used as demonstrations.

(Detach this part of syllabus and submit to Prof. Voigt by Mon. Jan. 7)

Student's Name_____

Title of Chosen Topic_____

Plan of presentation--Written_____ Oral_____.

Sources which you plan to use:

1.

2.

3.

4.

Baseball in American Culture--1985

A. Book Review Option.

1. A student opting to do a book review instead of a written (or orally
    presented) general study should follow these guidelines.
    --The report should be delivered orally and should be timed for
    about 12 minutes. All book reports will be delivered during the week
    of Jan. 25 on a day set aside for oral presentations.

2. In delivering the book review the following procedure is suggested:
    --Introduce the book and author
    --Give thesis of the book and a brief, overall summary.
    --Select a major topic for expanded treatment with illustrations.
    --Conclude the discussion by commenting on the significance of the
    book to the course and to the history of major league baseball.

3. The following eight books have been chosen for their significance to
    the course and to the general history of major league baseball. A
    student may nominate one of his own choices based on the same criteria.

    --G.H. Fleming, The Unforgettable Season (Holt, Rinehart, Winston, '81).
    --Jules Tygiel, Baseball's Great Experiment: Jackie Robinson and
                    His Legacy (Vintage, '83).
    --Peterson, Only the Ball was White.
    --Roger Kahn, The Boys of Summer (Signet Books).
    --L.Lowenfish and Tony Lupien, The Imperfect Diamond (Stein and Day, '80).
    --Ron Luciano and David Fisher, The Umpire Strikes Back (Bantam).
    --Roger Angell, 5 Seasons: A Baseball Companion (Popular Library).
    --Kevin Kerrane, Dollar Sign on the Muscle (Beaufort).

The choice of a book review should be indicated on this signup sheet. Priority
is on a first received basis. Deadline for receipt is 7 Jan. 85.

Name of Student_____

Title of Book_____

HIGHLIGHTS OF MAJOR LEAGUE BASEBALL HISTORY--the 19th Century

I. Three major eras of 19th century baseball.

   A. The Gentlemen's Era.

   1840s--Gentlemen's era of formalized amateur baseball underway. Formal men's
        clubs appear. Two styles of baseball vie for acceptance--Mass. vs. N.Y. games.
        Cartwright's modification (diamond infield) wins. The rise of N.Y. Knickerbockers.
   1857 --National assn of Base Ball Clubs Takes control of game from Knicks.
        (loose competition for national championships; "creeping commercialism.")

   1869 --H. Wright's Cincinnati Red Stockings.

   1871 --Natl Assn of Professional Base Ball Players--the first pro. major league, but
        not considered "major" by established publicists of today. NAPBBP was run by
        players under old amateur rules. Problems of NAPBBP included scheduling, drop-
        out clubs, umps, "revolving" players. Phila. A's win disputed '71 race.
   1872 --Wright's Boston Red Stockings win first of 4 consecutive NAPBBP flags.
        Wright's Reds tour England hoping to spread American baseball.
   1875 --NAPBBP hurting from Boston domination, dropout franchises. Wm. Hulbert plans
        new major league to be run by owners. Hulbert raids Boston of its "big 4."

   1876 --National League of Professional BB Clubs. Hulbert and A. Spalding father
        new league. New promoters seek profits, better mgt., player discipline.
   1877 -- NL's first major scandal--Louisville crooks; also an umpire scandal.
   1879 --Reserve Clause invoked.
   1881 -- pitching distance extended by five feet--now at 50'.

   B. Golden Age. (1880s sees dual major league system; World Series competition.)

   1882 -- Hulbert bans 10 players for drinking; Hulbert dies in April.
                                        Am. Assn. organized-Sunday ball, beer
                                        sales, 25c. admissions. Natl Agmt.
                                        promulgated. World Series Competition
                                        begins.
   1884 --overhand pitching Okd   Union Assn (lasts 1 yr).
   1885 --Owners try to fix $2000 salary limit
        (Players org. Brohood of BBP (1st Union)
   1886 --Sale of Kelly to Boston for $10,000   St. Louis Browns dominate Am. Assn.

   1887 --Walks count as hits; players no longer choose high or low strikes.
   1889 --modern rule on balls-strikes set
        (2nd overseas mission--Spaulding)   AA's Bklyn/Cincy jump AA for NL.

   1890 --NL vs. Players League. Great Strike. Am. Assn suffers in Pl War.
                                                        Players League

   1891 --modern rule on subs. NL wars with AA Am. Assn dies; end of first Natl Agmt.

   1892 -- NL and AA of Prof. BB Clubs organized; it's a single 12-club "big league."

C. The Feudal Age, 1892-1899
   (One single "big league" of 12 clubs--called NL and AA.)

   1893 --pitching distance set at 60' 6". Player salaries slashed; ceiling imposed.

   1895 --infield fly rule.

   1896 --Boston vs. Baltimore. Dirty ball controversy. Slugging game vs. "scientific" game.

   1898 --Umpire abuse at peak; Brush resolution seeks to blacklist rowdy players.

   1899 --NL drops 4 clubs at season's end (returns to 8 teams).

                            AM LEAGUE orgd by Ben Johnson
                            (formerly the Western Lg)
                            AL invades abandoned NL tour;
                            raids NL rosters (Lajoie, Cy Young
                            snagged).

                            New Natl Agmt concedes AL m.l. status

HIGHLIGHTS OF MAJOR LEAGUE BASEBALL HISTORY (1901-46)

I. <u>The Great Detente</u> (Features: Dual Majors--2 leagues, 8 teams each, W. Series, Stability

D. <u>Silver Age, 1901-1920.</u> Majors return to dual league structure; NL and Am. League
vie in profitable World Series encounters. No franchise shifts after 1903.
-style of play features "scientific ball," less scoring, more running, power pitching.
-Deadball Dynasties include AL's Chi, A's, Red Sox Tigers; NL--Pitt, Giants, Cubs.
-Ty Cobb superstar

1901--Am. League War rages. Players Assn. Formed (second Unionization attempt).
  02--Interleague war continues. 80 NL players jump to AL which outdraws NL in attdce.
  03--National Agreemnt ends interleague war. (AL recognized as major league; <u>Natl
      Commission</u> created to govern m.l. baseball (Johnson, Herrmann, Pulliam). First
      modern W. Series staged.
  04--Manager McGraw of Giants refuses to meet AL champs in W. Series.
  05--Peace comes to baseball. Era of stability begins. No franchise shifts till 1952.

1908--Year of Merkle boner.
  09--Cork-centered ball in--used from 1910 onward. Rise of slugging game.
  10--Pres. Taft throws out ball at Wash. Sens. opener; baseball's political flirtation.

1912--Players Fraternity formed (a third unionization attempt).
  13--Federal League War underway.   <u>Fed. League--lasts till 1915</u>
                                               (last incursion to date).
1917--Wartime baseball. Another of "baseball's time of troubles"
  18--Abbreviated season caused by W. War I. Ruth's first homer title. "Big bang"
      style coming on.

1919--Black Sox Series Scandal. Not publicized till 1920. Another of the "troubles."

E. <u>Second Golden Age</u>, 1920-45. Features big bang style; Ruth the super celebrity.
  -Judge Landis in as High Commissioner. Dynasties include AL Yanks, A's; NL include
   Giants, Cards, Cubs.
  -Innovations include radio, night ball.
  -Problems include Depression and War. Farm System policies transform minor lgs.
  -Era also includes the <u>Black Majors.</u> Negro Natl League under Rube Foster (1920-31;
   33-48) Negro AL, 1929, 1937-50. Black Leagues also include Eastern Colored League,
   Negro So. League, Negro East West League.

1920--Ray Chapman's death. Yanks buy Ruth from Ed Sox for $125gs. Landis in as Commissioner
      in aftermath of Black Sox expose (8 men tossed out). Spitter outlawed, but not
      <u>ex-post facto.</u>

  23--Yankee Stadium opens.
  27--Yankee superteam.
  30--Ruth gets paid $80gs a year.
  31--Branch Rickey's farm system thrives. Depression menaces baseball.
  33--Nadir of Depression. Radio baseball thrives.
  35--First night game played at Cincinnati (earlier versions at lower levels of play).
  36--Cooperstown Hall of Fame opens. Yanks win first of 4-straight W. Series titles.

1942--W.War II. Wartime baseball. Cardinal dynasty in NL.
  44--Landis dies; succeeded by A.B. "Happy" Chandler in 1945.
  45--War ends. Prosperity in 1945. Pale world series between Cubs and Tigers.
      Sentiment mounts to integrate baseball.

HIGHLIGHTS OF MAJOR LEAGUE BB HISTORY, 1946-85

. The Postwar Era, 1946-60.

946--First full postwar season; players return in droves to spring training camps.
   Players seek reforms--organize Players Guild (4th Union attempt). Strike threat;
   owners grant concessions (pensions promised). Mexican League Threat. Cards win
   NL in playoff with Dodgers.
47--Jackie Robinson--he wins rookie of yr; TV baseball growing--player pension fund tied
   to share of national radio (and TV) receipts.
48--peak yr. of postwar attdce boom. Cleveland (under owner Veeck) wins flag--Satch
   and Doby.
49--Yankee tyranny begins in AL--will produce 5 consecutive W. Series titles.
50--playing rules recodified.
51--Chandler ousted as Commissioner; weaklings follow (Frick 51-65; Eckert 65-69;
   Kuhn 69-84; Ueberroth current). O'Malley emerges as singular power in bb circles.
   Miracle Giants.
52--Pirates wear batting helmets.

53--First franchise shift in half a century (Braves move to Milwaukee).
54--AL Browns move to Baltimore. Players launch Major League Players Assn (Fifth
   Union attempt, it's destined to be the most successful).

55--Bonus baby era in high gear; talent shortage; some scouts combing Latin America

56--Don Larsen's W. Series perfect game
57--O'Malley takes his Dodgers to LA along with Stoneham and Giants. Dodgers to play
   at LA Coliseum 4 years until new Dodger Stadium is built.

59--Rickey and Bill Shea's Continental League threat forces owners to expand; new park
   building boom afoot (subsidized by public funds); new parks being built must conform to fixed outfiled dimentions--325' and 400' minimums.

. The Expansion Era Begins. First Phase 1961-69.

61--First expansion. AL goes to 10 teams and a 162-game sked; expansion draft and
   initiation fee for newcomers. (Senators and Angels added, as old Sens go to MINN).
   Maris hits 61 homers for Yanks (162 games).
62--NL expands to 10 teams, adding Mets and Astros. Wills steals 104 bases.
63--NL umps organize--in time org. becomes the powerful MLUA.

65--Free agent (rookie) draft established to deal with persisting talent shortage.
   Eckert in as Commissioner, but is ineffective. CBS buys Yanks.

66--MARVIN MILLER in as MLPA director; he soon wins bargaining and formal contract
   rights for orgd players. Milw. Braves jump to Atlanta and soon AL A's and
   Senators will move (A's go to Oakland and Sens go to Texas)--these are 2nd degree
   acts of carpetbaggery.

67--Baseball faces competition from rival sports--TV reshapes sports; the sports overlap.

68--Yr. of pitcher; bullpen rev. adding to batters' woes; batting aves. LOW this yr.
   (for 1969 pitching mounds to be lowered and the strike zone narrowed.)

1969--<u>Second Expansion Round</u>. Each maj. league expands to 12 clubs (162-game skeds and 6-team divisional play; playoff series to determine league champs). NL adds Expos and S.D. Padres; AL adds KC Royals and Seattle Pilots. Pilots prove to be financial bust; when bankrupt after this season, they go to Milw. as Brewers for 1970

72--Baseball enjoys boom decade. In 72 players strike over pension funding; new Basic Agmt allows agents and arbitration. Oakland A's win first of three consecutive world titles; Reggie Jackson becoming major celebrity.

73--AL unilaterally adopts DH rule. Clemente voted to Hall of Fame posthumously.
74--Aaron beats Ruth's lifetime hr mark; Brock steals 118 bases. Deeds of blacks and Latin Am. players shine. In Japan Sadaharu Oh touted as bb. superstar.

75--Arbitrator Peter Seitz casts deciding vote in Messersmith case. The decision effectively circuments reserve clause; owners lose Fed Court challenge and prepare to retaliate. Cowhide balls in; sewn in Haiti, m.l. pitchers call em voodoo balls

76--Owners lockout players; Kuhn orders s.t. camps opened. Squabble ends with 4th Basic Agmt which sets re-entry drafts for fall of 76. Six-year vets can opt for re-entry. This yr. sees spurious centennial of maj. league ball celebrated (includes 1 billionth paid admission since 1901.)
77--<u>Third Expansion</u> unilaterally pulled off by AL which adds Toronto and Seattle Mariners. AL now a 14-team league, but they retain two-div. system and 162-game sked.

78--Rose's 44-game hit streak ties Keeler's NL mark with old Orioles. Rose gets 800 g's a yr. as he joins Phils. <u>Salary boom afoot.</u>

79--Pirates "Family" wins W. Series in memorable comback-first of 4-straight for NL
1980--Phils finally win a W. Series.

81--<u>Great Strike</u>. Cuts out half the season; season restructured under a split season format (first since 1892). Issue in strike is owner demand for compensation for players lost to annual re-entry drafts. This is compromised with talent pool setup.

82--Baseball popularity surges; attendance up. Heroics include Perry's 300th win, Henderson base stealer. Cards win flag.

83--Kuhn fails to get re-election as Commis; new Comm. sought. Orioles beat out Phils to end NL skein. Carlton 300th win; Rose chasing Cobb mark.

84--Steinbrenner fires Martin for third time; Ray Kroc croaks. Padres win NL over swooning Cubs; Tigers win W. Series. Ueberroth replaces Kuhn. Ump strike in playoffs-Ueberroth arbitrates in umps favor. Miller back advising Don Fehl and MLPA as new contract looms. Strike threat for 85 possible. New expansion possible-distant threat of a third major league.

Summary of Expansion ERa thus far.
Black and Latin stars shine--homer records set--pitching and base stealing records set. Attendance up over 40 million for yrs 78-84 (81 excepted). Dodgers boast several 3 million paid seasons--TV money makes for salary revolution; TV contract with networks (local contracts still in) bring big money to baseball.
Salary rev. shows over 20 player millionaires--Carter, Winfield, Sutter, Schmidt, etc. Reggie Jackson top celebrity of the 70's.
Other features include equipment changes, new parks, turfed fields, domed stadia.

   BUT TV, EXPANSIONISM, UNIONISM ARE MAJOR THEMES.

Major League Baseball's 20th Century Expansion

A. 1903-53, following Am. League War, majors field same two, 8 team leagues.
   1. 1950's see franchise shifts--first changes within this traditional format.
   --NL--1953. Boston Braves to Milwaukee (Mil wins flags in 57,58)
     NL--1957. Giants and Dodgers to S.F. and LA (LA wins in 59, SF in 62)
   --AL--1954. Browns to Baltimore (O's win in 66)
     AL--1955. Phila. A's to KC (As Oakland A's they win 3 world titles, 72-74)

B. First true expansion--1961(AL), 1962(NL).
   1. Continental League invasion threat of 59 prods major leagues to expand to ten clubs in ea. league. So doing they preempt leading Con. League sites; major league decision announced on Oct. 17, 1960--each major to field ten clubs; schedule increased to 162 games.
   2. AL in 1961 added LA Angels and Washington Senators. (These new Sens added because originals, under owner Cal Griffith, demanded to move to Minn. where they became the Twins (rep. cities of Minneap.-St. Paul). A new Wash. franchise was added to cool outraged voices of Washingtonians.
      NL--1962 adds NY Mets and Houston Colt 45's. Houston in 1965 opens its all-wx Astrodome and changes team name to Astros. Mets lose 120 games in their 1962 debut.
   3. Other stirrings-In 1966 Milwaukee carpetbags to Atlanta; in 1968 Finley takes his KC Athletics to Oakland. Problem of runaway franchises becomes legal issue.

C. Second Expansion of 1969.
   1. This year ea. major league goes to 12 clubs; ea. league divides into two divisions; 162 game sked retained. But divisional playoff format set after regular season to determine W. Series contestants.
   2. AL in 1969 adds Kansas City and Seattle. By end of yr. Seattle bankrupt and is sold to Milwaukee interests; team moved to Milwauk. as Brewers in 1970. Soon after, owner Bob Shorts moves Sens out of Wash to Dallas-Ft. Worth where they surface as the Texas Rangers.
   3. NL in 1969 adds Montreal in the East and San Diego in the West.

D. Third Expansion--1977.
   1. In 1977 AL unilaterally expands to 14 clubs by adding Toronto and Seattle (Mariners) (AL retains its two divisional setup and the 162 game sked.)

E. Some seasonal highlights during these years.
   1. Yanks and Dodgers dominate from 1946-56 (AL interlopers are Cleve and Chi); NL interlopers include Giants, Braves, Phils, Cards.
   2. Yank domination of AL ends in 1964. Then come Twins-65, Balt-66, Boston-67, Tigers-68, Balt-69.
      NL winners at same time--Milwauk.-57-8, LA-59, Pirates-60, Reds-61, Giants-62, LA-63, Cards-64, LA-65-6, Cards-67-8, Mets-69.
   3. Dynasties of Seventies.
      AL--its Orioles, Oakland A's, and Yanks.
      NL--Dodgers, Pirates, Reds (Phils are an E. Div. mini dynasty, but can't win N. League).
   4. 1980--Phils win first world title!!
   5. 1979-82 NL reels off four straight world titles.
   6. 1983--Baltimore humbles Phils.

Pennant Winners, 1946 thru 1983

A. Postwar Era, 1946-61.

	AL	NL	World Champ
1946	Red Sox	Cards (playoff)	Cards
47	Yanks	Dodgers	Yanks
48	Indians (playoff)	B. Braves	Indians
49	Yanks	Dodgers	Yanks
50	Yanks	Phils	Yanks
51	Yanks	Giants (playoff)	Yanks
52	Yanks	Dodgers	Yanks
53	Yanks	Dodgers	Yanks
54	Indians (won 111)	Giants	Giants
55	Yanks	Dodgers	Dodgers
56	Yanks	Dodgers	Yanks
57	Yanks	M. Braves	Braves
58	Yanks	M. Braves	Yanks
59	White Sox	Dodgers (playoff)	Dodgers
60	Yanks	Pirates	Pirates

B. First Expansion Round, 1961-68

	AL	NL	World Champ
61	Yanks	Reds	Yanks
62	Yanks	Giants (playoff)	Yanks
63	Yanks	Dodgers	Dodgers
64	Yanks	Cards	Cards
65	Twins	Dodgers	Dodgers
66	Orioles	Dodgers	Orioles
67	Red Sox	Cards	Cards
68	Tigers	Cards	Tigers

C. Second Expansion Round 1969-83 (including AL Mini-Expansion of 1977)

	AL		NL		World Champ
69	Orioles	Twins	Mets	Braves	Mets
70	Orioles	Twins	Pirates	Reds	Orioles
71	Orioles	O.A's	Pirates	Giants	Pirates
72	Tigers	O.A's	Pirates	Reds	A's
73	Orioles	O.A's	Mets	Reds	A's
74	Orioles	O.A's	Pirates	Dodgers	A's
75	Red Sox	O.A's	Pirates	Reds	Reds
76	Yanks	Royals	Phils	Reds	Reds
77	Yanks	Royals	Phils	Dodgers	Yanks
78	Yanks(p)	Royals	Phils	Dodgers	Yanks
79	Orioles	Angels	Pirates	Reds	Pirates
80	Yanks	Royals	Phils	Astros(p)	Phils
81	Y/B	A's/KC(Yanks)	Ph/Exp	Dod/Ast(Dod)	Dodgers
82	Brewers	Angels	Cards	Braves	Cards
83	Orioles	White Sox	Phils	Dodgers	Orioles
84					

Baseball in American Culture--Test 1, 85

A. **Short ANSWER**. Use small sheet. Answer each question.

1. Which word best describes the way major league baseball came about? (1)invention (2)discovery (3)creation (4)evolution.

2. Which early form of organized baseball won out? (1)Massachusetts game (2)NY game.

3. One of these is not descriptive of the "dis-play" concept--which is it. (1)commercialized entertainment (2)spectators outnumber participants (3)paid performers (4)play.

4. Prior to the Cincinnati Reds of 1869 no ball player was ever paid for playing baseball.

5. The first professional league was the (1)Natl Assn of Base Ball Players (2)National League (3)Natl Assn of Professional Base Ball Players (4)American Assn.

6. In America Thru Baseball an essay argues that the first major league was the (1) Natl Assn of Professional Base Ball Players (2)National League (3)Am. Assn (4) Players League.

7. An essay in Am. Thru BB names which of the following as "father of Professional baseball?" (1)Wm. Hulbert (2)Harry Wright (3)Albert G. Spaulding (4)Abner Doubleday (5)Henry Chadwick

8. The myth of baseball's "single sin" refers to (1)the Black Sox scandal (2)the National League coup of 1876 (3)the reserve clause act (4)the player strike of 1890.

9. During the Natl Assn era (1871-75) all but one of the pennants went to the (1) Phil. Athletics (2)Boston Red Stockings (3)Cincy Red Stockings (4)NY Mutuals (5)NY Giants.

10. Which of the following illustrates the immaculate conception myth? (1)the Doubleday legend (2)Cincy Reds of 1869 (3)the National League coup of 1876 (4)all these (5)none.

11. In its first five years of existence the National League (1)controlled all of pro baseball (2)far exceeded the Natl Assn in profits (3)placed club interests ahead of player interests (4)did all of these (5)did none of these.

12. Major League Baseball of the 1880's featured (1)dual major leagues (2)stylistic experimentation (3)player sales (4)all of these.

13. Beer sales and Sunday ball were promotional gimmicks used by which league in the 1880's? (1)American League (2)Players League (3)American Assn (4)Natl League (5)Natl Assn.

14. Making a player contract with one major league team for an indefinite period was achieved by the (1)-re-entry draft (2)National Agreement (3)Players League (4) reserve clause.

15. Concerning the geography of major league baseball in the 19th century, it was (1) continental (2)limited to eastern and old northwestern regions (3)limited to northern and southern regions.

16. In monopolizing major league baseball in the 19th century, the National League eliminated all but one of these rivals (1)Am. Assn (2)Am. League (3)Players League.

141

17. "Official" recognition of major leagues and minor leagues is contained in (1) the reserve clause (2)syndicate baseball (3)national agreements (4)Natl Commission.

18. From 1892 to 1900 how many major leagues were there? (1)2 (2)2 (3)3.

19. Which of these defunct major league claimants was the last to field teams and to be recognized as major league by the Macmillan Encyclopedia? (1)Am. Assn (2) Natl Assn of Prof. BB Players (3)Continental League (4)Federal League.

20. The Chicago "Black Sox" Players were judged guilty and expelled under which code of law (1)baseball law (2)civil law.

21. As practiced in the 1890's "syndicate ball" referred to (1)Andy Freedman's trust scheme (2)an owner controlling more than one team (3)the farm system trend (4)pennant monopoly by the "three B" teams.

22. The Temple Cup of the 1890's was an attempt to rekindle the success of the World Series matches that were first staged in the 1880's.

23. The 19th century superstar whose $10,000 sale to Boston excited fans was (1)Pop Anson (2)Charley Radbourn (3)King Kelly (4)Harry Wright (5)Al Spalding.

24. Which of these stars holds the most batting titles? (1)Cobb (2)Ruth (3)Wagner (4)Kelly.

25. The style of offense associated with the "Silver Age" is the (1)scientific style (2)big bang.

26. The "Czar of Baseball" who made the American League into a thriving major league was (1)Ban Johnson (2)Harry Wright (3)Branch Rickey (4)Chris von der Ahe.

27. During the heyday of the American Assn most pennants were won by which team? (1)NY Mets (2)St. Louis Browns (3)Brooklyn Bridegrooms (4)Phil. Athletics.

28. From 1903 to 1952 major league baseball (1)experienced many franchise shifts (2) included franchises west of the Miss. (3)operated under a dual 16 club system.

29. Baseball's "Time of Troubles" (1913-1919) included all but one of these events – (1)World War I (2)Players League (3)Federal League war (4)Black Sox scandal.

30. Judge Landis succeeded in eliminating farm systems from baseball promotion.

31. The film "Glory of their times" focused on which era? (1)the 1880's (2)black majors (3)the 1920's (4)the Silver Age.

32. The 19th century innovator who codified rules, edited journals and histories, and devised the modern box score was (1)Harry Wright (2)Henry Chadwick (3)Al Spalding (4)John Ward (5)Chris von der Ahe.

33. John M. Ward (now a Hall of Famer) was associated with the Brotherhood of Pro. BB Players and led the players in the Players League war of 1890.

34. After the 1891 season the Am. Assn. was crushed by the National League; none of it teams were admitted into the National League thereafter.

35. Branch Rickey is best associated with which form of talent recruiting? (1)the farm system (2)the bonus baby era (3)purchasing players from independent minor league operators (4)the rookie free agent draft of 1965 and afterwards.

36. The film "The Sun Was Always Shining Someplace" made which point? (1)Negro major league teams played more exhibitions than scheduled games (2)Racketeers owned some Negro teams (3)Raids by Mexican and Latin Am. teams hurt the Negro majors (4)some players from Negro majors made the Hall of Farm at Cooperstown (5)all these points.

37. The Natl Agmt of 1903 recognized which league as major? (1)the Am. Assn (2)the Players League (3)the National League (4)the American League (5)the Federal League.

38. Baseball law differs from civil law in that baseball law was able to deny freedom of movement to players by such devices as blacklisting and the reserve clause.

39. To settle disputes between the two major leagues the Natl Agmt of 1903 set up the (1)High Commissioner post (2)reserve clause (3)Natl Commission (4)Players Assn.

40. According to the film "The Sun Was Always Shining" the mecca of black baseball was (1)Philadelphia (2)Chicago (3)New York.

41. The "big three" superstars of the black majors included all but one of the following: (1)Jackie Robinson (2)Cool Papa Bell (3)Stach Paige (4)Josh Gibson.

42. Once the white majors accepted black players the owners of the Negro major league clubs made hefty profit windfalls from sale of their players to the majors.

43. Old time players (those prior to 1920) enjoyed freedom of movement and better salaries during those times when invading major leagues tried to win acceptance.

44. It was under the National Assn of Prof. Base Ball Players that major league baseball achieved a set schedule of playing dates for all clubs to follow.

45. As the essay in Am. Thru Baseball shows, the "Black Sox" players of 1919 were the only players in major league history ever to have taken bribes to throw games.

46. By 1920 major league players had attempted at least three unionization efforts aimed at improving pay and correcting the reserve clause; however, none succeeded.

47. The era in baseball history that featured the big bang style, Ruth the super celebrity, Landis the High Commissioner, the first radio broadcasts of games, and the black majors was (1)the Silver Age (2)the Gentlemen's Era (3)the Golden 1880's (4)the Second Golden Age (5)the Feudal Age.

48. Baseball's "Unforgettable Season" which featured the Merkel boner and the Cub victory occurred during the 1920's.

49. Brandy Davis's scouting operations (with Philly and the Cubs) depended on the scouting bureau rather than their own enterprise.

50. According to Gene Benson it was he who popularized the "basket catch".

Name_____

B. <u>Written Answers</u>. Answer in space provided. You get a pt. for each factual sentence up to the limit listed behind each question. Answer in factual <u>sentences</u>.

1. What were the four eras of scouting as described by Kevin Kerrane: (2)

2. Show how Voigt divides major league history from the beginnings to 1945 into five distinct eras: (2)

3. Cite three major trends in American social life that are mirrored in major league baseball history (this is from Am. T. BB.) (2)

4. Cite three insights which you gained from Kit Crissey's talk on Japanese baseball: (2)

5. Pennant monopoly is a fact of life in major league baseball history. Defend by choosing any of the five eras: (2)

_____

<u>Longer Answer</u> (6 pts.)

Name the three great innovators of 19th century major league baseball and the three great innovators of 20th century m.l. baseball (to 1950) -- Also give a statement for each showing his significant contribution:

Baseball in American Culture, Final, 1985

A. <u>Short Answer</u>. Use small sheet. Answer each question.

1. During the "big bang" era of the 1920's (1)the Yanks outhomered most other clubs (2) the American League outhomered the National each year (3)at times Ruth outhomered some teams (4)all statements are true (5)all but one statement is true.

2. Under Rickey the Cardinal farm system eventually included more than 25 minor league teams.

3. During the Expansion Era (to date) which of these hitters won the most batting titles? (1)Rose (2)Carew (3)Mays (4)Aaron (5)Madlock.

4. The first league to expand to 10 teams was the National League.

5. The rookie draft instituted in 1965 had which of these effects? (1)scouts became talent evaluators (2)it started the bonus baby era (3)rich clubs monopolized all the talent (4)clubs no longer had to sponsor minor league teams.

6. Since the 1960's it can fairly be said that major league baseball has experienced a continuing "talent shortage."

7. The latest ballpark building boom was for the most part financed by private capital.

8. In vol. 3, the section "Baseball, Black and Beautiful" made the point that black players (including dusky Hispanics) (1)made up at least 20%of playing rosters since 1960 (2)dominated offensive categories (3)still encounter discrimination (4)fit all these descriptions.

9. The "dishonest season" mentioned in Vol. 3 was (1)1919 (2)1966 (3)1968 (4)1981.

10. Which form of television broadcasting currently brings most revenue to major league teams? (1)network (2)cable (3)local television contracts.

11. An essay in <u>American Through Baseball</u> upholds which nationalistic style as most characteristic of Amerca? (1)humanitarian (2)Jacobin (3)traditional (4)integral (5)liberal.

12. In the same book an essay on "the mission of America" argues that a strategy of professional advocacy successfully spread baseball into Latin American and Japan.

13. The essay on American baseball and the American dilemma deals with (1)player unions (2)the celebrity-making process (3)baseball corruption (4)racism in baseball.

14. The "manufactured villain" of American baseball was the (1)umpire (2)mercenary owner (3)rowdy fan (4)cruel Commissioner.

15. Another <u>ATB</u> essay argues that nowadays most baseball heroes are (1)consensus heroes (2)ethnic heroes (3)episodic heroes (4)folk heroes.

16. The film "A Touch of Royalty" dealt with the (1)1983 World Series (2)50 years of baseball memories (3)Roberto Clemente (4)the umpires.

17. Since baseball's 1969 expansion the only team to win 3 straight world series titles has been the (1)Yanks (2)Dodgers (3)Orioles (4)Athletics (5)Pirates.

18. According to <u>ATB</u> the double umpire system used in the majors was (1)first tried in the 1880's (2)not regularly used by both majors until 1911 (3)not used till after WWII (4)all true (5)all but one statement true.

19. Bill Klem was a (1)star pitcher (2)famous owner (3)inventive sportswriter (4) innovative umpire.

20. Over the past century major league baseball's player <u>celebrities</u> included (1)King Kelly (2)Babe Ruth (3)Reggie Jackson (4)all of these (5)none of these.

21. A <u>celebrity</u> player by Voigt's definition always has been the top performer at his position in his playing time.

22. According to <u>ATB</u> major league players tried five times to unionize before coming up with a strong, seemingly permanent union.

23. The umpires of today have no union counterpart of the Major League Players Assn.

24. The postwar franchise move which ended 50 seasons of major league stability was undertaken by the (1)Braves (2)Athletics (3)Dodgers (4)Giants.

25. The first Expansion of the major leagues came when (1)each major league expanded to 10 teams (2)the majors adopted divisional play with 12 teams in each league (3)when O'Malley moved to LA with his Dodgers.

26. The first major league club to relocate a second time was the (1)Braves (2)Athletics (3)Senators.

27. In the years 1949-1967 the Yankees were the only American League team to win a world series.

28. The Expansion franchise that went bankrupt after its initial 1969 season was the (1)Milwaukee Braves (2)Washington Senators (3)Seattle Pilots (4)KC Athletics.

29. From 1966 through 1984 the winningest team in major league baseball was the (1) Yanks (2)Dodgers (3)Cardinals (4)Orioles.

30. The American League took unilateral action during the 1970's in all but one of the following incidents. Which is the exception? (1)the DH rule (2)building new parks (3)expanding to 14 teams.

31. The "union ethic" described in <u>ATB</u> is an all out force in American society that engulfs nearly every individual American.

32. During the 1960's and until 1977 the American League consistently outdrew the National League and also led the Nationals in offensive performances.

33. Joy Risner's presentation on <u>Boys of Summer</u> quoted author Kahn as saying that a ballplayer dies twice--as an athlete and as a human being.

34. The flamboyant hero of <u>The Umpire Strikes Back</u> was (1)Darth Vader (2)Jim Honochick (3)Ron Luciano (4)Babe Pinella (5)Bill Klem.

35. According to the student presentation on fads and manners of fans, the promotional giveaways used so much by major league clubs are limited strictly to kids.

36. The student presentation on life in the minors pointed out that today the rights of minor league players are protected by their memberships in the Maj. League Players Assn.

146

37. The presentation on Baseball Economics stated that major league baseball has been called a monopoly for all but one of the following reasons. The exception is-- (1)baseball's policy on signing rookie free agents (2)the reserve clause (3)franchise allocations (4)scheduling interleague championship games (5)granting territorial rights to teams.

38. The great player triptych of the Postwar Era (according to Voigt) included all but one of the following--(1)Ted Wms (2)Joe DiMaggio (3)Warren Spahn (4)Stan Musial.

39. The triptych that succeeded the above included all but one of these--(1)Rod Carew (2)Pete Rose (3)Hank Aaron (4)Willie Mays.

40. The first relief ace to be voted into the Hall of Fame was (1)Joe Page (2)"Iron Man" McGinninity (3)Mike Marshall (4)Hoyt Wilhelm (5)Rollie Fingers.

41. The best estimate of the amount of real action occurring in a 1 and ½hr. baseball game is (1)30 min (2)an hour (3)ten minutes (4)an hour and a half.

42. Jimmy Piersall, Steve Blass, Kevin Saucier are examples of what kind of nuts? (1)genuine (2)jesters (3)ludicrous role performers (4)overconformers.

43. Over the past two seasons (83 and 84) the strongest division in m.l. baseball has been the (1)NL west (2)NL east (3)AL east (4)AL west.

44. In the wake of m.l. baseball's strike season of 1981 attendance has dropped and has remained below the pre-1981 levels.

45. The current acting director of the Major League Players Assn is (1)Marvin Miller (2)Ken Moffett (3)Don Fehr.

46. Under the terms of baseball's latest network TV pact (negotiated for six years and beginning in 1984) each club gets $4 a season.

47. The new Commissioner of baseball is (1)Landis (2)Kuhn (3)Frick (4)Miller (5)Ueberroth.

48. Concerning baseball's salaries which statement is true? (1)there are at least 20 million dollar a year players (2)in 84 Schmidt was the reigning plutocrat at 1.9 mill (3)the average salary of 1984 neared 300,000 a year (4)all statements are true (5)none are true.

49. The 1981 major league baseball strike lasted longer than the 1890 one.

50. Compared with past eras baseball today has (1)more outstanding shortstops (2)the leading strikeout pitchers (3)far more wealthy clubowners (4)all of these (5)none of these.

Name_____

B. **Short Sentence-Type Questions**. Answer each in <u>factual, complete sentences</u>. 2 pts. each.

1. Name the great triptych of Postwar Players; also name the great triptych of early Expansion Era players. (6 pts.)

2. Identify 3 films shown since the last test and give statement of significance for each:

3. From the essay on baseball's changing dimensions identify and give a descriptive statement for each of the four:

4. Identify and briefly describe each of the three phases in baseball's expansion:

5. What are some characteristics of the "new breed of ballplayers?":

C. <u>Longer Essay</u>. Answer in complete, factual sentences.

Baseball (major league) is a long established institution that mirrors changes and trends in the culture at large. Explain: (six points)

VI. SPORT AND LITERATURE

AND FILMS

BASEBALL FICTION FOR ADULTS 1973-1985

Andersen, Richard. <u>Muckaluck</u>. New York: Delacorte, 1980.
    Cloth. One chapter on baseball.

Bell, Marty. <u>Breaking Balls</u>. New York: Signet, 1979. Paper.

Brady, Charles. <u>Seven Games in October</u>. Boston: Little, Brown,
    1979. Cloth.

Brashler, William. <u>The Bingo Long Traveling All-Stars and Motor
    Kings</u>. New York: Harper and Row, 1973. Cloth. New York:
    Signet, 1975. Paper.

Carkeet, David. <u>The Greatest Slump of All Time</u>. New York:
    Harper and Row, 1984. Cloth.

Charyn, Jerome. <u>The Seventh Babe</u>. New York: Arbor House, 1979.
    Cloth. New York: Avon, 1980. Paper.

Clifton, Merritt. <u>A Baseball Classic</u>. Richford, Vermont:
    Samisdat, 1978. Paper.

Craig, John. <u>All G.O.D.'s Children</u>. New York: Morrow, 1975.
    Cloth. New York: Signet, 1976. Paper.

_____. <u>Chappie and Me</u>. New York: Dodd, Mead, 1979.
    Cloth.

Cronley, Jay. <u>Screwballs</u>. New York: Doubleday, 1980. Cloth.

DeAndrea, William L. <u>Five O'Clock Lightning</u>. New York: St.
    Martin's, 1982. Cloth.

Donohue, James F. <u>Spitballs and Holy Water</u>. New York: Avon,
    1977. Paper.

Engelman, Paul. <u>Dead in Centerfield</u>. New York: Ballantine,
    1983. Paper.

Everett, Percival L. <u>Suder</u>. New York: Viking, 1983. Cloth.
    A baseball player is the focus.

Foster, Alan S. <u>Goodbye, Bobby Thomson! Goodbye, John Wayne!</u>
    New York: Simon and Schuster, 1973. Cloth. New York:
    Signet, 1974. Beginning section relates to baseball.

Frank, Murry. <u>Every Young Man's Dream: Confessions of a
    Southern League Shortstop</u>. Chicago: Silverback Books,
    1984. Cloth. 1985, Paper.

Graham, John Alexander. <u>Babe Ruth Caught in a Snowstorm</u>. Boston:
    Houghton Mifflin, 1973. Cloth.

Greenberg, Eric Rolfe. *The Celebrant*. New York: Everest House, 1983. Cloth.

Harris, Mark. *It Looked Like For Ever*. New York: McGraw-Hill, 1979. Cloth. New York: McGraw-Hill, 1984. Paper.

Hays, Donald. *The Dixie Association*. New York: Simon and Schuster, 1984. Cloth.

Hegner, William. *The Idolaters*. New York: Trident, 1973. Cloth.

Hemphill, Paul. *Long Gone*. New York: Viking, 1979. Cloth.

Herrin, Lamar. *The Rio Loja Ringmaster*. New York: Viking, 1977. Cloth.

Honig, Donald. *The Last Great Season*. New York: Simon and Schuster, 1979. Cloth.

Jordan, Pat. *The Cheat*. New York: Villard Books, 1984. Cloth.

Kahn, Roger. *The Seventh Game*. New York: New American Library, 1982. Cloth.

Keifetz, Norman. *The Sensation*. New York: Atheneum, 1975. Cloth.

Kennedy, William. *Ironweed*. New York: Viking, 1983. Cloth. Penguin Books, 1984. Paper.

Kinsella, W. P. *Shoeless Joe*. Boston: Houghton Mifflin, 1982. Cloth. New York: Ballantine Books, 1983. Paper.

Kinsella, W. P. *The Thrill of the Grass*. Penguin Books, 1985. Paper.

Kluger, Steve. *Changing Pitches*. New York: St. Martin's, 1984. Cloth.

*Kowett, Don. *The 7th Game*. New York: Dell, 1977. Paper.

Magnuson, James. *The Rundown*. New York: Dial, 1977. Cloth.

Mayer, Robert. *The Grace of Shortstops*. Garden City, NY: Doubleday, 1984. Cloth.

Morgenstein, Gary. *Take Me Out to the Ballgame*. New York: St. Martin's, 1980. Cloth.

_____. *The Man Who Wanted to Play Centerfield for the New York Yankees*. New York: Atheneum, 1983. Cloth.

Neugeboren, Jay. *Sam's Legacy*. New York: Holt, Rinehart and Winston, 1974. Cloth.

*Lorenz, Tom. *Guys Like Us*. New York: Viking, 1980. Cloth. Softball.

O'Connor, Philip F. _Stealing Home_. New York: Knopf, 1979.
 Cloth.

Parker, Robert B. _Mortal Stakes_. Boston: Houghton Mifflin,
 1975. Cloth.

Paulos, Sheila. _Wild Roses_. New York: Dell, 1983. Paper.

Platt, Kin. _The Screwball King Murder_. New York: Random House,
 1978. Cloth.
*

Powers, Ron. _Toot-Toot-Tootsie, Good-bye_. New York: Delacorte,
** 1981. Cloth.

Quarrington, Paul. _Home Game_. Toronto: Doubleday, 1983. Cloth.

Rice, Damon. _Seasons Past_. New York: Praeger, 1976. Cloth.

Ritz, David. _The Man Who Brought the Dodgers Back to Brooklyn_.
*** New York: Simon and Schuster, 1981. Cloth.

Roth, Philip. _The Great American Novel_. New York: Holt, Rinehart, and Winston, 1973. Cloth. New York: Bantam, 1974.
 Paper.

Rothweiler, Paul R. _The Sensuous Southpaw_. New York: Putnam,
 1976. Cloth.

Sayles, John. _Pride of the Bimbos_. Boston: Atlantic/Little,
 Brown, 1975. Cloth.

Schiffer, Michael. _Ballpark_. New York: Simon and Schuster,
 1982. Cloth.

Small, David. _Almost Famous_. New York: Norton, 1982. Cloth.

Stein, Harry. _Hoopla_. New York: Knopf, 1983. Cloth.

Vogan, Sara. _In Shelly's Leg_. New York: Knopf, 1981. Cloth.
 Softball.

Willard, Nancy. _Things Invisible to See_. New York: Knopf,
 1985. Cloth.

Winston, Peter. _Luke_. New York: Manor Books, 1976. Paper.

Wolff, Miles J. _Season of the Owl_. New York: Stein and Day,
 1980. Cloth.
****Zacharia, Irwin. _Grandstand Rookie_. Canoga Park, CA: Major Books, 1977. Paper.

 *Pomeranz, Gary. _Out at Home_. Boston: Houghton Mifflin, 1985. Cloth.

 **Puechner, Ray. _A Grand Slam_. New York: Warner Books, 1973. Paper.

 ***Rosen, R.D. _Strike Three, You're Dead_. New York: Walker and Company, 1984. Cloth.

Books Omitted by Grobani

Beckham, Barry. <u>Runner Mack</u>. New York: Morrow, 1972. Cloth.
New York: Popular Library, 1972. Paper. Washington, DC:
Howard University Press, 1984. Paper.

Green, Gerald. <u>To Brooklyn With Love</u>. New York: Trident
Press, 1967. Cloth.

Karlins, Marvin. <u>The Last Man Is Out</u>. Englewood Cliffs, N.J.:
Prentice-Hall, 1969. Cloth.

Mendelsohn, Felix Jr. <u>Superbaby</u>. Los Angeles: Nash, 1969.
Cloth.

Nye, Bud. <u>Stay Loose</u>. Garden City: Doubleday, 1959. Cloth.

Potok, Chaim. <u>The Chosen</u>. New York: Simon and Schuster, 1967.
Cloth. Contains an account of a ball game between two Jewish
parochial schools that turns into a holy war.

154

Robert J. Higgs, East Tennessee State University
Sports Literature
2nd Period, MWF
Fall, 1985

Texts: (1) <u>Sports in the Western
World</u>, ed. William J.
Baker, Rowan & Little-
field, Totowa, NJ, 1982.

(2) <u>The Sporting Spirit:
Athletes in Literature
and Life</u>, eds. Robert
J. Higgs and Neil D.
Isaacs, Harcourt Brace,
Jovanovich, 1977.

January

8   Discussion of Course Requirements & Objectives

10   Baker, Introduction & "The Compulsive Impulse," pp. 1-13

13   Baker, "Organized Greek Games," 14-27; Higgs, "Plato," 221-224, &
     Pindar & Euripides, 7-8.

15   Baker, "The Decline & Fall of Athletics," 28-41; Higgs, Edith Hamilton,
     & Toynbee 243-246

17   Baker, "Medieval People at Play," 42-56

20   Martin Luther King, Jr. Holiday

22   Baker, "The Day of the Scholar Athlete," 59-71; Higgs, "Castiglione,"
     141-143

24   Baker, "Frowning Puritans," 72-84

27   First-In-Class Essay

29   Baker, "New Standards for Old Sports," 85-98; Higgs, Henry Adams, 247-249

31   Baker, "Varieties of Football," 119-137; Higgs, Theodore Roosevelt,
     144-150

February

3   Baker, "Boys of Winter," 155-170; Higgs, Dennis Trudel, 52-54

5   Baker, "Bats, Balls & Business,: 138-154; Higgs, Mark Twain &
     Gregory Corso, 11-13

7   Baker, "Individualism Rugged & Refined," 171-188; Higgs, Veblen, 250-255

10   Baker, "Days Dark & Golden," 209-228; Higgs, "Gene Tunney, My Fights
     with Jack Dempsey," 124-132

155

12 Baker, "Coping with Depression," 229-244; Higgs, Thorstein Veblen, 257-258, Damon Runyan, 258-259

14 Baker, "Testing the Super Race," 245-260; Higgs, "Jesse Owens," 95-102, Budd Schulberg, 191-199

17 2nd In-Class Essay

19 Baker, "East-West Games," 263-282; Higgs, Henry Morton, 211-213

21 Baker, "Breaking Barriers through Sports," 283-303; Higgs, Edwards, 185-189 & Dugan, 190-191

24 Baker, "Sports Biz," 304-329; Higgs, Mumford, 259-262

26 Baker, "Sports in Perspective," 330-340; Higgs, Huizinga, 228-242

The Remaining Selections are From

The Sporting Spirit

28 J.F. Powers & William C. Williams, 13-27

March

3 Irwin Shaw & Jarrell, 29-40

5 Thurber & Updike, 41-43 & Mencken, 110-113

7 Updike, 45-52

10 In-Class Essay #3

12 Virgil & Schulberg, 54-60

14 McCullers, 61-65

17 Houseman & Hemingway, 66-75

19 Lardner, Robinson, & Auden, 76-90

21 Yukio Mishima, 103-109; Don Johnson, 263-264

24-28 SPRING BREAK

31 Diana Nyad, 114-116 & Maxin Kumin, 200-202

April

2 Eleanor Matheny, 202-210; Juvenal & Jim Wayne Miller, 140-141

4 Jerry Kramer & Gary Gildner, 117-123

7 Mike Spino, 133-136

9 Byron R. White, 151-159 & Xenophanes, 139

11   Kenneth Patchen & Norman Mailer, 151–163

14   William Faulkner, 164–165

16   In–Class Essay #4

18   Robert Frost, 166–168

21   Marianne Moore & George Plimpton, 169–177

23   Marshall McLuhan, 264–267

25   Weiss & Rilke, 264–273

Course Requirements:

1. Four In–Class Essays

2. Three Out–of–Class Essays (4 pgs. handwritten)

3. One Oral Report on Assigned Book

4. All Work Kept in Harbrace Folder

5. Class Attendance

English 210 First Semester, 1985-1986

The Athlete in Twentieth Century Literature and Life

Tuesday and Thursday, 2-3:15

R. Johnson
Office: 382 Bachelor; Phone: 6508
Office Hours: Tuesday and Thursday, 12:45-1:45

Texts

William Blinn, Brian's Song
John Brady and James Hall, Sports Literature (Abbreviated Sports)
Robert Coover, The Universal Baseball Association
Don DeLillo, End Zone
Peter Gent, North Dallas Forty
Robert Higgs and Neil Isaac, The Sporting Spirit (Abbreviated Spirit)
Roger Kahn, The Boys of Summer
W.P. Kinsella, Shoeless Joe
Ring Lardner, You Know Me, Al
Bernard Malamud, The Natural
Philip Roth, The Great American Novel
Burt Standish, Frank Merriwell's Schooldays

Assignments

1) Two hour exams.
2) Regular class attendance and participation in discussion.
3) A journal reflecting your observations, reactions to the readings and
to current events in the world of sports.
4) A final exam.
5) A short paper (approximately five pages) detailing your personal reactions
to and comments on one of the novels read during the semester. You should try
to convince your assumed reader to read this novel or for your instructor to
drop this novel from the reading list. You may discuss a novel not included
on the reading list, but please check the title with me before you take this
option.

Class Schedule

August 29 Introduction to Course: Expectations and definitions.

September 3 Slusher, "Sport as a Human Absurdity," in Spirit, 274-280; Plato,
"The Republic," in Spirit, 221-224; Huizinga, "Play-Element," in Spirit, 228-
243; Goodman, "Don Larsen's Perfect Game," Humphries, "Polo Grounds," Peck,
"TKO," in Sports, 20-24.

September 5 Read Kumin "400-Meter Freestyle," Dickey, "In the Pocket,"
Lattimore, "Sky Diving," Wallace, "The Double Play," in Sports, pp. 48-52;
Brown, "I'm a Dedicated Man, Son," in Sports, 76-89.

September 10 Read Kahn, "The Crucial Part Fear Plays in Sports," in Sports, 54-63; Gardner, "Chuvalo," Collier, "On Chuck Hughes, Dying Young," in Sports, 110-138; Housman, "To an Athlete Dying Young," in Spirit, 66-67; Hemphill, "The Last Days of Ernie Banks," in Sports, 25-33; Mailer, "The Death of Benny Paret," in Spirit, 160-164.

September 12 Read Gayle Sayers, "Pick" and Tom Meschery, "As It Should Be," in Sports, 163-179, 187. Read Brian's Song.

September 17 Read Edwards, "The Myth of the Racially Superior Black Athlete," in Spirit, 185-190.

September 19 No class today.

September 24 Read Frank Merriwell's Schooldays.

September 26 Continue Merriwell

October 1 Read Lardner, You Know Me, Al and "A Caddy's Diary," in Spirit, 76-88.

October 3 Continue Lardner

October 8 Read J.F. Powers, "Jamesie," in Spirit, 13-27 and Updike, "Ace in the Hole," in Spirit, 45-52; Mercer, "The Only Way to Win," in Sports, 90-106.

October 10 Hand in journal. Read W.P. Kinsella, Shoeless Joe.

October 15 Continue Kinsella.

October 17 Exam

October 22 Read Coover, The Universal Baseball Association.

October 24 Continue Coover.

October 29 Read Roth The Great American Novel.

October 31 Continue Roth.

November 5 Read Malamud, The Natural. If you have seen the movie, be prepared to discuss the very different endings of the two works.

November 7 Continue Malamud.

November 12 Read Meggysey, "Football and Education," and Stafford, "He Tries Hard," in Sports, 238-250; 266-267; White, "Athletics: . . . Unquenchably the Same?" in Spirit, 151-158; Dunn, "Athletic Recruiting: A Campus Crisis," and Paterno, "Opinion," in Sports, 251-256; 260-265.

November 14 Read Juvenal, "Female Athletes," in Spirit, 140; Fasteau, "Giving Women a Sporting Chance," in Sports, 220-228; Collins, "Billie Jean King Evens the Score," and Gibson, "We Weren't Bad, Just Mischievous," in

Sports, 201-215; 2-15; Metheny, "Symbolic Forms of Movement: The Feminine Image in Sports," in Spirit, 202-210.

November 19   Exam.

November 21   Read Updike, "Ex-Basketball Player," and Petrie, "The Old Pro's Lament," in Sports, 180-82; Shaw, "The Eighty-Yard Run," in Spirit, 29-39; Schulberg, "The Crowd Pleaser," in Spirit, 55-60.

November 26   Read Kahn, The Boys of Summer.

December 3   Continue Kahn.

December 5   Read DeLillo, End Zone.

December 10   Continue DeLillo. Start Gent, North Dallas Forty. Hand in journal.

December 12   Finish Gent. Short paper due.

English 210   February 24, 1984   First Exam

A) In the last chapter of The Universal Baseball Association the baseball park
is depicted as American house of worship. In Shoeless Joe W.P. Kinsella also
suggests that baseball is a religion and its fans are a congregation. First
describe how each author develops or uses this baseball/religion metaphor and
then compare and contrast how this metaphor is important to our understanding
of each novel.

B) Michael Oriard has described two criteria for judging a sports novel:
    1) The good sports novelist understands and demonstrates that baseball
        itself is "about" more than "baseball," football about more than the
        game on the field. The point is not for the novelist to recognize
        that baseball and football players are people too, but that as football
        and baseball players they are particular kinds of people whose necessary
        concerns and activities touch their culture in important ways.

    2) Good sports novels also exploit the potential inherent in the specific
        sports with which they deal. Rabbit, Run could only be about basketball.
        The Universal Baseball Association could not have been about an
        imaginary football league.

Short Answer
Write on four of the five questions

1) List three differences between sport and play and show how your understanding
of these differences allows you to read with more insight the excerpts from one
of the following: Slusher, Huizinga, or Weiss.

2) How do you account for your different reactions to the death of a young
athlete depicted by Housman and to the death of either Brian Piccolo (Sayers)
or Chuck Hughes (Collier)?

3) In what way does reading Kahn's essay, "The Crucial Part Fear Plays in
Sports," help us better understand Gardner's portrait of George Chuvalo?

4) How effectively does one of the following poets capture the thrill of the
sport in his or her poem: Kumin, Dickey, Littimore, or Wallace?

5) What sport, if any, could you substitute for lacrosse in Brown's story,
"I'm a Dedicated Man, Son?" Develop briefly your argument.

161

2/26/85

Part One. You must write on A or B.

A

Both Coover and Roth use the perfect game as an integral part of the novel
or an episode in the novel. First explain what the perfect game represents
and then compare and contrast how each author uses this idea to develop that
particular episode. Be sure to recognize the different intent of each author.

B

First explain how the spirit of fair play is an essential part of the play
or game experience and then discuss how this idea is used by both Burt
Standish and Ring Lardner. Be sure that you recognize the different purposes
of the two authors and make clear to your reader your conclusion about
Lardner as either a comic or satiric writer.

Part Two. You must write on two of the four questions.

1) Given your understanding now of play, game, and sport, how do you react
to Chuvalo's criticism of Ali: " 'He doesn't bother me, he said. 'But he
seems kind of like a kid, you know? It's unprofessional.'" (Sports, p. 111).

2) One theme running through Hemphill's essay on Ernie Banks is that there
is something sad, even pathetic, about the aging athlete. But Ernie Banks
is not simply representative of all aging athletes. What are the particular
characteristics of Banks which make his story unique or especially poignant.
Be sure to recognize the somewhat symbolic nature of Banks.

3) Do you consider Mumford ("Sport and the 'Bitch-goddess'") or Slusher
("Sport as a Human Absurdity") the more perceptive commentator on sport?
In your answer draw on your own experience and refer to at least two poems,
essays, or stories we have read so far this semester.

4) I would insist that Coover could not substitute any other sport for
baseball in his novel, The Universal Baseball Association. However, Lardner's
hero, Jack Keefe, could also have played football or basketball. Support
or argue with this statement.

162

English 210 Final Exam 5/7/85

Part One (Required Question)

This summer you may very well find yourself in a conversation about sports and athletics with an old friend and find that your attitude about the subject is markedly different from that of your friend. For the sake of argument, let us pretend that this person represents you back in January. First show how your attitude or understanding of sports has changed since January and then recommend a minimum of five works (one of them must be a novel) which would best bring your friend to the same understanding that you now have. Be specific when you refer to the readings and make sure that the individual works can also be subsumed under a general thesis which you are trying to develop.

Part Two (Write on two of the four questions)

A) Defend the statement that End Zone is a better sports novel than North Dallas Forty.

B) Using Billy Cox or Roy Campanella and two other Dodgers explain what Kahn means by the distinction between baseball players and baseball playing men.

C) Explain how your knowledge of history and myths of baseball and your understanding of the game itself are essential to an intelligent reading of either The Natural or Shoeless Joe.

D) I would think that many, if not all of us, share a delight in the athletic experience. I know I look back with warm nostalgia on my years of playing college football, and I now relish my attempts to master the so-called life-time sports such as tennis. But many of our readings this semester suggest that the athletic experience can be a flawed or negative one. Other factors can work against that positive experience. From your readings identify first the positive aspect of athletics (refer to at least two separate works), and then identify some of these negative elements (refer to at least three works).

163

Final Exam English 210.2 5/8/84

Part 1   Essay Question

One of the themes of Roger Kahn's "The Boys of Summer" is that one is a different person because of the experience he or she has had. Kahn's boyhood experiences in Brooklyn, his work on the Herald Tribune, all contributed to his writing of this particular book. The members of the 1952-53 Brooklyn Dodgers are also different in significant ways, both because of their shared experiences as members of the team and because of their unique backgrounds. If we apply this idea to ourselves, all of us are different because of this course and the readings and discussion. In an integrated and coherent essay discuss how your perceptions of athletics and athletes, sport and game, and/or competition have changed in the last few months. You must refer to at least four specific readings, and you must advance a specific thesis. As a starting point, you might consider how, in some cases, your journal entries have reflected a significant change in your attitudes. The important point is that you personalize the essay and that you show that you understand the readings that you have selected.

Part 2   Short Answer
Write on four of the five questions

1) At the end of "North Dallas Forty," Bob Beaudreau, who has just killed Charlotte and David, calls Phil Elliott crazy. From the point of view of the Dallas football team Phil is indeed crazy. Define the measures of sanity in the world of this novel and explain, therefore, why Phil, despite his own excessive actions, is a sympathetic protagonist.

2) How do you explain the fact that when we read Roth's "The Great American Novel" we laugh at events and jokes that from another perspective can not be considered comical: racial stereotypes, physical handicaps, mental illness, etc.?

3) Discuss the significance of the following sentence from Kahn's book (p. 194): "It was then, in Frost's last decade, that I began to consider the Dodgers not as baseball players but as baseball-playing men, as some are poetry-writing men, or painting men or men who make decisions of state."

4) The visit of Dr. Harry Edwards to Miami should have forced you to confront a basic question about sport and game. If game and/or sport and athletic competition are intrinsically appealing and beneficial, what is the societal or psychological effect of restricting access to that competition because of racial, economic, or sexual differences? You may, of course, choose to argue against this idea.

5) The theme of the last part of the course was "capturing the past," a particularly appropriate topic today, May 8, my 46th birthday. Drawing on the readings of the last few weeks (or readings throughout the semester), distinguish between the destructive and the constructive influences of the past.

English 202: Sports and Literature

Jim O'Donnell
Office: 2250 FOSS
Hours: 8:30-9:20 am
    and just prior
    to class
Telephone: 546-4796

This course meets in Room
425 on Thursday nights from
6 to 10. Class attendance is
imperative because of this
once-a-week format.

Required Texts: <u>The Sporting Spirit: Athletes in Literature and Life</u>, edited
by Robert J. Higgs and Neil D. Isaacs; one novel chosen from
the instructor's approved list.

Course Requirements: Two examinations (mid-term and final)
                    One paper (750-1200 words) relating to novel chosen by
                      student
                    Class participation

Grading: Each exam counts ¼ of the course grade; both the paper and class
participation count ¼ of the course grade as well.

Course Objectives: English 202 does not require a previous literature course.
                    Students will read fiction, poetry, and drama related to
                    sports, especially by authors who have made major contri-
                    butions to American literature, e.g., William Faulkner,
                    Ernest Hemingway, F. Scott Fitzgerald, Philip Roth, and
                    John Updike; the course will also include classical authors,
                    such as Homer and Vergil. Through lecture and discussion,
                    students will learn about the perceptions writers have had
                    on the relationship between sports and society. Because,
                    for many students, this is an introduction to literature,
                    literary terms--theme, character, plot, imagery, symbol,
                    to name a few--will be defined in the process of examining
                    the texts. Basic knowledge of these aspects is expected
                    as the course develops.

                    Films and guest speakers will be scheduled when feasible.

See attached sheet for the approved reading list.

Works Approved for Course Paper

Baseball

Robert Coover, The Universal Baseball Association

Bernard Malamud, The Natural

Philip Roth, The Great American Novel

Football

Peter Gent, North Dallas Forty

Don DeLillo, End Zone

Frederick Exley, A Fan's Notes

Basketball

John Updike, Rabbit, Run

Hunting

Ernest Hemingway, The Green Hills of Africa

William Faulkner, The Bear

Bullfighting

Ernest Hemingway, The Sun Also Rises

Fishing

Norman Maclean, A River Runs Through It

Golf

Michael Murphy, Golf in the Kingdom

Athletic Contests

Homer, The Illiad and The Odyssey

Jim O'Donnell
Home: 632-2255
Office: 771-1625 (Lynnwood 426)

125 Mountlake Terrace Hall
Monday and Wednesday, 7-9:40pm

Required text: Fielder's Choice: An Anthology of Baseball Fiction, Holtzman
Optional texts: The Natural, Malamud; The Great American Novel, Roth; Bang
the Drum Slowly, Harris; The Universal Baseball Association
etc., Coover

June 23--Introduction

Part I: The Team (The Individual in Society)

June 25--Ring Lardner: "Hurry Kane," "My Roomy," and Horseshoes"

June 30--Lardner: "Alibi Ike," FC, pp. 28-46; John Cheever: "The National Pastime"

July 2 --William Brashler: excerpt from The Bingo Long Traveling All-Stars and Motor
Kings, FC, pp. 132-142; Eliot Asinof: "The Rookie," FC, pp. 256-270.

July 7 --Arnold Hano: "The Umpire Was a Rookie," FC, pp. 334-348; Mark Harris:
excerpt from Bang the Drum Slowly, FC, pp. 53-61; William Carlos Williams:
"At the Ball Game" (poem)

July 14--Chaim Potok: excerpt from The Chosen, FC, pp. 97-121; Richard Hugo:
"Missoula Softball Tournament" and "The Freaks at Spurgin Road Field" (poems)

Part II: The Hero (A Champion of the People)

July 16--Ernest Lawrence Thayer: "Casey at the Bat"; John Updike: "Hub Fans Bid
Kid Adieu" (nonfiction); Laurence Lieberman: "My Father Dreams of
Baseball" (poem)

July 21--First Exam; Greg Corso: "Dream of a Baseball Star"; J.F. Powers:
"Jamesie""; W.C. Heinz: "One Throw," FC, pp. 47-52; Robert Fitzgerald:
"Cobb Would Have Caught It" (poem); Marianne Moore: "Hometown Piece
for Messrs. Alston and Reese" (poem)

July 23--Robert Coover: excerpt from The Universal Baseball Association, FC,
pp. 6-27; Bernard Malamud: excerpt from The Natural, FC, pp. 380-395.

Part III: The Dream ("America, America . . . ")

July 28--Philip Roth: excerpt from The Great American Novel, FC, pp. 158-180;
John Updike: "The Slump"; Damon Runyon: "Baseball Hattie," FC, pp. 153-155.

July 30--William Price Fox: "Leroy Jeffcoat," FC, pp. 71-80; John Sayles: excerpt
from Pride of the Bimbos, FC, pp. 208-217; James Thurber: "You Could Look
It Up," FC, pp. 81-96.

August 4--Andres Dubus: "The Pitcher," FC, pp. 329-365; Stanley Frank: "The Name
of the Game," FC, pp. 304-320; David Huddle: "Jeep Alley, Emperor of
Baseball" (poem)

August 6--Two plays: Bleacher Bums and Damn Yankees

August 11--paper due; other works; summary

August 13--Second Exam   167

English 276--Baseball Literature

A 750-1250 word paper is due August 11. Choose one of the four characters below
and describe the conflict which affects him and his love of baseball. What are
his goals? Does he achieve them by the end of the book? Is he the same person
at the end of the story as he was at the beginning? How does he relate to others
around him? Can you sympathize with him? Does this book have any special
significance for you? Does the significance go beyond baseball?

1. Henry Wiggen in Bang the Drum Slowly by Mark Harris.

2. J. Henry Waugh in The Universal Baseball Association by Robert Coover.

3. Roy Hobbs in The Natural by Bernard Malamud.

4. Gil Gamesh or Word Smith in The Great American Novel by Philip Roth.

If you decide to type your paper, you should figure on 3-5 typewritten pages
as a limit. A handwritten paper would probably be longer, but estimate the
number of words to be sure you meet the requirements of the assignment.

ENGLISH 347 Literature and Film
Dr. Noverr and Kathy Hadley and Marcie Lassota (Graduate Teaching Assistants)
Spring term 1986
MW 7-8:50 p.m. B104 Wells
  and 2 hrs. arr.

I. REQUIRED COURSE TEXTS

William J. Baker and John M. Carroll, eds. Sports in Modern America. St. Louis:
  River City Publishers Limited, 1981.

Mark Harris. Bang the Drum Slowly. University of Nebraska Press paperback.
  Novel originally published in 1953.

Bernard Malamud. The Natural. Avon paperback. Novel originally published
  in 1952.

Peter Gent. North Dallas Forty. New American Library Paperback. Novel
  originally published in 1973.

Wheeler, Robert W. Jim Thorpe: World's Greatest Athlete. University of
  Oklahoma Press paperback, 1979.

Randy Roberts. Papa Jack: Jack Johnson and the Era of White Hopes.
  The Free Press, 1983.

II. COURSE DESCRIPTION

This course will consider the relationship between sports literature and sports
films by examining four sports (baseball, football, boxing, and the Olympics)
in their American historical and social context. Specific concerns include:
the dynamics of hero and sports legend creation, kinds of sports heroes,
differences between professional and amateur athletes, the minority experience,
sports as secular myth and ritual, and other themes. The class will be taught
by the lecture-discussion method with the nine feature films and the assigned
course readings serving as the basis for discussion.

III. COURSE EVALUATION

The final grade in the course will be based on two examinations (mid term and
final) and on an 7-10 page research paper on sports literature. The examinations
will be objective, short answer, and a short essay. Students must take both
examinations and submit the required research paper. Failure to complete all
course requirements will result in a 0.0 grade for the course. The final grade
will be calculated in the following way:

Midterm Examination	30%
Termpaper	30%
Final Examination	40%

IV. COURSE TERMPAPER

The termpaper should be 7-10 typed pages in length (double-spaced with standard
margins). At least five different sources (other than footnotes to primary
sources) should be cited in the footnotes. These secondary sources can include
sports history books, biographical reference sources, general historical and
cultural history sources, journal and periodical articles, specialized literary
studies, book and film reviews, etc.. Students may use the MLA in-text citation

format with the "Works Cited" page serving as the bibliography/footnote references, or they can use the standard system of footnote numbers in the text, the footnotes page, and the alphabetical bibliography page. A termpaper prospectus (completed on the form provided) must be submitted by <u>Monday,</u> <u>April 28th</u>. Termpapers will be due according to the following schedule and system.

    May 7 (W) 1st third of students on final class list
    May 14 (W) 2nd third of students on final class list
    May 21 (W) 3rd third of students on final class list

Students with termpapers due on May 14th or May 21st can hand in their termpapers on the previous dates if they wish. Any extension of a termpaper due date <u>must have</u> the approval of Dr. Noverr, and a request for an extension must be made at least a week before the assigned due date.

V.   THE 2 HRS ARRANGED

The 2 hours arranged requirement for ENG 347 will be handled in the following manner. Extra sessions will be scheduled for further small group discussions of the three novels assigned in the course, and two supplementary programs will be scheduled, including a showing of "There Was Always Sun Shining Someplace: Life in the Negro Baseball Leagues" videotape and a screening of <u>The</u> Jackie Robinson Story (1950). Dates and places for these sessions will be announced as soon as arrangements are complete. Students will be given credit under the 2HRS ARR for the library and research work they do for their termpaper. There will be one Tuesday evening screening, that of "Chariots of Fire" on May 27th.

VI. CLASS AND READING ASSIGNMENT SCHEDULE

    March 26 (W)   Course introduction and course aims

    March 31 (M)   Discuss career of Lou Gehrig and essays by James Harper
                    "Baseball: America's First National Pastime" and Charles
                    T. Summerlin "The Athletic Hero in Film and Fiction" in
                    <u>Sports in Modern America</u> (pp. 53-62 and 77-87). This
                    text is abbreviated as SMA hereafter in the syllabus.

    April 2   (W)   Screening of <u>Pride of the Yankees</u> (1942)

    April 7   (M)   Screening of <u>Bank the Drum Slowly</u> (1973)

    April 9   (W)   Discussion of Mark Harris novel <u>Bang the Drum Slowly</u>

    April 14 (M)   Screening of <u>The Bingo Long Travelling All-Stars and</u>
                    <u>Motor Kings</u> (1976)

    April 16 (W)   Discussion of William W. McDonald's "The Black Athlete in
                    American Sports" in SMA (pp. 88-98)

    April 21 (M)   Screening of <u>The Natural</u> (1984)

    April 23 (W)   Discussion of Bernard Malamud novel <u>The Natural</u>

    April 28 (M)   Midterm examination (1 hour) and screening of <u>Jim Thorpe -</u>
                    <u>All American</u> (1951)

    April 30 (W)   Discussion of Jim Thorpe biography and Jack W. Berryman and
                    Stephen H. Hardy's "The College Sports Scene" in SMA (pp. 63-76).

May 5	(M)	Screening of <u>North Dallas Forty</u> (1979)
May 7	(W)	Discussion of Peter Gent novel and Harry Jensen's "The Big Business of Sports" and Douglas A. Noverr and Lawrence E. Ziewacz's "Violence in American Sports" in SMA (pp. 101-114 and 129-145)
May 12	(M)	Screening of <u>The Great White Hope</u> (1970)
May 14	(W)	Discussion of film, Randy Roberts' <u>Papa Jack</u> biography, and Randy Roberts "Boxing and Reform" in SMA (pp. 27-38)
May 19	(M)	Screening of <u>Raging Bull</u>
May 21	(W)	Discussion of <u>Raging Bull</u> and issue of a possible ban on boxing.
May 26	(M)	No class - Memorial Day
May 27	(Tu)	Screening of <u>Chariots of Fire</u>
May 28	(W)	Discuss <u>Chariots of Fire</u> and William J. Baker and John M. Carroll's "The Politics of the Olympics" and Joan S. Hult and Roberta J. Park "The Role of Women in Sports" in SMA (pp. 159-172 and 115-128)

Monday, June 2nd   FINAL EXAMINATION PERIOD
8-10 p.m.
(2 hour exam)

ENG 347 Literature and Film
Dr. Noverr
Spring quarter 1986

THE BINGO LONG TRAVELING ALL-STARS AND MOTOR KINGS

QUESTIONS

by Douglas A. Noverr

1. Discuss <u>Bingo Long Traveling All-Stars and Motor Kings</u> as an effective star and talent vehicle for remarkable black performers, notably James Earl Jones, Billy Dee Williams, Richard Pryor, and others. How is it significant that this was a Motown Production, produced by Berry Gordy?

2. Analyze how the Bingo Long All-Stars team comes together as a barnstorming team and develops team solidarity.

3. Discuss <u>Bingo Long</u> as a tribute to the careers of such star performers of the Negro Leagues as Josh Gibson, Satchel Paige, Cool Papa Bell, John Henry Lloyd, Martin Dihigo, and others. What social and economic conditions brought about the development of the Negro Leagues in the 1920s? How did the Negro Leagues survive in the Great Depression and the 1930s? For information about the Negro Leagues, see Robert Peterson, <u>Only the Ball Was White: A History of Legendary Black Players and All-Black Professional Teams</u> (1974), and William Brashler's <u>Josh</u> (A Biography of Josh Gibson), and Donn Rogosin, <u>Invisible Men: Life in Baseball's Negro Leagues</u> (1983).

4. What role does Sallie Potter play in the film? How is he the "power behind the scenes" who controls the League and the business arrangements? How is this character based on the real-life characters of Andrew "Rube Foster and Nat C. Strong? For information, see Peterson's <u>Only the Ball Was White</u> and Douglas A. Noverr and Lawrence E. Ziewacz, <u>The Games They Played: Sports in American History, 1865-1980</u> (1983).

5. Describe the style of play developed by the Bingo Long All-Stars team. How did the players combine solid baseball skills and smooth team play with crowd-pleasing antics, routines, and stunts? How did the players feel about "playing up" to the white audiences in small-town America? Did they feel they were forced to "perform" in ways that were degrading or insulting? Why did they have to entertain and amuse first and foremost?

6. Why were black baseball teams so important to the identity and pride of black communities in the urban areas? How did the style of play differ from that in the counterpart white professional major leagues? Why was it important to black people to know that black athletes could do the same things that white athletes did, even though blacks were barred from directly competing against white professionals (except in after-season exhibition games or tours)?

7. How does the film deal with elements of white racism and prejudice? Does the film understate the ugly realities of racism as it limited and hindered the hopes and abilities of black people in America?

8. In terms of travel, accommodations, food, what were the difficulties that blacks faced when traveling in the United States? Why did whites insist on segregation and make it law as well as social custom?

9. Discuss the importance of mobility and free, unhindered movement as part of the black dream of equality in America. How is this treated in the film?

10. The game of baseball depends on non-verbal and verbal communication for effective team play. How did the black players communicate with their own special language, signs, and body signals? Did whites understand this complex system by which blacks communicated their emotions and feelings in the presence of whites? How does this system of communication change when blacks were relating in their own culture and society?

11. Compare and contrast the personalities and characters of Bingo Long and Leon Carter in the film. How does their friendship develop and deepen? What do they learn from each other?

12. Analyze the theme of black pride in the film. Or discuss the theme of the recovery of black history as treated in the film.

13. Why and how did integration of major league baseball come about in post-World War II America? Can this "breaking of the color line" be explained solely by the fact that white management had come to recognize the talents of black players and were now more enlightened and willing to accept them (notably Branch Rickey, Jr.)? How long did full integration take after Jackie Robinson played his first full season with the Brooklyn Dodgers in 1947?

14. What did integration do to the Negro Leagues? How were they a passing phenomena that left a rich heritage and tradition?

15. Discuss the role of Charlie Snow/Carlos Nevada (Richard Pryor) in the film. Why were native Americans (Indians) and Spanish-speaking baseball players (Cubans and others) acceptable in the major leagues while black players were not? What famous American Indians played major league baseball? Check on such individuals as Jim Thorpe, Chief Lon Meyers, Charles Albert "Chief" Bender, and others.

16. Analyze the film's treatment of white middle-America (Ohio and Indian) and small town or village America. Are any stereotypes applied to whites? If so, which ones? Are any black stereotypes used? If so, which ones?

17. Analyze the use of historical time references in the film: the reference to Franklin D. Roosevelt, the Depression, the newspapaer headline reading "German Army Invades Poland," the radio shows playing over the radio when Bingo steals the Packard car, and the reference to the breaking of the "color line" in major league baseball with the signing of Esquire Joe Callaway.

18. Discuss the film's treatment of black women and their role in black culture, including Mrs. Bertha DeWitt (the only woman owner of a black baseball franchise), Pearline, and Violet.

19. Discuss the film's use of the old Universal newsreel to introduce the movie and its historical context.

20. Analyze the film's effective mix of comedy, sentimental melodrama, farce, satire, nostalgia, and seriousness.

21. Discuss the contrasting and complementary acting styles and screen images of Billy Dee Williams and James Earl Jones in their respective roles as Bingo Long and Leon Carter.

22. Duscuss the film's use of music (the contributions of William Goldstein, Ron Miller, and Berry Gordy), especially the theme music of "Razzle Dazzle" and "Steal On Home."

23. Analyze the "crossover" appeal of this film with reference to white audiences and black audiences.

24. Compare and contrast Bingo Long with The Natural (1984) as a baseball film. Or compare and contrast Bingo Long with a classic baseball film such as The Pride of the Yankees (1932), which was about Lou Gehrig and starred Gary Cooper.

25. How do Bingo and Leon react when they realize that they are too old to crack the major leagues and that the Negro Leagues are doomed to extinction as integration takes place? Was age always a factor in determining what black players made the major leagues? What about Satchel Paige and Jackie Robinson? How did the film base its central characters on noted black players, with Leon Carter based on Josh Gibson, Bingo Long based on Satchel Paige, and Esquire Joe Callaway based on Jackie Robinson and Willie Mays?

26. Discuss the role of Rainbow in the film as a test of the friendship and solidarity between Bingo Long and Leon Carter.

27. What are the names of the eight baseball teams in the Negro League in the film? How do these names compare and contrast with the actual names of black baseball teams? How were names significant, and how did they symbolize certain black attitudes?

28. Discuss the Technicolor look and tone of the film in terms of the atmosphere conveyed in the film.

29. It is often said that laughter and high-spirited fun can hide pain and mask bitter disappointment. Discuss the relation of this concept to the idea of "shining" or clowning for the whites.

30. Discuss the importance of the following references in the film: "Seize the means of production," "brotherhood of athletes," W.E.B. DuBois's injunction, "Be your own man," a full share and a half-share.

31. Discuss the significance of Bingo Long's inclusion of a midget catcher (who replaces Leon after he leaves the team) and a one-armed first baseman on the All-Stars team.

32. In Films in Review (October 8, 1976), Frank Jackson noted that Bingo Long "never really condemns white society" for segregation and racial discrimination. Is this true? If it is, what explains this lack of anger?

33. Discuss the film as a commentary on blacks in show business and entertainment. What happened to black actors and actresses or to black musicians and singers during this same period of time?

34. Compare and contrast the Sidney Poitier screen image and acting style in In the Heat of the Night with that of James Earl Jones or Billy Dee Williams in Bingo Long.

35. Compare and contrast the presentation of the black experience in Bingo Long with that of Soldier's Story (1984).

36. Compare and contrast James Earl Jones's portrayal of Leon Carter in Bingo Long with his portrayal of Jack Johnson, the black heavyweight boxing champion, in The Great White Hope (1970).

37. Discuss the importance of notable black athletes to black pride and identity, specifically the importance of Joe Louis, heavyweight boxing champion, and Jesse Owens, noted Olympic performer.

SUGGESTED TERMPAPER TOPICS

1. Ring Lardner's baseball fiction: You Know Me Al (1916) and Lose with a Smile (1933)

2. Mark Harris's Henry Wiggen baseball novels: The Southpaw (1953), Bang the Drum Slowly (1956), A Ticket for a Seamstitch (1957), and It Looked Like For Ever (1979)

3. The demythologizing of baseball in Robert Coover's The Universal Baseball Association, Inc., J. Henry Waugh, Prop. (1968) and Philip Roth's The Great American Novel (1973)

4. Jim Bouton's self-revealing saga in Ball Four, Plus Ball Five, (1970), I'm Glad You Didn't Take It Personally (1971)

5. the mythology of the Brooklyn Dodgers: Roger Kahn's The Boys of Summer (1971), Peter Golenbeck's Bums: An Oral History of the Brooklyn Dodgers, Bill Borst's The Brooklyn Dodgers, 1953-1957: A Fan's Memoir

6. Jim Brosnan's The Long Season (1960) and Pennant Race (1962) as sports history and personal chronicle

7. The baseball pennant race book as sports history: Sparky Anderson, God Bless You Boys, Diary of Detroit Tigers' 1984 Season, Roger Craig's, Inside Pitch, Roger Craig's '84 Tiger Journal, Lou Sahadi, The LA Dodgers

8. Recent baseball fiction: David Carkeet, The Greatest Slump of All Time, John Alexander Graham, Babe Ruth Caught in a Snowstorm (1973), Barry Beckham, Runner Mack (1972), Paul Hemphill, Long Gone (1979), Donald Hays, The Dixie Association (1984), Eric Rolfe Greenberg The Celebrant (1986), Harry Stein, Hoopla (1986)

9. The baseball superstar autobiography: Reggie Jackson, Reggie, Mickey Mantle, Mick: Mickey Mantle's Autobiography, and others.

10. Baseball and humor: Jay Johnstone's Temporary Insanity, Bill Lee, The Wrong Stuff, Jim Bouton, Ball Four, Bob Uecker, Catcher in the Wry

11. Earlier baseball novels: Eliot Asinoff, Man on Spikes (1955), Heywood Broun, The Sun Field (1923), Lucy Kennedy The Sunlit Field (1950)

12. Babe Ruth's major biographers: Robert W. Creamer, Marshall Smelser, and others.

13. The journalist's view of baseball: Alison Gordon, Foul Ball: Five Years in the American League and Jim Kaplan, Pine-Tarred and Feathered, A Year on the Baseball Beat

14. Roger Kahn's baseball writings; The Boys of Summer (1971), The Summer Game, Good Enough to Dream, The Seventh Game (novel)

15. The "inside" baseball book: Graig Nettles' _Balls_, Geoffrey Stokes, _Pinstripe Pandemoniam: Behind the Scenes with the New York Yankees_, Bill Lee, _The Wrong Stuff_, Ron Luciano's _Strike Two_

16. Roger Angell's baseball writings: _Late Innings: A Baseball Companion_, _The Summer Game_, _Five Seasons_

17. The evolution and development of a notable American baseball sports writer: Red Smith, Jimmy Cannon, Frank Graham, Fred Lieb

18. Self revelation autobiographies of fallen sports heroes with substance abuse problems: Bob Welch's _Five O'Clock Comes Early_, _A Ballplayer's Battle with Alcoholism_ and Darrel Porter's _Snap Me Perfect: The Darrell Porter Story_

19. W.P. Kinsella as baseball fiction writer: _The Thrill of the Grass_ and _Shoeless Joe_

20. Peter Gent's fiction on professional football: _North Dallas Forty_, _Texas Celebrity Turkey Trot_, and _The Franchise_

21. Recent football novels: Don DeLillo, _End Zone_ (1972), Frederick Exley, _A Fan's Notes_, Dan Jenkins, _Semi-Tough_ (1972), Gary Cartwright _The Hundred-Yard War_ (1968), Eliot Berry, _Four Quarters Make a Season_ (1973)

22. Life after Sports: The Novel of Post Sports Adjustment - Jay Neugeboren's _Big Man_ (1966), James Whitehead's _Joiner_ (1971), John Updike's _Rabbit Run_ (1960), Al Young, _Ask Me Now_ (1980)

23. The boxing novel: Budd Schulberg, _The Harder They Fall_ (1947), Leonard Gardner, _Fat City_ (1969), W.C. Heinz, _The Professional_ (1958), William Riley Burnett, _Iron Man_ (1930), Robert Lipsyte, _The Contender_ (1967), Jack London, _The Game_ (1905)

24. Recent basketball novels: Lawrence Shainberg, _One on One_ (1970), Charles Rosen, _Have Jump Shot, Will Travel_ (1975), and _A Mile Above the Rim_ (1976), Todd Walton, _Inside Moves_ (1978)

25. The black perspective on sports in Harry Edwards's _The Revolt of the Black Athlete_ (1969) and _The Struggle That Must Be_ (1980)

26. The autobiographies of Billie Jean King and Martina Navratilova

27. Babe Ruth and Lou Gehrig: Contrasting American Sports Heroes

28. Ty Cobb and Pete Rose as Competitive Individualists

29. Joe Louis or Jessie Owens as national black sports heroes

30. The juvenile sports fiction of Frank O'Rourke, Zane Grey, or Jackson V. Scholtz

31. William "Bill Bill" Tilden's tennis fiction

32. Fishing in the fiction of Ernest Hemingway

33. The meaning of the team in selected sports fiction

34. Muhammad Ali as a black sports hero

35. Hagiography and the biographies of Lou Gehrig

36. The creation of boyhood sports heroes in the biographies of Guernsey Van Riper, Jr. (Lou Gehrig, Knute Rockne, Babe Ruth, and Jim Thorpe)

37. The black sports novel: William Brashler's The Bingo Long Traveling All-Stars and Motor Kings (1973), Barry Beckham, Runner Mack (1972), Al Young, Ask Me Now (1980)

38. The tennis novel: Jane and Burt Boyar, World Class (1975), Gary Brandner The Players (1975), and William Brinkley, Break Point (1978)

39. Books about Pete Rose and his chase of Ty Cobb's hit record

40. The autobiographies of Jackie Robinson (I Never Had It Made) and Roy Campanella (It's Good to be Alive 1959)

41. The journalistic and sports reporter career of Howard Cosell (see Cosell and I Never Played the Game)

42. Autobiographies of Negro League baseball players who made the Major Leagues: Leroy "Satchel" Paige's Maybe I'll Pitch Forever (1962) and Quincy Trouppe, 20 Years Too Soon (1977)

43. Thomas Boswell as an observer and analyzer of baseball: How Life Imitates the World Series and Why Time Begins on Opening Day

44. Jerry Kramer's writings on professional football

45. Pete Axthelm's writings on professional basketball - The City Game (1970), Newsweek columns, etc.

46. The modern sports revelation and indictment book: Paul Hoch, Rip Off the Big Game (1972), Leonard Shecter, The Jocks (1970), and Bernie Parrish, They Call It a Game (1971)

47. George Plimpton's sports books written from the point of view of the outsider

48. Dan Jenkins's Billy Clyde Puckett as character in Semi-Tough and Life Its Ownself (1985)

ENG 347 Literature and Film
Dr. Noverr
Spring quarter 1986
Study Guide for <u>Pride of the Yankees</u> (1942)

1. How does this film, directed by Sam Wood (who also directed <u>The Stratton Story</u>, 1949, another baseball film) and produced by Sam Goldwyn, present Lou Gehrig as a self-made success story and American hero? What were Gehrig's qualities of heroism and greatness?

2. How authentic or realistic are the baseball playing scenes in the film? A number of former New York Yankees, specifically the notable members of the famed 1927 Yankees Murderer's Row (Babe Ruth, Bob Meusel, and Mark Koenig), and actual baseball players (Bill Dickey, who joined the Yankees in 1928 and was Gehrig's roomate, and (Peanuts Lowrey) make up the supporting cast of the film.

3. How is it important to note that Gehrig was not a natural fielder at first base and that he had to overcome his awkwardness by hard work, concentration, and self-discipline?

4. How does the film present Gehrig's relationship with Babe Ruth, the Yankee star and home run hitter? How did Gehrig have to play in Babe Ruth's shadow as all the press attention was lavished on the colorful, controversial, and popular Ruth? Why did Gehrig and Ruth have a falling out in 1933 and refuse to speak to each other for almost three years until Ruth left the Yankee organization after the 1934 season and joined the Boston Braves? Does the film suggest any of the tensions between Ruth and Gehrig? How might the aging Ruth have resented and envied Gehrig, who was steady, dependable, and admired? How did Gehrig have his greatest year in 1934, when he hit .363, 49 home runs, and had 165 RBIs, and claimed the Triple Crown honor?

5. How did Gehrig claim his own stardom after Ruth left the Yankees and help bring the Yankees back to domination of the Major Leagues? The Yankees won the World Series in 1936, 1937, and 1938. How was Gehrig one of the great World Series performers with a .361 batting average in seven World Series and a .997 fielding average with only one error in 322 chances?

6. How does the film present the drama and achievement of Gehrig's (the Iron Horse, as he was called) remarkable record of 2,130 consecutive games from June 1, 1925 to April 30, 1939? What factors made this record so remarkable and noteworthy? How did the record reflect the character of Gehrig, his commitment to strict conditioning, his dedication to the team, and his professionalism?

7. How does the film present Gehrig's family life, his German ethnic background, his relationship with his mother, Christina Gehrig, and his father, Henry Gehrig? How does Lou go through the process of Americanization and assimilation as the son of first generation German immigrants who came to the United States in 1900?

8. How does <u>Pride of the Yankees</u> present Lou Gehrig's love affair with Eleanor Twichell, whom Gehrig married in 1933? Is this dramatization overdone and typically Hollywood formula in treatment?

9. Babe Ruth was the popular sports hero of the Roaring Twneties, while Lou Gehrig was the more acceptable sports hero of the 1930s. Why? How did Gehrig never make the money that Ruth did? Note: The highest salary Gehrig was ever paid was $39,000 for the 1938 season, while Ruth made $85,000 in his best salaried season.

10. How were Gehrig's shyness, insecurity, and self-deprecation both assets and liabilities? How was he the symbol of the quiet hero?

11. How does the film present Gehrig's life at Columbia University from 1922 to 1923?

12. How was Yankee Manager Miller Huggins (who managed the Yankees from 1918 to his death at age 50 in 1929) influential in Gehrig's development as a player?

13. How does the film treat these three key events in Gehrig's career?

    a. Gehrig replacing Yankee first baseman Wally Pipp, who had been the regular first baseman for the Yankees from 1915 to 1925, on June 1, 1925.

    b. Gehrig removing himself from the Yankee lineup on May 2, 1939 at Detroit

    c. Lou Gehrig Appreciation Day at Yankee Stadium on July 4, 1939

14. How was Gehrig's speech on July 4, 1939 characteristic of the man and his personality? How was Gehrig's fate tragic, but how did he face his fate with courage and quiet resignation?

15. How was Gary Cooper, in many ways (other than athletic ability), a good choice to play Lou Gehrig? Note that Cooper had played Sergeant Alvin York, the WWI America war hero, in Sergeant York just the previous year and had won the Academy Award for best actor in that role.

16. How Lou Gehrig symbolized the kind of national hero that the United States needed in 1942 as it was now involved in a war struggle against the forces of Japanese military imperialism, Nazism, and Facism? If Gehrig was the Pride of the New York Yankees, how was he also the pride of American Yankees? What messages are contained within this wartime film?

17. How would you evaluate the screenplay for Pride of the Yankees done by Herman J. Mankiewicz, who just the previous year had collaborated with Orson Welles on Citizen Kane (1941) and shared the Oscar with Welles for best screenplay?

18. How was Gehrig's friendship with Bill Dickey, who caught for the Yankees from 1928-1946, important? Note: Dickey wrote the preface entitled "My Roommate, Lou Gehrig" to Paul Gallico's Lou Gehrig: Pride of the Yankees (1942).

19. What are the inherent problems of a sports film biography as these are evident in Pride of the Yankees? How does this film differ from The Babe Ruth Story (1948) or The Jackie Robinson Story (1950) as sports film biographies?

ENG 347 Literature and Film
Dr. Noverr
Spring quarter 1986
Study Guide for Mark Harris's <u>Bang the Drum Slowly</u> (1956)

1. In an interview Mark Harris said his "baseball books are written out of a rebellion against formal language." How does Henry Wiggen, the first person pitcher narrator, use the vernacular and ungrammatical English? How is his style of speaking related to his background and education?

2. How does Henry Wiggen react to the news that Bruce Pearson, his roommate on the New York Mammoths, is dying of Hodgkin's Disease? How is he able to keep the knowledge to himself up to the point that he tells Goose Williams, another catcher on the Mammoths?

3. How does Bruce Pearson handle the reality of his fatal disease? Why is the fact of his condition more troublesome to Henry Wiggen, Bruce's roommate and friend, than to Bruce?

4. Why didn't the 1955 New York Mammoths jell together as a team? How were they divided by jealousy, antagonism, racial feelings, and insensitivity? How and why do they lack respect for each other?

5. Why is it important that while Bruce Pearson is dying the Wiggens are having their first child, a daughter, Michelle, who is born just after the All-Star game break?

6. How is Holly Wiggen, Henry's wife, a strong, sensitive, and caring person? How is she Henry's conscience? How does she care deeply for Bruce and show her caring? Why did Holly agree with her husband that Katie, Bruce's prostitute girlfriend, should not be named beneficiary in the $50,000 Arcuturus insurance policy?

7. Discuss the importance of the stories within the novel's main action: Goose Williams' last season in baseball at age 35, Sid Goldman's assault on Babe Ruth's home run record for the season, and the pennant race with the Washington team.

8. How is "ragging" part of baseball? Why do the members of the Mammoths "rag" on Bruce Pearson and ride him unmercifully? Why does Henry Wiggen end the novel by stating: "From here on in I rag nobody."?

9. How are the 1955 New York Mammoths struggling with problems of racial integration? Note that four players on the team are black: Perry Simpson, the shortstop, Jonah Brooks, a catcher, Lysander Washington, an infielder, and Keith Crane, a relief pitcher. Why is it important to note that Henry Wiggen had roomed with Perry Simpson during the 1952 season? How do the black players feel about Bruce Pearson?

10. How does Mark Harris blend the comic and the serious? How do Mike Mulrooney and Red Traphagen represent different points of view about death? Why are Mike and Red called back to the Mammoths after the entire team learns of Bruce's condition?

181

11. How does Henry Wiggen mature in the course of the novel? How does he learn what his values and principles are? How does he learn to appreciate his friendship with Bruce? How does he learn the importance of being nice to people because life is so tentative and conditional? How does he develop responsibility for Bruce? How are the scenes where he holds Bruce and gives him comfort important to the bonding between the two men?

12. How does Henry realize that Bruce knows things that Henry does not, and how does Henry build up Bruce's confidence? How does Bruce improve and develop as a hitter, especially after the team begins to support him? What does the novel say about the way people of lesser or more limited talents are held back from development because others convince them they cannot do something?

13. How is Dutch Snell, the manager of the new York Mammoths, a comic character as well as an intelligent and experienced manager? Why is Dutch so determined to get to the bottom of the Wiggen-Pearson matter?

14. How is the evening of Goose Williams's 35th birthday and of Henry Wiggen's 20th victory in the 1955 season (August 26th) the time that Henry knew the Mammoths had won the pennant, even though it took them some time to clinch it after that date? See Chapter 16. How do they come together as a team off the field first?

15. Why does Mark Harris include detailed biographical information (following Chapter 6, pp. 89-92) on the Mammoths' team? How many of the team's players are veterans of WWII? the Korean War?

16. How does the novel describe the 1955 travel conditions (mostly train travel with some plane travel) and playing conditions (mostly day games with some night games)?

17. Why does Piney Woods, the young, daredevil catcher from Good Hope, Georgia, sing the song ("The Streets of Laredo") in the clubhouse that is Bruce Pearson's death dirge? How is this a poignant and meaningful moment for the team? How does this song become the team's song during the latter part of the 1955 season?

18. When does Henry Wiggen begin to write this novel, and when does he finish it? How are Holly Wiggen and Red Traphagen involved in the writing of the novel? Why does Henry refer a number of times to his first book, The Southpaw?

19. What does the novel say about the way we take life for granted? the way we waste time?

20. Why didn't Henry send Bruce the World Series program from Detroit? How does Author realize he is "just like the rest"? Why is Henry upset that the Mammoths club did not send a representative to Bruce's funeral in Bainbridge, Georgia?

21. How does the novel present the inside skills and strategies of baseball, such as flashing signs, hitting, juggling the lineup, keeping the book, etc.?

22. Bruce Pearson is largely inarticulate and is considered to be a "dumb" country boy by many. But how is he also intelligent? How does he learn to enjoy doing the simplest of things?

23. How do women in the novel have some of the best statements? For example, Holly Wiggen says "Then you have got to go." and Patricia Moors says "Such a thing can be not only hate but also love."

24. How does Sid Goldman, the home run power hitter of the Mammoths, represent selfish individualism and self-absorption as a star while Henry Wiggen learns to be unselfish and unconcerned about his records?

25. How does Mark Harris avoid sentimentalism in the treatment of Bruce Pearson's illness and death? What are the stages of Henry Wiggen's acceptance that Bruce will die?

ENG 347 Literature and Film
Dr. Noverr and Kathy Hadley and Marcie Lassota
Spring term, 1986
Study Guide for Bernard Malamud's <u>The Natural</u> (1952)

1. How does Bernard Malamud consciously recognize the underlying myths (particularly
    the myth of the hero and his exploits) of baseball? How is baseball a rich source
    of folklore, popular myths, legends, and folk tales? How are myths important
    to a nation that has a relatively short history and an absence of mythic
    literature?

2. How is the character of Roy Hobbs based in many ways on the real life exploits,
    personality, and character of George Herman "Babe" Ruth, especially Ruth's
    power hitting, his tremendous appetite for food, his record setting and record
    breaking, his sexual dissipation, his emotionally immaturity, and his selfishness?

3. Why does Roy Hobbs want and need to be a hero and a legend of the game of baseball,
    but how does he lack the necessary character and self-discipline needed to
    develop into an admirable hero? Why is he unable to learn from experience
    and to develop maturity?

4. What happened to Roy Hobbs in the fifteen years that intervened between the
    time he was shot and wounded by Harriet Bird in the hotel room in Chicago and
    his arrival at the stadium of the New York Knights at the age of 34? How is
    it significant that he returns to the professional game as a hitter-outfielder
    whereas he had gone to the Chicago Cubs at the age of 19 as a pitcher?

5. How is <u>The Natural</u> a story of lost innocence and the pursuit of an adolescent
    dream that cannot be realized or fulfilled in reality?

6. What does Roy Hobbs conceive of as happiness, well-being, and self-satisfaction?
    How does Roy feel that the game of baseball owes him something for all the
    years he has waited for his chance and for all the years he toiled in obscurity
    in semipro baseball for teams like the Oomoo Oilers? How does Hobbs have confused
    personal values?

7. How is the story of the New York Knights season and struggle to win the National
    League pennant loosely based on the 1914 Boston Braves who came from last place
    to win the pennant? How is Judge Goodwill Banner loosely based on Judge Emil
    Fuchs, the owner of the Boston Braves in the 1930s who had the Braves' franchise
    taken away from him by the National League when Fuchs wanted to convert Braves
    Field into a greyhound racing track?

8. Why is Roy Hobbs so attracted to Memo Paris, the niece of Pop Fisher, who manages
    the New York Knights and is part owner? How is Roy torn between Memo Paris
    and Iris Lemon? How does Memo Paris emasculate Roy Hobbs and take away his
    strength? How is Memo involved in Roy's corruption as he agrees to fix the
    playoff game between the New York Knights and the Pittsburgh Pirates? Why
    couldn't Roy accept the fact that Iris was a grandmother?

9. In what ways is Roy Hobbs a "natural"? How did his original strength come
    from his connections to rural America, to nature, to idealized dreams and goals,
    to natural abilities? How is Roy corrupted by the city, by money, by success,
    and by sex? How does Roy want the wrong things, and how is he willing to sacrifice
    his natural virtues to obtain these things?

10. What is the significance of Roy's miracle bat, Wonderboy? How is this bat
    his connection back to his past and his roots? Why does Roy plant his shuttered
    bat, hoping it will grow into a tree?

11. How is what happens to Roy Hobbs a kind of metaphor for the American national experience in terms of the movement from the rural to the urban and the transition from the natural to the mechanical? How was baseball thought to be a game that was natural, indigeneous, and incorruptible? How could this game be corrupted by greed (Judge Goodwill Banner) and by gambling (Gus Sands)?

12. How is Roy's failure inevitable, but how do his failure and his disgrace bring him some degree of self-knowledge? How does Roy Hobbs realize the truth about himself?

13. How does Malamud use the following patterns of imagery and symbolism in The Natural: dark and light, water, trains and train trips, forests, flowers, and birds? How are these patterns related to the game of baseball?

14. How is Roy Hobbs the symbol of the failed and fallen hero? How are his potential and promise unrealized? What do we have to learn from such heroes? How did Roy Hobbs have the natural power to shape and direct his destiny, yet how was this natural power misdirected, wasted, and dissipated?

15. How does baseball provide a context where heroes rise up, star, command attention and adulation, and then are replaced? How is Herman Youngberry, the relief pitcher for the Pirates who strikes out Roy Hobbs in the playoff game, the new star when Hobbs sinks into disgrace and obscurity? How is this mythic pattern of new heroes replacing old heroes important?

16. How does Malamud use situations or incidents that echo historical events in baseball history? These include:

    a) the "fix" in the 1919 World Series Black Sox scandal and Shoeless Joe Jackson
    b) the shooting of Eddie Waitkus by Ruth Ann Steinhagen in 1949
    c) Chuck Hoestetler falling down in the 1945 World Series and Pop Fisher's "flop"

17. How is Roy Hobbs characterized or connected with the following heroes: Achilles, Odysseus, an Arthurian knight in quest of the Holy Grail?

18. Why was Memo Paris unable to forget Bump Baily, who had died as a member of the New York Knights baseball team and who was replaced in left field by Roy Hobbs? How does Memo taunt and tease Hobbs and help set him up for the fall? How does Iris Lemon try to help Roy Hobbs, but why does he resist her help?

19. When Roy Hobbs goes into a severe slump, what are the causes or reasons? How does he try to break the slump and regain his power? How are superstitions an important part of the game of baseball?

20. How is it significant that Judge Goodwill Banner lives in a dark tower high above the Knights Field? What happens during Roy Hobbs's three encounters with Judge Banner?

21. What does The Natural say about dreams and ideals? How must the sporting hero take satisfaction in working toward the dream, give to the game and honor its traditions, learn self-knowledge and accept one's limitations, and avoid corruption? Why was Roy Hobbs unable to become a true sporting hero whereas Henry Wiggen in Bang the Drum Slowly was able to do these things because of his commitment to Bruce Pearson, the game, and the team?

22. Why does Roy Hobbs have such an uncertain sense of personal identity? How did he feel about his personal past? How is he insecure?

23. How would you evaluate Malamud's descriptions of baseball action compared with those of Mark Harris in Bang the Drum Slowly?

24. Discuss the theme of sterility and fertility as developed in Malamud's novel.

25. Discuss the importance of the following individuals to Roy Hobbs's career; Sam Simpson, Pop Fisher, and Max Mercy.

26. Discuss the significance of the following events in The Natural: a) Roy Hobbs striking out Whammer Wambold on three pitches; b) Doc Knobb's sessions with the New York Knights; c) Roy's catching a canary in his glove; d) the wreck of the Mercedes when Roy takes Memo to Long Island; e) the moonlight swimming scene with Roy and Iris Lemon; f) Roy'e bashing the clock on the right field wall in Ebbets Field; g) Memo Paris's party for the team.

27. How does Malamud show that Americans have ambivalent feelings and attitudes about their sports heroes? How do the fans demand and expect much from their heroes? Why is a fan named Otto Zipp important to the action in the championship playoff game?

28. How does the Barry Levinson directed film The Natural capture the mythical dimensions, mythical allusions, and mythical texture of Malamud's novel? For example, how is the contest between Roy Hobbs and Whammer Wambold presented in visual terms?

29. Evaluate the acting performances of Robert Redford as Roy Hobbs, Glenn Close as Iris Lemon, Robert Duvall as Max Mercy, Wilford Brimley as Pop Fisher.

30. How does the action of the film take place in 1939, and how does the film recreate the authenticity and atmosphere of this late 1930s period?

31. Why do you think the screenwriters for The Natural, Roger Towne and Phil Dusenberry, changed the bitter and downbeat ending of Malamud's novel to an upbeat and positive ending? What is the effect of this change, and the added sequence at the beginning of the film that develops a youthful romantic and sexual relationship between Roy Hobbs and Iris Lemon before Roy heads off to Chicago for his big tryout? How does the film's ending reflect a more optimistic and positive outlook and self-determination and the realization of one's dreams?

32. Bernard Malamud said in an interview that he was happy with the 1984 film version of his novel because it enabled him "to be recognized once more as an American writer - and that is a kind of triumph." What are the American qualities of The Natural?

ENG 347 Literature and Film
Dr. Noverr
Spring quarter 1986

Study Guide for <u>North Dallas Forty</u> (novel by Peter Gent and film screenplay by Peter Gent, Ted Kotcheff, and Frank Yablans)

1. In the Gent novel Phil Elliott observes that professional football runs on the adrenalin of "intense and constant" fear, anger, and hatred. Does the 1979 film adaptation capture this prevailing visceral tension of fear, anger, and hatred? In the novel, what does Phil Elliott fear, and why can't he face these fears?

2. How does the film characterize the owners, executive management, and coaching staff of the Dallas professional team? How do these individuals (Conrad Hunter, the owner; Clinton Foote, the general manager; and B.A. Quinlan, the head coach) view the game and sport of football as contrasted to the ways the players experience it? How does the corporate business mentality control the sport and its operations?

3. In his review of Peter Gent's 1973 novel, Roger Kahn said <u>North Dallas Forty</u> is a "passionate book about evil." How is evil of the novel (violence, brutality, duplicity, hypocrisy, immorality) different in degree and pervasiveness from the evil evident in the film? In the Gent novel, how is evil destructive, deep rooted, and endemic to an American society in 1970?

4. How does the film treat the topic of racism and racial relations on the Dallas team? How is this theme muted and downplayed in the film?

5. What is the significance of the <u>title</u> of Gent's novel in terms of the team's roster and the new Texas Stadium being built in north Dallas? What's wrong with the title of the film?

6. The Gent novel is clearly and solidly set in the context of 1970 during the Nixon administration and the later years of the Vietnam War. The novel is also located in the context of widespread violence in American society at large due to the war, the war protest movement, and racial violence. Is this context of cultural upheaval, dislocation, and revolution evident in the film?

7. In what ways is Gent's novel about Dallas and about Texas as well as about a football team? How does Phil Elliott feel about living in Dallas and in Texas?

8. In what ways is this a story about power and sex--the two great "turn-ons" of modern life? How are power and sex connected and interrelated? How is this same theme treated in such television series as <u>Dallas</u>?

9. How does Phil Elliott realize that professional football is learning how to deal with pain, increasingly physical limitations, and debilitating injuries? Why does Phil Elliott accept the need to use prescription drugs provided by the football organization, and why does he also smoke grass?

10. How is the Phil Elliott of Gent's novel a man obsessed with survival? Why does he see his career and life as a dead-end? How does Phil play out of pure self-interest rather than any motives of team play?

11. How are the following important to Gent's novel: John David the crow, Uncle Billy Bunk, Frank Gifford and Sam Huff, references to such professional greats as Red Grange and Bronko Nagurski?

12. What does Gent's novel say about the psychology of certain professional football players and their penchant for drug and sex rituals, physical and verbal intimidation, sadism, and exhibitionism? How does the sport cause these players to become cases of arrested development or boys-men who lack maturity?

13. How is the Phil Elliott of the film different from the novel's Phil Elliott in terms of his personality and temperament, his maturity, his ability to see the realities of his life, and his love of football?

187

14. Why does Gent's novel clearly indicate that this Dallas professional team plays in the National Football League (NFL) against the well-known players such as Fran Tarkenton of the New York Giants? Why does the film call the North Dallas team the Bulls and the team they play the Chicago Marauders?

15. How is Gent's novel grimly deterministic, brutally realistic, and deeply pessimistic? How are the murders by Beaudreau shocking but not entirely unexpected? How is Phil a kind of existential hero trying to survive in an insane and absurd world?

16. How do the novel and film differ in the following areas or points?
    a. Phil Elliott's relationship with Seth Maxwell
    b. the reasons the Dallas team wants to get rid of Phil
    c. Phil's relationships with Joanne Remington and Charlotte Caulder
    d. reasons Phil accepts the end of his career
    e. the Dallas-New York Giants game and the Dallas Bulls-Chicago Marauders game

17. Discuss the meaning and significance of the following quotes from the film.
    a) Seth Maxwell "Well, we're all whores anyway. We might as well be the best."
    b) Phil Elliott to Charlotte Caulder "The meanest and the biggest get to make all the rules."
    c) B.A., the coach "No one of you is as good as that computer."

18. In the film how is Phil Elliott's relationship with Charlotte Caulder important to his maturity, his ability to love someone, and his acceptance that there is a life beyond and after football? Why is it important that Phil has bought a twenty acre farm in the country and has planned to build a house on it? In the novel how does Phil Elliott realize that returning to the land is just a fantasy (see novel, p. 170)?

19. Pete Gent has said: "Man is the only animal in the universe who continually reorganizes time and space. I write out of that urge. There are no new things, only new relationships and different understandings of those relationships and each man's responsibility is to be true to his belief." How does North Dallas Forty provide a perspective on professional football and our cultural fascination with it? In what ways is the game of football a reorganization of time and space?

20. How does professional football mirror the modern world with its emphasis on power, aggressiveness, critical decision making and planning, bureaucratic organization, execution of a game plan, and decisive outcome?

WESTERN LITERATURE AND SPORT
P.E. 597D--M.W.F. 11:15-12:05
with Ronald A. Smith and James G. Thompson

Basic Course Outline

The seminar course, Western Literature and Sport, will involve reading
important Western literature and discussing the impact of the literary
thoughts on the development of sport and physical activity in Western
civilization. A written project and oral presentation will culminate the
seminar.

Readings

BOOKS

1. Homer, ODYSSEY (ca. 720 B.C.)

2. Plato, REPUBLIC (ca. 380 B.C.)

3. THE BIBLE (King James Version)
   Genesis and I Corinthians

4. William Penn, NO CROSS, NO
   CROWN (1682)

5. Jean Jacques Rousseau,
   EMILE (1762)

6. Thomas Hughes, TOM BROWN'S
   SCHOOLDAYS (1857)

7. Thorstein Veblen, THE THEORY
   OF THE LEISURE CLASS (1899)

8. Karl Marx and Fredrick Engles,
   COMMUNIST MANIFESTO (1848)

9. David Young, THE OLYMPIC MYTH
   OF GREEK AMATEUR ATHLETICS
   (1984)

ARTICLES

1. Homer, "Book XXIII" of ILIAD
   (ca. 750 B.C.)

2. Thucydides, "Funeral Speech" of THE
   PELOPONNESIAN WAR (431-411 B.C.)

3. Galen, "Exhortations for Medicine"
   and "Exercise with the Small
   Ball" (ca. 180 A.D.)

4. Ben Franklin, "Essay on Swimming"
   (1743)

5. Alfred Russell Wallace, "Darwinism"
   (1889)

6. Andrew Carnegie, "Gospel of Wealth"
   (1889)

7. Raymond Murphey, "National
   Socialism--25 Points" (1920)

8. Hitler, excerpts from MEIN KAMPF
   (1927)

9. Carl Becker, "Modern Democracy"
   (1941)

(The books listed are in paperback at the Penn State Book Store.)

Written Project

A written, graduate level semester project will be presented at the end
of the semester.   Possible subject areas related to the course are:
1. Compare and contrast several of the books and readings,
2. The influence of an idea or a person on the development of sport,
3. How writers have viewed the following: religion and sport; social
   class and sport; sex and sport; race and sport; ideology and sport;
   freedom and sport; human character and sport; virility and sport;
   war and sport; mind, body, and sport; or sport as enjoyment or
   sport as competition.

Gregory S. Sojka
Wichita State University
AN ANNOTATED SPORTS SHORTS FILMOGRAPHY:
VISUAL TEXTS FOR SPORTS CULTURE CLASSES

Perhaps no subject lends itself better to the use of film to illustrate
historical occurrences or thematic concerns than sports culture studies.
Surely the visual media have contributed greatly toward the universal
recognition of sports heroes. But a lack of comprehensive texts has sent
teachers of sports courses scurrying through film catalogs in search of
supplemental instructional materials. When films are used as "visual
texts"--students "read" them by taking notes and listening to introductory
remarks and participating in discussion afterwards--students of today's
"media-oriented generation" respond positively and retain facts well for
examination questions. "One picture is worth a thousand words" is a shop-
worn cliche, but the successful use of films in sports culture classrooms
is a fact. This filmography includes non-feature length films (both
dramatic and documentary) screened reglarly in an "American Sports Culture"
class. Rental prices constantly change, but distributors' addresses remain
fairly consistent. The "sports studies" teacher should not overlook feature
length films such as "One on One," "North Dallas Forty," "The Bingo Long
Traveling All-Stars and Motor Kings," and "The Bad News Bears" as additional
discussion "visual texts."

"STICKY MY FINGERS, FLEET MY FEET" - 23 mins. 1972. color. Time-Life
    Films, 43 W. 16th St., NY, NY 10011. Adapted from Gene Williams'
    NEW YORKER short story, John Hancock's film portrays Norman, a week-
    end touch-football player, whose ego is crushed by a skinny schoolboy
    named Wesley. Most useful in dramatizing the evils of the Lombardi
    school of "competing to win."

"OF SPORTS AND MAN" - 60 mins. 1961. b&w. McGraw-Hill Text Films.
    330 W. 42nd St., NY, NY 10036. Narration by French philosopher
    Roland Barthes provides a distinctive European perspective to bull-
    fighting, Grand Prix auto racing, Tour de France bicycle race, ice
    hockey and soccer. Barthes stresses sportsmanship, skill and courage
    used by men who battle animal instinct, mother nature, time, gravity
    in contests where man gains distinction, contrasted to the American
    man versus man "win at all costs" attitude.

"BODY AND SOUL: PART I, BODY" - 24 mins. 1968. color. BFA Educational
    Media. 2211 Michigan Ave., P.O. Box 1795, Santa Monica, CA 90406.
    On the eve of the black demonstrations at the 1968 Mexico City Olympics,
    Harry Reasoner considers unresolved race conflict in athletic competition.
    Interviews with Harry Edwards, Tommie Smith, Jim Hines, Ralph Boston,
    Lee Evans and Charlie Greene indicate the complexity of the 1968
    situation.

"JESSIE OWENS RETURNS TO BERLIN" - 54 mins. 1965. b&w. McGraw-Hill Text
    Films. 330 W. 42nd St., NY, NY 10036. Bud Greenspan utilizes Owens'
    ,return to Berlin in 1951 to flashback to the 1936 Nazi Olympic games
    where the American's four gold medals punctured the myth of Aryan
    superiority and black inferiority.

"JEFFRIES-JOHNSON 1910" - 21 mins. 1971. b&w. McGraw-Hill Text Films. 330 W. 42nd St., NY, NY 10036. Many original photographs and action film dramatize the heavyweight championship fight in Reno, Nevada, between racist Americans' "Great White Hope" Jim Jeffries and "uppity nigger" Jack Johnson, who drives sportscars, marries white women and spends money freely.

"THE LONG HAPPY RACE" - 25 mins. 1962. color. General Motors. 3044 W. Grand Blvd., Detroit, MI 48238. This promotion film, an early 60's period piece narrated by Lorne Greene, preaches the virtues of sportsmanship, international goodwill, educational merits, and developmental process experienced by young boys who build their own cars from scratch. An interesting contrast to Richard Woodley's account of the cheating scandal which permanently damaged the Soap Box Derby's credibility.

"GATEWAY TO OPPORTUNITY" - 20 mins. 1964, and "SIDELINE OF STARTING LINE?" 22 mins. 1964, present more of the same by General Motors.

"RUNNING" - 20 mins. 1970. color. CCM Films, c/o MacMillan Films, NY, NY 10022. Philip Kearney's film utilizes the occasion of a Long Island high school crosscountry meet to make a wordless statement about the beauty, necessity and nature of competition.

"ROOKIE OF THE YEAR" - 43 mins. 1975. color. Time-Life Films. 43 W. 16th St., NY, NY 10011. Jodie Foster plays Sharon Lee, a 12 year old girl playing on a boys' Little League team.

"SPORTS CHALLENGE" - 24 mins. 1978. color. Women's Athletic Dept., Wichita State University, Wichita, KS 67208. This film features women ahtletes (including Lynette Woodard, 1981 female college basketball player of the year) gaining the traditional values and benefits associated with women's athletics.

"MAJOR LEAGUE BASEBALL: THE NOW CAREER" - 26 mins. color. Major League Baseball, Film Division. 41 E. 42 St., NY, NY 10017. Narrator Chuck Connors describes baseball as a wonderful career opportunity for young men with talent. A piece of propaganda with all the exaggerated touches.

"BASEBALL VS DRUGS" - 25 mins. color. Major League Baseball, Film Division. 41 E. 42nd St., NY, NY 10017. Commissioner Bowie Kuhn with aid from Wes Parker, Pete Richert and Reggie Smith persuade American youth against the evils of drug use.

"SECONDS TO PLAY" - 28 mins. 1976. color. Films Inc. 733 Green Bay Road, Wilmette, IL 60091. This behind the scenes look at an ABC broadcast of a 1975 Ohio State University-UCLA game dramatizes the relationship between sports and the media, particularly the influence of television upon a college football game.

"YOUTH SPORTS: IS WINNING EVERYTHING?" - 28 mins. color. 1980. Barton Cox Jr. Films. P.O. Box 769, San Mateo, CA 94401. This sane film examines the "winning is everything" philosophy of American sports and its destructive effect on youth sport programs.

191

"COACHING KIDS TO COMPETE" - 23 mins. color. 1980. Barton Cox Jr. Films. P.O. Box 769, San Mateo, CA 94401. More of an instructional film which offers youth sports coaches information concerning the physiological, psychological and social needs of pre-adolescent children.

"THE ANCIENT GAMES" - 28 mins. color. 1972. ABC Media Learning Resources. 1330 Avenue of the Americas, NY, NY 10019. Bill Toomey and Rafer Johnson recreate the original pentathlon while they document the history of the ancient Olympics.

"A WINNER NEVER QUITS" - 20 mins. color. 1972. Lynbrook Films, c/o Ralph Taragan. 170 E. 4th St., Brooklyn, NY 11218. Focuses on a high-pressured high school football program with footage of summer camps and game highlights.

"DEFENSE! DEFENSE!" - 30 mins. color. 1975. Cally Curtis Co. 1111 N. Las Palmas, Hollywood, CA 90038. Coach Don Shula and former player Merlin Olsen explain classic defensive strategy in relation to business world strategy: demonstrates how sports reflect society's values.

"IT'S ALL IN THE GAME" - 27 mins. color. 1975. Iowa State University. Media Resource Center, 122 Pearson Hall, Ames, IA 50010. Propaganda presentation of traditional justification for interscholastic sports. In twenty years this film will be to sport what "Reefer Madness" is now to drug education.

"SPORTS: THE PROGRAMMED GLADIATORS" - 22 mins. color. 1977. University of California Extension Media Center. 2223 Fulton St., Berkeley, CA 94720. Enlightened look at increased commercialization of U.S. sports and its effect upon athletes.

"JACKIE ROBINSON" - 30 mins. b&w. 1963. Wolper Productions. 8489 W. 3rd St., Los Angeles, CA 90048. Mike Wallace narrates Robinson's struggle to break the color barrier in Major League Baseball.

"PIGS VS THE FREAKS" - 15 mins. color. 1974. University of California Extention Media Center. 2223 Fulton St., Berkeley, CA 94720. Comic look at the annual football game between long-haired Michigan State students and the local police force. Can sports provide a common ground to resolve political differences?

"FABULOUS HARLEM GLOBETROTTERS" - 9 mins. color. 1972. ROA Films. 1696 N. Astor St., Milwaukee, WI 53202. Highlights Globetrotter success entertaining audiences--primarily white spectators, however. Tests claim that the Globetrotters reaffirm all the racial stereotypes associated with blacks.

VII. SPORT AND SOCIOLOGY

Sociology of Sport
Joan Ferrante Wallace
Department of Sociology
Northern Kentucky University

Texts: <u>Social Aspects of Sport</u> (1983) by Eldon Snyder and Elmer Spreitzer

<u>The Breaks of the Game</u> (1981) by David Halberstam

<u>Out of the Bleachers: Writings on Women and Sport</u> (1979) edited by Stephanie Twin

I. Introduction

A. The state of sociology of sport

1. Sociology of sport has not yet become a mainline specialty; the area is still considered somewhat esoteric and unacceptable.

a. Sport is viewed as primarily physical rather than social interaction--thus not sociologically significant.
b. Sport is perceived as separate from the "real" world.
c. Analysis of sport is considered "beneath" a serious scholar.

2. Sport has as much claim to legitimacy as more conventional specialties such as family, education, deviance, etc.

a. Sport is a cultural universal.
b. Sport is an important social institution of society.

B. Characteristics of Sport (as contrasted to play)

1. Explicit rules and regulations govern positional inter-relationships allowing less individual discretion.
2. Individual is accountable for quality of performance.
3. The outcome of the sporting event extends beyond the participants in the physical activity.
4. Sport is an activity with formally recorded history and traditions.
5. Physical and mental demands exceed leisure and recreational motivations.

C. Two Central and Interrelated Questions Investigated by Sociologists.

1. What is the nature of sport as a social institution and how is sport related to other institutions?

[Example: The Relationship of Sport to Education]
a. High schools and colleges in the United States assume

responsibility for providing the public with sports
entertainment.
b. Relatively few schools have intercollegiate programs
that are self-supporting; the rationale for the loss is
to view it as an advertising expense (e.g., alumni attach-
ment, school spirit, enrollment, etc.)
c. Research suggests that status in school comes from
athletic achievement rather than academic achievement.
d. Athletic achievement is a road to educational mobility
and as a result social mobility.

2. What is the Function of Sport and What Social Values Does
It Promote?

    a. Sport functions imperfectly
      --to transmit social values.
      --to facilitate the mastery of skill achievement
        and physical fitness.
      --to maintain societal order by using athletes
        as models of good and bad behavior.
      --to encourage social mobility.

    b. Slogans in dressing rooms highlight the values
promoted by sport.
      --"A quitter never wins, a winner never quits."
      --"If it doesn't matter if you win or lose, why
        keep score."
      --"Winning isn't everything, it's the only thing."

II. Sport in the Life Cycle

    A. Children and Organized Sport

    1. Organized sport puts children in situations where he/she
must learn to perform a skill under pressure (e.g., stop
someone from scoring) before he/she is comfortable with the
sport.
    2. Children who are exposed to adult organized sport lose the
benefits of participation in spontaneous play: the development
of interpersonal skills and the enjoyment of a game as an end in
itself rather than a means to victory.
    3. There are several areas that can potentially produce stress
in childhood sports: (a) losing, (b) being a substitute,
(c) peer pressure, (d) fear of getting hurt, and (e) the
child who wants to quit but can't because of peer pressure or
parents won't let them.

    B. High School Experience

    1. Much of the research suggests that status in high school
comes from athletics and not academic achievement.
    2. There are no consistent findings about the relationship
between sports involvement and academic achievement.

3. There is almost no research on the psychological and social impact of summer athletic camps for high school students.

    a. Feeder camps or general camps designed to improve skills of any athlete with a means of transportation and money.
    b. High exposure camps designed for the athlete who has aspirations of attending college. Athletes (about 300 to 400 at a time in a given camp) are exposed to intense competition for a week, a top 30 team is selected; college scouts from around the country attend and the sponsoring scouting service sends scouting reports to member colleges.

4. Another area lacking serious investigation is the role high school sports play in small town settings where there are no other forms of live sport entertainment. [Note: The movie The Big Game: in the Middletown series is very enlightening on this issue]
5. There has been little research on the transition or lack of transition from high school to college sport.

C. College Experience

1. Most media attention focuses on big-time schools so perception of college sports may be biased and distorted.
2. Diversity of programs make it hard to generalize about the relationship between sport and higher education.
3. USA Today published graduation rates of Division I basketball programs. Rates ranged from 11 percent (Memphis State) to 100 percent (Harvard). In evaluating figures one has to ascertain whether graduation rates for athletes are better or worse than those of non-athletes.
4. Opportunities for upward mobility.

    a. Professional mobility is very limited.
    b. Findings suggest that athletes are less likely to earn degree than non-athletes.
    c. Athletes are less likely to drop out for financial reason than non-athletes.
    d. College athletics prepare one to be a coach.
    e. Contacts are usually made if person is both a good athlete and student.

5. The athlete and "institutionalized powerlessness": this means that within the structure of college sports, athletes have no legitimate decision-making power.

    a. The school is not required to guarantee financial assistance for more than one year; they may notify the athlete as late as July 1 prior to fall semester.
    b. An athlete must sit out for a year if the individual decides to transfer. Although this prevents the superstar from transferring, what about athletes seeking better programs in their field of study?

D. Professional Athlete

1. Pressures on the Modern Athlete (Halberstam's book <u>The</u>
<u>Breaks of the Game</u> is excellent on this issue).

a. Invasions of privacy are common by media and fans.
b. Obnoxious taunting and hostile treatment by fans
are common if the athlete is in a slump.
c. Injuries are a source of great anxiety among professional athletes who depend regularly on being able
to push their bodies to high levels of exertion.
--restorative drugs are overused to alleviate pain.
--addictive drugs are used to induce better performances.
d. Particular pressures are placed on aging veterans,
rookies and marginal players trying to establish or maintain a career.
e. Retirement problems are common because it is difficult
for athletes to maintain psychological and material rewards
of professional sport.

2. Economic Rewards for Modern Athletes

a. Well publicized figures give us a distorted and
inflated view of incomes.
b. When counting all professional sports there is
considerable discrepancy among pay schedules.

III. Social Stratification Aspects of Sports

A. Social differentiation in sport mirrors that of larger society.

1. Social scientists have long noted the patterning of
leisure activities across class lines (e.g., bowling--working
class; tennis--middle class).
2. Sport, however, does cut across class lines (e.g., Super
Bowl, World Series).
3. Racial and sexual discrimination reflects that of larger
society.

B. Social Mobility and Sport

1. It is commonly believed that the U.S. is an open class
system and this belief extends to the world of sport.
2. There are definite limitations to social mobility
through sport.

C. Racial Discrimination in Sport

1. Is the Black Athlete Superior to the White Athlete?

a. Genetic Explanation: there is a connection between
race and athletic behavior.

198

b. Cultural differences between the two groups may provide some clues.

c. Social Structure Explanations: Blacks, especially disadvantaged Blacks, perceive opportunities for mobility to be confined to sport and therefore channel more of their energies in that direction.

2. Racial discrimination in sport is manifested through stacking; that is, central positions (e.g., quarterback, pitching, point guard) are disproportionately held by whites.

a. Coaches' attitudes toward Blacks may provide an explanation.

b. Blacks are socialized to play non-central positions.

c. Genetic reasons might be involved if the physical attributes of Blacks just happen to match physical attributes of non-central positions.

d. Role models are in non-central positions so phenomenon of discrimination is accidentally perpetuated.

3. Racial discrimination is often practiced when whites are retained for marginal positions over blacks (e.g., subs, bench players).

4. Consequences of Discriminatory Practices

a. Loss of income since 3/4 of TV, radio and newspaper spots go to players in central positions.

b. Loss of media coverage during game.

c. Shorter careers of non-central positions.

d. Athletes in central positions are more likely to continue their athletic career through coaching college or professional sports.

Note: Good Film on Black Athlete is <u>Hard Road to Glory</u> by Arthur Ashe.

D. The Female Athlete

1. Sources of sexism in sport are many.

a. Historically, Western cultures have taught us that females are by nature physically inferior.

b. Other influences that affect the development of female athletic skills include parent-child rearing practices, lack of role models, and the mass media.

2. Consquences of Sexism

a. One consequence of sexism has been the perpetuation of myths about the female.

--athletic competition masculinizes females.

--sport participation is harmful to the health of females.

199

                        --women are not interested in sport and do
                        not perform well enough to be taken seriously.
                    b. Negative attitudes discourage participation.
                    c. Unequal facilities and opportunities exist
                    despite Title IX.

            3. A crucial question needs to be addressed if we want to
            assess accurately the athletic potential of women: Has women's
            potential been limited by a social construct of femininity?
            In other words, do women limit themselves so that they do not
            depart from this construct?

Note: An exceptional film on this issue is Pumping Iron II: The Women

IV. Problems, Dilemmas and Controversies in Sport

        A. The interrelationship between sport and the mass media
        B. Dehumanization of athletes
        C. Cheating and hypocrisy in sport
        D. Drugs and alcohol in sport
        E. Violence in sport

V. Technology and Sport (Improving or altering human performance through
technical means)

        Examples:
        --Computer programs that analyze the motion of every limb and
        muscle and suggest how the athlete might alter movements for
        optimal performance.
        --Diagnostic tests to identify potential world-class athletes.
        --Electrodes that literally program an athlete's muscles with
        electrical signals.
        --Biofeedback devices that measure physiological features such
        as pulse rate to help the athlete fine tune performance.

VIII. THEMATIC AND TOPICAL
COURSES IN SPORT HISTORY

Hispanic Sports in Texas and The Southwest

by Mary Lou LeCompte
The University of Texas at Austin

Various equestrian sports were introduced into Mexico by the conquistadores in the early sixteenth century. However, these elite Spaniards had retained for themselves the exclusive right to own and ride horses. To flaunt their status and skills they organized elaborate contests both on their ranches and in the cities on festive occasions. Many of these contests were held as part of or in conjunction with <u>corridas</u> (bullfights).

The first Mexican bullfight was organized by Crotez himself in 1525, and the sport has remained popular in Mexico ever since. In the sixteenth-century corridas, gentlemen on horseback used lances to fight the bulls. Other contests were soon added to the program. These included <u>jaripeo</u>, in which the object was to ride the bulls to death, and <u>sortijas</u>, in which the speeding horsemen tried to spear rings that were suspended overhead.

Soon, Mexican cattle began to multiply so rapidly over such a vast area that men on foot had no hope of controlling them. Rather than take up this menial work, Spaniards from the ranching areas successfully pressed for new laws permitting Indians and <u>Mestizos</u> (a mixture of Spanish and Indian) to ride, and the <u>vaquero</u> (cowboy) was born. This new group of Mexican horsemen became excellent cowhands, perfecting the use of lasso and many of the ranching techniques still used today. They also developed their own unique style of horsemanship and dress. The most successful among them became known as <u>charros</u>, widely recognized for their ostentatious attire and skills in roping and riding. Their fame and status were greatly enhanced by the Mexican war for independence from Spain in which the charros played a leading role.

The charros and vaqueros adopted and adapted the sports of the conquistadores and developed many new contests of their own. Some, like capturing and riding wild bucking horses and roping cattle and horses were derived from utilitarian skills, while others, like the charro version of jaripeo, the coin game, and many races were simply challenging contest for man and horse and an excellent opportunity for gambling.

These sports, known collectively as <u>charreria</u>, (see chart; 19th century charro sport) became an integral part of the Mexican culture and were included at such hacienda events as roundups, auctions and brandings, as well as at the numerous fairs and fiestas that took place year round in village and cities all over Mexico. They moved north with the cattle ranches, and were well established from Texas to California when the first Anglo settlers arrived. Many Anglo-Texans and Californians joined in these festivities and sometimes entered the contests.

However, the Anglo-Texan victory over Mexico and the establishment of the Republic of Texas in 1836 bought about rapid changes in the social order, leaving the <u>Tejanos</u> (Hispanic-Texans) virtual strangers in their own land. Many of the Tejano ranchers abandoned their land and cattle and fled to Mexico.

Taking advantage of Texas laws pertaining to stray cattle, the Anglo Texans then hired the remaining vaqueros, rounded up the abandoned cattle, and established the Anglo-Texan cattle business as an integral part of the economy. Thereafter, Anglo and Hispanic hands worked together and Anglo

19th Century Charro Sports & Their Origins

American Names

EVENTS ORGINATING WITH CONQUISTADORES

Sortijas	Ring tournaments
Jaripeo	Bull/steer riding
Colear	Bull/steer tailing, wrestling
Bullfights from horseback	-------------

EVENTS DERIVED FROM RANCH WORK

Jineteos	Bronc Busting, Bronc riding
Paso de muerte	-------------
Terna	Team Roping
Florear la reata	
Piales	Trick & Fancy Roping
Manganas	

RACES & GAMES ON HORSEBACK

Correr el gallo	Chicken race, chicken pulling
Coin games	Picking up objects
rayar	ride to the line

cowboys adopted the techniques, dress, equipment, and lingo of the vaqueros. As the folk games of an equestrian, ranching society, the diverse contests of charreria passed from Hispanic to Anglo as well, becoming popular at fairs and festivals of both groups through out the southwest.

Gradually, the contests became more organized and professionalized, but through the time of the first World War, contestants from the United States and Mexico competed and won in both countries. However, following the Mexican Revolution and World War I, drastic changes took place.

In Mexico, the haciendas were broken up, and the lifestyle in which charreria flourished was ended. To preserve the rich cultural heritage of the sport, former charros in 1921 established the National Charro Association, and soon thereafter, charreria became the official national sport of Mexico. It is organized as an amateur sport in which contests are staged between two club teams. Because contests are now limited to Sunday afternoons, rather than taking place at three to four-day hacienda fiestas, games and races are no longer included.

American rodeo, a direct outgrowth of charreria, was organized much later, beginning with the 1936 formation of the Cowboys Turtle Association, now the Prorodeo Cowboys Association. Over the years, rule changes have served to exaggerate the differences between rodeo and charreria, but a look at the standard contests included today shows that the two sports remain essentially the same (see chart: Standard Events).

REFERENCES

LeCompte, Mary Lou. "The Hispanic Influence on the History of Rodeo 1823-1922," Journal of Sport History 12 (Spring, 1985), 21-38.

"The First American Rodeo Never Happened," Journal of Sport History 9 (Summer, 1982), 89-96.

STANDARD EVENTS

CHARREADA	PRCA RODEO

MEN

Cala de caballo: horsemanship	
Jineteos: riding until the animal calms down; usually 2-3 minutes	Rough Stock Events: 8 second ride
Jineteo de novillo.	Bull riding
	Bareback bronc riding
Jineteo de yeguas	Saddle bronc riding
Paso de muerte	
Colear: Bull tailing: speed & style	Steer Wrestling: timed event
Roping on foot & on horseback: style and accuracy	Calf Roping: timed event
	Steer Roping: timed event
Manganas: roping the forelegs running mare	
Piales: roping the hind legs of a running mare	
Tiron de muerte: roping with the lasso tied around your neck	
Terna: team roping	Team Roping: timed event

WOMEN

Escaramuza: team event, presicion and style	Barrel Racing: timed event

206

NINETENTH-CENTURY CHARRO SPORTS

1) **Colear:** wrestling a bull or steer to the ground by twisting its tail. Originally a method of capturing wild cattle, **colear** quickly became a popular sport as well as a form of bull fighting. It was first described in 1586.

2) **Jaripeo:** riding wild bulls. Originally a form of bull fighting in which the object was to ride the beast to death, **jaripeo** became a popular sport among charros where it became a test of riding skill.

3) **Jineteos:** riding wild bucking horses was a necessity as well as a sport, and was described in Mexico as early as 1621.

4) **Paso de Muerte** (pass of death): a charro riding full gallop jumps from the back of his own horse to a wild horse that is galloping alongside, and rides it bareback until it has calmed down. Originally a method of capturing a breaking wild horses.

5) **Roping:** Mexicans were the world's greatest ropers, and had many skills and contests both on foot and from horseback, including standing on the back of the horse. Speed and accuracy were most important, but fancy loops and flourishes with the rope were also stressed.

   Florear La Reata: Making shapes with the rope
   Piales: Roping and animal by the hind legs
   Manganas: Roping an animal by the forelegs

6) Equestrian games and contests

   Correr el gallo (called by Anglos the "chicken race") was probably the most popular game, and was commonly run in the streets of San Antonio, Santa Fe, and Los Angeles in the nineteenth century. The rules varied from place to place, but in all cases a rooster was the object. The live bird might be buried neck deep in the sand, suspended from a tree, or held by a non-participant. The contestants, riding full speed, tried to snatch the bird. The one who got it took off and was pursued by all the other horsemen who tried to take it away. Whoever held the rooster as he crossed the finish line was the winner. In some cases, the game lasted all day, until there were no more roosters in the town.

   Sortijas (ring tournaments): horsemen riding full speed attempted to spear with a lance rings suspended overhead. The rider spearing the most rings was the winner.

   Coin Games (there seems to be no common Spanish name for these contests). Horsemen riding full speed attempt to pick up tiny object from the ground. The most popular were silver dollars, but handkerchiefs, gloves, arrows, and even potatoes were used. The rider collecting the greatest number of objects was the winner.

   Rayar Horseman ride full speed up to a line and then stop and literally slide their horse attempting to come as close to the line as possible without crossing it.

207

COURSE: PHYSICAL EDUCATION 39: "Healthy, Moral and Strong": Athleticism in the Late 19th Century"

INSTRUCTOR: Roberta J. Park, Professor, Department of Physical Education

UNIT VALUE: Three (3) Units

FORMAT: Pro-Seminar (3 Hours Per Week); Freshman/Sophomore Limited Enrollment Course

COURSE SIZE: 15 Freshman and/or Sophomore students

DESCRIPTION: One of the first things which a student might notice when arriving on the Berkeley campus in the early fall is the amount of space in The Daily Cal which is devoted to athletics--especially football. On several Saturday afternoons thousands of spectators will file into Memorial Stadium, where the boom of the cannon and the roar of the crowd will signal "Golden Bear" touchdowns.

College athletics have formed an important part of student life at American universities for a century. Across the nation they rose to prominence in the 1880s and 1890s, and impacted both college communities and the broader communities in which the campuses were located. Many important American values were-and still are-dramatically reflected in American college sports.

This course will focus upon American views of bodily fitness, physical culture, and college athletics as models for moral and physical regeneration in the period from 1870 to 1915. Some attention will be given to British and selected European events:

(1) Changing concepts of health and fitness, 1870-1915

(2) Assumed relationships of physical strength and well-being, intellectual development, and moral rectitude

(3) The "healthy body" as a metaphor for the well-ordered society

(4) Play and games as agents of socialization

(5) Similarities and differences in ideological origins of 19th century intercollegiate athletics and physical education

(6) Nineteenth century English "muscular Christianity" and "athleticism compared to and contrasted with American college athletics

REQUIRED TEXTS: Daniel Rodgers, The Work Ethic in Industrial America: 1850-1920 (Chicago, 1974)
F.N. McCoy, Researching and Writing in History: A Practical Handbook for Students (Berkeley, 1974)

ASSIGNMENTS: Students will be expected to discuss in class a variety of primary and secondary source readings dealing with these topics. Additionally, students will be expected to investigate some very narrowly defined historical question drawn from the broader topics of the course and prepare a research paper (6-10 pages) on that question. This research will involve the use of the main (Doe) Library, the Bancroft Library, and the libraries of local historical societies.

208

PHYSICAL EDUCATION 39: "Healthy, Moral and Strong: Athleticism in the
Late 19th Century"

Reading Assignments:

Fellman, Anita C. and Fellman, M. Making Sense of Self: Medical Advice
    Literature in Late Nineteenth Century America. University of
    Pennsylvania Press, 1982. Chapters 1,2,3.

"Science, Society and Social Thought," in Charles E. Rosenberg (Ed.) No
    Other Gods: ON Science and American Social Thought. Johns Hopkins
    University Press, 1976.

"Philosophy in the Gymnasium," in Charles C. Whorton, Crusaders for Fitness:
    A History of American Health Reformers. Princeton University Press,
    1982.

"Are Americans Less Healthy Than Europeans?" Galaxy, 5 (1872), 630-640.

Douglas, Mary, Natural Symbols. Pantheon Books, 1982. (Preface, and Introduction
    to the New 1982 edition.)

Higham, J. "The Reorientation of American Culture in the 1890s," in John
    Higham (Ed.) Writing American History: Essays on Modern Scholarship.
    Indiana University Press, 1972, pp. 73-102.

Wiebe, Robert H. The Search for Order: 1877-1920. Hill and Wang, 1967.
    Chapter 6.

Rodgers, Daniel T. The Work Ethic in Industrial America: 1850-1920. University
    of Chicago Press, 1974. Chapters 4 and 5.

Higgenson, Thomas W. "Saints and their Bodies," The Atlantic Monthly, I
    (March 1858), 582-595.

"The Health and Physical Habits of English and American Women," Scribner's
    Magazine, 128 (1879), 511-525.

Mergen, Bernard, "The Discovery of Children's Play," American Quarterly, 27
    (1975), 399-420.

Cavallo, Dominick, Muscles and Morals: Organized Playgrounds and Urban
    Reform, 1880-1920. University of Pennsylvania Press, 1981.
    Chapters 1 and 3.

Park, Roberta J. "Too Important to Trust to the Children: Freedom and Order
    in Children's Play, 1900-1917," in John Loy (Ed.) The Paradoxes of
    Play. Leisure Press, 1982.

Fitz, George W. "Conditions and Needs of Physical Education," American
    Physical Education Review, 4:4 (December 1896), 337-399.

Park, Roberta J. "Measure and Order: Concern for Anthropometric Studies in
    American Physical Education, 1885-1905." (Manuscript)

Sargent, Dudley A. "The Physical Proportions of the Typical Man,"
    Scribner's Magazine, 2:1 (July 1887), 3-17.

Sargent, Dudley A. "The Physical Proportions of the Typical Woman,"
    Scribner's Magazine, 2:

Hartwell, Edward M. Physical Training in American Colleges and Universities,
    Bureau of Education. Circular No.5-1885. Washington, D.C.:
    Government Printing Office, 1886.

Stocking, George W. Race, Culture and Evolution: Essays in the History
    of Anthropology. University of Chicago Press, 1982. Chapter 8.

"College Athletics: From Student to Faculty Control," In John A. Lucas
    and Ronald Smith, Saga of American Sport. Lea and Febiger, 1978.

Lawson, Hal A. and Alan G. Ingham, "Conflicting Ideologies Concerning the
    University and Intercollegiate Athletics: Harper and Hutchins at
    Chicago, 1892-1940," Journal of Sport History, 7:3 (Winter 1980),
    37-67.

Needham, Henry Beach, "The College Athlete: How Commercialism Is Making
    Him a Professional," McClure's Magazine, 25:2 (June 1905), 115-128.

Park, Roberta J. "Boys Into Men, State Into Nation: Rites of Passage In
    Student Life and College Athletics, 1890-1905." In The Masks of Play
    eds. Brian Sutton-Smith and Diana Kelly-Byrne (Leisure Press, 1984), chpt. 5.
Newsome, David, Godliness and Good Learning. London, 1961. Chapter 8.

Haley, Bruce, The Healthy Body and Victorian Culture. Harvard University
    Press, 1978. Chapters 7 and 8.

Mangan, James A. "Social Darwinism and English Upper Class Education,"
    Stadion, 6 (Autumn 1982), 92-115.

Tozer, Malcom, "From 'Muscular Christianity' to 'Esprit de Corps':
    Games in the Victorian Public Schools of England," Stadion, 7
    (Spring 1983), 117-130.

American Studies 350
American Sports Culture

Dr. G.S. Sojka
Fall, 1982

Office: 406 Jardine Hall
         689-3148
Hours: M-F, 8:30-9:30
and by appointment

Texts

Baker & Carroll, Sports In Modern America
James Michener, Sports In America
Peter Gent, North Dallas Forty
Also, the films we see in the course are our "visual texts" for which you are
responsible. In addition, guest speakers might occasionally lecture about
their personal experience in sports.

Format

Combination lecture, discussion: all material should be read for the date
noted on the syllabus so that you can be actively engaged in the learning
process during our scheduled classes. Attendance is expected as a positive
correlation exists between good grades and attendance.

Evaluation

Three exams equally spaced during the semester will determine course grades.
The examinations will test your knowledge of assigned readings, lecture
material, and film presentations. The examinations will contain both
objective (multiple choice) and subjective (essay) evaluations.

Educational Philosophy

As an educator, I am here to help you learn; no mere dispenser of information,
I do need your cooperation as learning is a two-way process. Thus, I will
challenge you by asking you questions that deal with the "whys" not just the
"whats" of sports in America. Strive to understand the significance of the
people, places and ideas we discuss in the class, not merely the facts.

Course Themes

Sports as businesses; evolution of minorities in American sports; the business
of intercollegiate athletics; women in sports--separate or equal?; sports
build character or characters?--sports and/or the media?; and others.

Aug   23 Introduction; "War Games" (film)
      25 Baker & Carroll, 1-15
      30 "Sport and Man" (film)
Sept   1 Baker & Carroll, 101-114; Michener, 15-32
       6 Labor Day, NO CLASS
       8 Gent ND40, 1-80
      13 Gent ND40, 181-294
      15 ND40 (film: part 1)
      20 ND40 (film: part 2)
      22 FIRST EXAMINATION

Sept	27	Minorities; Baker and Carroll, 88-98
	29	Michener, 183-217
Oct	4	films, "Jeffries vs. Johnson" and "Only the Ball Was White"
	6	film "Body & Soul," part IV and Michener, "The Black Athlete"
		Baker & Carroll, 159-172
	11	Women; Baker & Carroll, 115-128
	13	Michener, 155-182
	18	film, Michener's "Women & Sports"
	20	film, "Sports Challenge"
	25	SECOND EXAMINATION
	27	College Sports: film "Scandal in College Sports"
Nov	1	Baker & Carroll, 63-75 and Sojka lecture
	3	Michener, 219-280
	8	Sojka lecture
	10	Media: Michener, 355-415
	15	Baker & Carroll, 63-76
	17	film, "Seconds To Play"
	22	Sojka lecture on "T.V. Trashsports"
	24	Thanksgiving vacation--NO CLASS
	29	Baker & Carroll, 129-146
Dec	1	Baker & Carroll, 147-158
	6	film "Breaking Away" part 1
	8	film "Breaking Away" part 2
	13	FINAL EXAMINATION 5:40-7:30

Akers, Dwight. <u>Drivers Up: The Story of American Harness Racing</u>. New York: 1938.

Allen, Lee. <u>The National League Story</u>. <u>The American League Story</u>.

Ali, Muhammad, with Richard Durham. <u>The Greatest: My Own Story</u>. New York: Random House, 1975.

Angell, Roger. <u>The Summer Game</u>.

Asinof, Eliot, <u>Eight Men Out</u>. New York: Holt, Rinehart, and Winston. 1963.

Auerbach, Arnold "Red" and Sann, Saul. <u>Red Auerbach: Winning the Hard Way</u>.

Axthelm, Pete. <u>The City Game</u>.

Barber, Red. <u>The Broadcasters</u>. New York: Dial Press, 1970.

Beckham, Barry. <u>Runner Mack</u>.

<u>The Best Sports Stories</u>. New York: E.P. Dutton, 1945.

Betts, John R. <u>America's Sporting Heritage</u>.

<u>Blacks Sports</u> published by Black Sports, Inc., 386 Park Avenue South, New York, New York 10016.

Bledsoe, Jerry. <u>The World's Number One, Flat-Out, All-Time Great Stock Car Racing Book</u> (New York: Bantam Book, 1976.)

Bouton, Jim. <u>Ball Four</u>.

Bradley, Bill. <u>Life On the Run</u>.

Brokow Al. <u>Golf's Golden Grind</u>.

Brosnan, Jim. <u>The Long Season</u>.

Chipman, Donald, Randolph Cambell, and Robert Calvert, <u>The Dallas Cowboys and and the NFL</u>. Norman: University of Oklahoma Press, 1970.

Cohen, Richard M., David S. Neft, and Roland T. Johnson, text by Jordan A. Deutsch. <u>World Series</u>. Dial Press: New York, 1976.

Cosell, Howard. <u>Cosell</u>. New York: Pocket Books, 1974.

Cosell, Howard. "If Local Team Belongs to the Fan', as a Baseball Official Says, Why Do Those Teams Move So Often?," <u>Letter</u>, New York Times, May 16, 1976.

Creamer, Robert W. <u>Babe: The Legend Comes To Life</u>.

Danzing, Allison, and Peter Brandwein, eds., The Great Sport Stories from the New York Times. New York: A.B. Barnes.

DeLilio, Don. End Zone.

Denny, Reuel. The Astonished Muse. Chicago: University of Chicago Press, 1957.

DeWitt, Robert M. The American Fistiana, Showing the Progress of Pugilism in the United States, From 1816 to 1973. New York: 1973.

Durant, John and Bettman, Otto. Pictorial History of American Sports.

Durso, Joseph. The All-American Dollar. The Big Business of Sports. Boston: Houghton-Mifflin, 1971.

Editors of Sports Illustrated, The Best of Sports Illustrated Boston: Little, Brown & Company, 1973.

Edwards, Harry. The Revolt of the Black Athlete. New York: The Free Press, 1969.

Engle, Kathleen. "The Greening of Girls' Sports" The Nation's Schools 1973.

Emery, Edwin. The Press and America: An Interpretative History of the Mass Media. 3rd ed. Englewood Cliffs, New Jersey: Prentice Hall, Inc., 1972.

Fischler, Stan. Slashing.

Fleischer, Nathaniel S. The Heavyweight Championship.

Falls, Joe. The Boston Marathon. New York: Macmillan Publishing Co., Inc., 1977.

Fox, Larry. Illustrated History of Basketball.

Foster, Alan S. Goodbye Bobby Thomson, Goodbye John Wayne.

Gittelson, Bernard. Biorhythm Sports Forecasting. New YOrk: Arco Publishing Company, Inc., 1977.

Gocher, W.H. 3 Vols. Pacealong, Trotalong, Racealong.

Gilmore, Al-Tony. Bad Nigger!

Gent, Peter. North Dallas Forty.

Hart, M. Marie. Sport and American Society.

--------------- Sport in the Socio-Cultural Process.

Harris, Mark. The Southpaw.

--------------- Bang the Drum Slowly.

Hemphill, Paul. _The Good Old Boys_.

Hildreth, Samuel C. and Crowell, James R. _The Spell of the Turf: The Story of American Racing_.

Honig, Donald. _Baseball: When the Grass was Real_.

Hoch, Paul. _Rip Off the Big Game_.

Isaacs, Neil. _All the Moves_.

Grobani, Anton. _Guide to Football Literature_.

Guttmann, Allen. _From Ritual to Record_.

Grella, George. "Baseball and the American Dream," _Eastern Review_ (April 1977): 39-41, 56-57. Reprinted from _The Massachusetts Review_, 1975.

Huizinga, Johan. _Homo Ludens: A Study of the Play Element in Culture_.

Johnson, William O., Jr. _Super Spectator and the Electric Lilliputians_. Boston: Little, Brown and Company, 1971.

Jares, Joe. _Basketball: The American Game_.

Johnson, William O., Jr., "Television and Sport," _Sports Illustrated_. 3 parts (Jan. 5, 19, 26, 1970).

Johnston, Alexander. _Ten and Out: The Complete Story of the Prize Ring in America_.

Jordan, Pat. _Broken Patterns_. New York: Dodd, Mead & Company, 1977.

-------------- _False Spring_.

Journal of Health, Physical Education, and Recreation published by the American Association for Health, Physical Education, and Recreation, 1201 Sixteenth Street, N.W. Washington, D.C. 20006.

Journal of Leisure Research published by the National Recreation and Park Association, 1700 Pennsylvania N.W., Washington, D.C. 20006.

Journal of Popular Culture.

Journal of Sport History. North American Society for Sport History.

Kahn, Roger. _The Boys of Summer_.

Klafs, Carl, and M. Joan Lyon. _The Female Athlete: Conditioning, Competition & Culture_. St. Louis: C.V. Mosby Co., 1973.

Kaye, Ivan N. _Good Clean Violence: A History of College Football_.

Leach, George B. _The Kentucky Derby Diamond Jubilee_. New York: 1949.

Koppett, Leonard. _The New York Times Guide to Spectator Sports_. New York: Quadrangle, 1972.

--------------- _24 Seconds to Shoot: An Informal History of the NBA_.

Kramer, Jerry, _Instant Replay_.

--------------- _Lombardi: Winning is the Only Thing_.

Lardner, Rex. ed. _The Best of Sports Fiction_. New York: Grossett and Dunlap, 1966.

Leonard, George. _The Ultimate Athlete_.

Leonard, George. "Winning Isn't Everything. It's Nothing," from the Esalen Sports Symposium, reprinted in _Intellectual Digest_. October, 1973, pp. 45-41.

Lewis, Guy. "_The American Intercollegiate Football Spectacle, 1868-1917_." Ph.D. Dissertation.

Lipsyte, Robert. _Sports World: An American Dreamland_. New York: New York Times Book Co., 1975.

Lucas, John A. "The Modern Olympic Games: Fanfare and Philosophy 1896-1972." in _Maryland Historian_ IV, No. 2 (Fall 1973): 76-87.

McKay, Jim. _My Wide World_. New York: Macmillan Publishing Co., Inc., 1973.

McQuaid, Clement. ed. _Gambler's Digest_. Chicago: Follett Publishing Co., 1971.

Malamud, Bernard. _The Natural_.

McWhirter, Norris and Ross McWhirter, _Guinness Sports Record Book_, 4th edition. 1976.

Manchester, Herbert. _Four Centuries of Sport in America, 1490-1890_.

Mandell, Richard R., _The Nazi Olympics_. New York: Macmillan Publishing Co., 1971.

Meggyesy, Dave. _Out of Their League_.

Merchant, Larry. _The National Football Lottery_. New York: Holt, Rinehart, and Winston, 1973.

Miller, Stuart. "New Directions in Sport," _Intellectual Digest_ (1973).

Merchant, Larry. _Ringside Seat at the Circus_. New York: Holt, Rinehart and Winston, 1976.

Murray, Thomas J. "The Big, Booming Business of Pro Football," _Dun's Review and Modern Industry_, (1964).

Michener, James A. _Sports in America_. New York: Random House, 1976.

216

Newcombe, Jack. The Best of the Athletic Boys. (Jim Thorpe).

Noll, Robert G. Government and the Sports Business.

Novak, Michael. The Joy of Sports.

Ogilvie, Bruce C. and Tutko, Thomas A. "Sport: if you want to Build Character Try Something Else," Psychology Today, (1971).

Olson, Jack. The Black Athlete: A Shameful Story (1st pub. in Sports Illustrated July 1964).

Naismith, James. Basketball, Its Origin and Development.

Obojski, Robert. Bush League.

Page, Charles H. Sports & Society: An Anthology.

Parr, Jeanne. The Superwives. New York: Avon Books, 1976.

Palmer, Arnold. Go for Broke.

Parrish, Bernie. They Call it a Game. New York: The Dial Press, 1971.

Paxton, Frederick. "The Rise of Sport," Mississippi Valley Historical Review 4 (Sept. 1917) 144-168.

Petty, Richard. King of the Road. (N.Y.: Rutledge Book-MacMillan Publishing Co., Inc., 1977).

Pepitone, Joe with Staimback, Barry. Joe , You Coulda Made Us Proud.

Peterson, Robert. Only the Ball was White. New York: Prentice-Hall, Inc., 1970.

Physical Educator.

Pluket, H.W. and Finley, M.I. The Olympic Games--The First Thousand Years.

Pooley, John C., "Ethnic Soccer Clubs in Milwaukee: A Study in Assimilation," reprinted in M. Marie Hart, ed., Sport in the Socio-Cultural Process Dubuque, Iowa: William C. Brown Company Publishers, 1972: 328-345.

Powell, Harford, Jr. Walter Camp: The Father of American Football. Boston: Little, Brown & Company, 1926.

Pye, Lloyd. That Prosser Kid.

Queen, Ellery, ed. The Great Sport Detective Stories. Gardner City: Blue Ribbon Books, 1946.

Rentzel, Lance. When All the Laughter Died in Sorrow: An Autobiography. New York: Bantam Books, Inc. 1972.

<u>Research Quarterly</u>, published by the American Association for Health, Physical Education, and Recreation, 1201 Sixteenth Street, N.W., Washington, D.C. 20036.

Rice, Grantland. "The Other Babe and Women in Sports," in <u>The Tumult and the Shouting</u>. New York: Dell Publishing Company, Inc., 1954.

Riesman, David and Reuel Denny. "Football in America: A Study in Cultural Diffusion," <u>American Quarterly</u> 3 (Winter 1951): 309-25.

Robinson, Jackie, as told to Alfred Duckett. <u>I Never Had it Made</u>. Greenwich, Conn.: Fawcett Crest Books, 1972.

Ross, Murray. "Football Red and Baseball Green," <u>Chicago Review</u> (Jan.-Feb., 1971): 30-40. This article was reprinted with the title "Football and Baseball in America," in John T. Talamini & Charles H. Page, eds., <u>Sports & Society: An Anthology</u>. Boston: Little, Brown, and Company, 1973.

Roth, Philip. <u>The Great American Novel</u>.

<u>Rules of the Game: The Complete Illustrated Encyclopedia of All the Sports of the World</u>. (New York; Paddington Press, Ltd., 1974).

Russell, Bill. <u>Go Up For Glory</u>. New York: Coward McCann, 1966.

Sabol, Ken. <u>Babe Ruth and the American Dream</u>.

Sage, George H., ed., <u>Sport and American Society</u>, 2nd ed. Reading, Mass: Addison-Wesley Publishing Company, 1974.

Samson, Jack. <u>The Sportmen's World</u>. New York: Holt, Rinehart and Winston, 1976.

Savage, Howard J. <u>American College Athletics</u>.

--------------- <u>An Illustrated History of the Olympics</u>.

--------------- <u>The Perfect Jump</u>.

Schaap, Richard, comp. <u>Quarterbacks have all the fun: the good life and hard times of Bart, Johnny, Joe, Francis, and other great Quarterbacks</u>. rev. ed. Playboy Press, 1975.

Shaw, Gary, <u>Meat on the Hoof: the Hidden World of Texas Football</u>. 1972.

Schickel, Richard. <u>The World of Tennis</u>. Random House, 1975.

Scott, Jack. <u>The Athletic Revolution</u>. Free Press. 1971.

Silverman, Al. comp. <u>The Best of Sport, 1946-1971</u>. Viking, 1971.

Smelser, Marshall. <u>The life that Ruth Built: A Biography</u>. Quadrangle, 1975.

Smith, Robert Miller. <u>Illustrated History of Baseball</u>. Madison Square Press, 1973.

---------------- Pro football: The History of the Game and the Great Players. Doubleday, 1963.

Smith, Walter Wellesley. Out of the Red, by Red Smith. Knopf, 1950.

Sobol, Ken. Babe Ruth & the America Dream. Random House, 1974.

Sorell, Richard S. "Sports and Franco Americans in Woonsocket, 1870-1930," Rhode Island History 31 (Fall 1972): 117-26.

Sport. 1946- . McFadden Bartell Corp., 205 E. 42nd St., N.Y. 10017.

Sporting News. 1886- . 1212 N. Linbergh Blvd., St. Louis, Mo. 63166.

Sports Illustrated. 1954 - . Time, Inc., 541 N. Fairbands Court, Chicago, Ill. 60611.

Stewart, Jackie and Peter Manso. Faster! A racer's diary. Farrar, Straus & Giroux, 1972.

Stone, Gregory P. "Wrestling--the great American passion play," in Eric Dunning, ed. The sociology of sport. Cass, 1971.

Suits, Daniel and Maureen Kallick. "Gambling in the United States: a summary report." Institute for Social Research, University of Michigan, 1976. (Not yet published. Also expected to be published by G.P.O. as Appendix I to the Final Report of the U.S. Commission on the Review of the National Policy toward Gambling, directed by Peter Reuter.)

Sumner, William Graham. Folkways: a study of the sociological importance of usages, manners, customs, mores, and morals. Dover, 1959 (orig. pub. in 1906).

Talamini, John T. and Charles Hunt Page, comps. Sport & society: an anthology. Little, Brown, 1973.

Tannenbaum, Percy C. and James W. Noah. "Sportugese: a study of sports page communication." Journalism Quarterly 36 (1959): 163-170.

Thorn, John. A Century of Baseball Lore.

Treat, Roger L. The official National Football League football encyclopedia. 14th ed. by Pete Palmer. A.S. Barnes, 1976.

Turkin, Hy and S.C. Thompson. Official encyclopedia of baseball, 8th ed. rev. by Pete Palmer. A.S. Barnes, 1976.

Tutko, Thomas A. and William Bruns. Winning is everything and other American myths. Macmillan, 1976.

Umphlett, Wiley Lee. The sporting myth and the American experience: studies in contemporary fiction. Bucknell, 1975.

Vass, George. George Halas and the Chicago Bears. Regnery, 1971.

Veblen, Thorstein. The Theory of the leisure class. Macmillan, 1899.

Voigt, David Quentin. <u>American baseball</u>. 2v. Oklahoma, 1966-70.

Wagenheim, Kal. <u>Babe Ruth: his life and legend</u>. Praiger, 1974.

Wallace, Francis. <u>Knute Rockne</u>. Doubleday, 1960.

Webb, Bernice Larson. <u>The Basketball Man: James Naismith</u>. Kansas, 1973.

Weyland, Alexander M. <u>The Saga of American football</u>. Macmillan, 1955.

Williamson, Nancy and Gilbert, Bill. "Women in Sports" in <u>Sports Illustrated</u> (May and June, 1973).

Wolf, Dave. <u>Foul! The Connie Hawkins story</u>. Holt, Rinehart and Winston, 1972.

Wooden, John and Tobin, Jack. <u>They Call Me Coach</u>. Word Books, 1972.

<u>Womensports</u>. 1974-1978. 1660 S. Amphlett Blvd., San Mateo, Cal. 50306.

Woodward, Stanley. <u>Sports page</u>. Greenwood, 1968 (orig. pub. by Simon & Schuster, 1949).

Young, Andrew Sturgeon Nash. <u>Negro Firsts in Sports</u>. Johnson, 1963.

Zaharias, Mildred Babe Didrikson. <u>This life I've had; my autobiography</u>, as told to Harry Paxton. A.S. Barnes, 1955.

Course Outline
for
Children and Organized Sport:
A Focus on First Experiences in Organized Sport

by
Joan Ferrante Wallace
Department of Sociology
Northern Kentucky University

I. Historical Overview of Organized Sports for Children (Berryman, 1975)

   A. Prior to the late 1920's or early 1930's sport for preadolescents was part of school curriculum.
   B. After 1930, sport for children was organized independent of the school on the community level.
   C. By the 1940's children's sports were nationally organized and administered.
   D. Several factors contributed to the organization of youth sports independent of the school system.

      1. The schools refused to sponsor competitive sport for young boys.

         a. Physical educators denounced the overt emphasis on winning.
         b. Educators were concerned about the physical and emotional stress accompanying competitive sport.
         c. They refused to organize competition into leagues for championships.
         d. They wanted all children to participate, not only the best athletes.
         e. Sport for children was organized on a community level by volunteer groups, the members of which had no educational training in child psychology and development.

      2. Childhood became recognized as an important stage in the development of an adult and sport was viewed as important to development.
      3. With the end of child labor, children have more leisure time and an activity was needed to occupy their free time.

   E. By the 1960's sports for children were fully organized and and administered on a national/international level (e.g., Little League baseball, Pop Warner Football, Biddy Basketball, Pee Wee Hockey, Little Rodeo Britches, Midget Lacrosse, Junior Ski Jumping, etc.)

221

II. The model for youth sport is an adult professional model (Bower, 1979).

    A. Winning and emulating professionals rather than enhancing the experience of the child-athlete are emphasized.

    B. With the adult professional model as a guide, the experience becomes a highly competitive and stressful one.

    C. Organized sport puts children in a situation where they must learn to perform a skill under pressure before they are comfortable with a sport (Tutko and Bruns, 1979).

> [e.g., The child who just wants to learn to pick up
> a ground ball and throw it correctly to first base
> is confronted by the fact that he has to throw a
> runner out and kill a rally.)

    D. Children who are exposed primarily to adult-organized sport lose the benefits of participation in spontaneous play (Coakley, 1979).

        1. Skill-development and competitiveness are emphasized at the expense of the development of interpersonal skills.
        2. The game is viewed as a means to victory rather than for enjoyment as an end in itself.

    E. "Little Leaguism" or adult-organized play robs children of the fun and valuable learning experiences that result from children's spontaneous play (Devereux, 1976).

    F. Children indicate that they would like sports scaled down to a child's level rather than one they perceive as an adult-level: make the games easier, cut down the length of games, making playing areas smaller (Orlick and Botterill, 1979).

III. Early Social Experiences and Athletic Participation

    A. Childrearing Systems and Athletic Behavior (Cratty, 1981).

        1. In authoritarian systems the child learns to accept authority without question.

        In sports a child reared in this system is happiest with an authoritarian coach, works hard, accepts strategies without reason, and believes in the good of athletics without question.

        2. Children reared in capricious systems are likely to be mistrustful of authorities, as they have been able to coerce their parents. They are also likely to have a rebellious attitude toward unexplained demands and they lack stable guidelines to behavior.

In the sport setting this child may be difficult
to coach. They may be easily led by dissident
members of team and may change allegiance to
team, goals of the team or coach as the season
progresses.

3. Child reared in such a system are manipulative of
   authority figures. They experience unrealistic feelings
   of power and omnipotence over situations, as parents
   have led them to believe that about themselves.

   In the sports setting such children may not do well
   under the stress of competition, particularly if
   they fail. They have a tendency to do well in
   team sports rather than individual sports because
   patterns of overindulgence do not prepare them for
   independent action. They need constant approval
   from coach.

4. Children raised in exploration systems are able to
   function well in abstract, ambiguous, or confusing
   situations. The child is capable of examining
   alternatives, is flexible intellectually, and is
   open and sensitive to others.

   In the sport setting this child will not become
   easily rattled if a change in strategy is required
   nor will he/she have difficulty accommodating to
   new teammates or coaches.

B. Tutko and Bruns (1976) identify family "styles" likely to
have strong negative influence on the child in sport.

   1. Perfectionistic families require that the child be
      a winner and play "perfect."
   2. Authoritarian families require that the child make
      the team.
   3. Families that place emphasis on sports achievement
      when the child is a non-athlete can be negative.
   4. The sports experience can be negative for the
      child if the mother uses her child's sport
      involvement to work out her competitive needs
      vicariously.

C. Brosnan (1963) believes that parental influence is the main
impediment to realizing the aims (e.g., build character, social
relationships, etc.) of organized sport programs for children.

IV. Studies About Stress and Emotion in Children's Sport

A. Hanson (1967) found Little League players expressed high emotional stress while at bat as manifested by rapid heart beat. Researchers recorded upward shifts of 110 per minute to 160 per minute. Players reported, however, they did not experience nervousness while at bat. Hanson believes that Little League players refuse to or are unable to acknowledge this tension.

B. Simon and Martens (1979) studied 468 boys between the ages of 9 and 14 participating in one of the following sports: baseball, ice hockey, gymnastics, swimming or wrestling. Based on the results of an anxiety inventory (e.g., Competitive State Anxiety Inventory), individuals playing a team sport generally have lower anxiety prior to competition. In essence the findings indicate that an important determinant of stress is whether a child athlete is participating in an individual or team activity.

C. Skubic (1965) surveyed 100 boys participating in Little League and found that slightly over 50 percent (N=100) evidence signs of at least temporary emotional upset. Among the signs reported by parents were disruption of normal sleeping patterns and mood shifts. Skubic found reports of emotional instability were more often experienced after winning contests than after losing contests.

D. Tutko and Bruns (1976) defined five major areas that can produce stress in children's sport: losing, being a substitute, peer group pressures, fear of getting hurt and forced participation.

E. Horn (1977) summarizes findings from interview of 1000 players, parents and coaches in Little League Baseball programs in Utah and New Mexico. Twenty-five percent of the players and 53 percent of the coaches believed participation was a product of parent urgings. Fifty percent of players responded that parents chewed them out if they played poorly.

V. Effects of Team and Individual Failure on Child Participants

[Note: Findings are mixed]

A. Dishman (1985) addresses the debate surrounding the impact of sport on children's psyches. One side (supporters of children's sports) hail social values: teamwork, courage, character and self-esteem as the outcome. Opponents counter that physical and metal stress result. Dishman concludes that both sides have exaggerated their case--"neither the worst fears nor the best hopes of the youth sport debate have been confirmed."

B. Iso-Ahola (1977) studied 300 Little League players and found that team failures decreased players' evaluation of team ability but did not reduce ratings of personal ability or effort.

    1. Players judge their own abilities and efforts high, regardless of the team's repeated poor performance.

2. Players' own perceptions of their own internal
   qualities are not vulnerable to team failure.

C. Learned helplessness may be the result depending on how the
child-athlete assigns responsibility for the failure (Iso-Ahola, 1980).

   1. The child may assume personal responsibility for
      failures and therefore think that lack of personal
      ability was one of the main causes of losing.

      a. Generalized helplessness may result if the child
         believes that, as a result of poor sports perfor-
         mance, personal inability to bring about positive
         outcomes holds true for most of life's activities,
         not just Little League.
      b. Discriminated helplessness may result if the
         child believes that personal inability is limited
         to sport performance.

   2. [or] The player may assign causality of failure to
      such situational factors as incompetent umpires or
      teammates' poor performance.

      a. Repeated failure is viewed as determined by
         forces outside those associated with personal
         performance.
      b. Such situational attributions are rarely
         followed by feelings of helplessness.

D. Scanlan (1982) defines young athletes' reactions to competitive
situations as dependent on several interrelated influences.

   1. The Objective Competitive Situation or the real
      factors in the environment contribute to a
      competitive situation.
   2. The Subjective Competitive Situation or how an
      individual perceives, appraises and accepts the
      competitive situation (e.g. threatening, non-
      threatening) is an important dimension.
   3. Response or the direct behavioral reaction of
      the child-athlete influence the character of the
      situation.
   4. Consequences or the short or long term effects
      of the competitive event which may be positive,
      negative, or neutral must also be considered.

E. Being cut from a team can leave emotional scars (Greene, 1984).

VI. The Coach

   A. Results of a study (Rejeski, et. al.) 8 of 14 coaches and 71 male
youth basketball players ranging in age from 8 to 12 suggest that a
"pygmalion effect" operates.

        1. High expectancy children receive more reinforcement
            from the coach.
        2. Low expectancy children receive more general technical
            instruction.

   B. Children's attitudes toward coaches tend to be positive when
the coach's style is characterized by reinforcement and technical
instruction (as opposed to yelling). Win-loss record seems unrelated
to attitudes toward coach (Smith, et. al., 1979).

   C. Coaches participating in "coaching effectiveness training"-- a
program designed to assist them in relating more effectively to children--
were evaluated more positively by their players than were those coaches
who did not participate (Smith, et. al., 1979).

        1. Players who played for trained coaches exhibited an
            increase in general self-esteem.
        2. The greatest differences in attitudes toward trained
            and untrained coaches were found among child low in
            self-esteem. Such children appeared more sensitive
            to variations in coaches' use of encouragement,
            punishment and technical instruction.

   D. There are five coaching issues organized sport face and need
to resolve if there is to be a healthy sports environment for children
(Zucher, 1985).

        1. The majority of people working with kids in sport
            make a gross assumption--that kids are adults.
        2. Although national organizations provide guidelines
            for appointing coaches, individual leagues are
            responsible for appointing them.
        3. A problem in children's sport is finding enough
            coaches, let alone qualified coaches.
        4. Some sport organizations such as American Youth
            Soccer are attempting to raise the level of compe-
            tency of coaches through instructional training programs.
        5. Under the right leadership organized sports are
            wonderful for kids. Under poor leadership, they can
            be devastating.

VII. Coed Sports (Monagan, 1983)

   A. Advances made in the area of co-ed sports have been few.

B. One reason for this is that there is an unresolved debate about the effects of co-ed sport for children.

    1. One side believes that coed sport is not developmentally positive.

        a. Early failure while competing against the opposite sex can be psychologically humiliating for many youths, especially boys.
        b. Sports has traditionally been a grounds to help establish sexual identity and mixing of the sexes confuses this process.

    2. The other side maintains that coed sports is developmentally positive.

        a. Mixed competition will pay off by producing more "androgynous adults"--more assertive women and more sensitive men.
        b. Boys would view women in more equal terms.

Bibliography

Berryman, J.W.
   1982   "The Rise of Highly Organized Sports for Preadolescent Boys."
           pp. 2-15 in R.A. Magill, M.J. Asch and F. Smoll (eds.)
           Children in Sport Illinois: Human Kinetics Publishers.

Brosnan, J.
   1963   "Little Leaguers Have Big Problems--Their Parents."
           Atlantic Monthly March: 117-120.

Brower, J.J.
   1979   "The Professionalism of Organized Youth Sport: Social and
           Psychological Impacts and Outcomes." Annals AAPSS
           September: 39-46.

Cratty, B.J.
   1981   "Early Social Experiences and Later Athletic Participation."
           in Social Psychology in Athletics. Englewood Cliffs,
           New Jersey: Prentice-Hall.

Dishman, R.
   1985   "Big Stress for Little Athletes?" Sports Fitness June:
           73-75+.

Greene, B.
   1984   "Cut: The First Time It Happens Leaves Scars That Don't
           Heal." Esquire July: 10-11.

Horn, J.C.
   1977   "Parent Egos Take the Fun Out of Little League." Psychology
           Today 11 (September): 18-22.

Iso-Ahola, S.E.
   1977   "Effects of Team Outcome on Children's Self Perception."
           Journal Of Psychology 18:38-42.

   1980   "An Attributional Model of Learned Helplessness With
           Particular Reference to Little League Sports." pp. 121-122
           in The Social Psychology of Leisure and Recreation. Iowa:
           WCB Publishers.

Monagan, D.
   1983   "The Failure of Coed Sports." Psychology Today March: 58+.

Orlick, T. and C. Botterill
   1979   "What's Best for Kids?" in D. Stanley Eitzen Sport in
           Contemporary Society: An Anthology New York: St. Martin's
           Press.

Rejeski, W., C. Darrocott and S. Hutslas
   1979   "Pygmalion in Youth Sports: A Field Study." Journal of
           Sport Psychology 1:211-219.

Scanlan, T.K.
   1982 "Social Evaluation: A Key Developmental Element in the
        Competition Process." in R.A. Magill, Michael Asch and Frank
        Small (eds.) <u>Children in Sport</u> Illinois: Human Kinetics
        Publishers, Inc.

Simon, J.A. and R. Martens
   1979 "Children's Anxiety in Sport and Non-sport Evaluative
        Activities." <u>Journal of Sport Psychology</u> 1:160-169.

Skubic, E.
   1965 "Emotional Responses of Boys to Little League and to Middle
        League Competitive Baseball." <u>Research Quarterly</u> 35:118-125.

Smith, R.E., F.L. Small and B. Curtis
   1978 "Coaching Behavior in Little League Baseball." in F. Small
        and R. Smith <u>Psychological Perspectives in Youth Sport</u>
        Washington, D.C.: Hemisphere.

   1979 "Coaching Effectiveness Training: A Cognitive-Behavioral
        Approach to Enhancing Relationship Skills in Youth Sport
        Coaches." <u>Journal of Sport Psychology</u> 1:59-75.

Tutko, T. and W. Bruns
   1976 "Dealing With the Emotions of Childhood Sports." in
        <u>Winning is Everything and Other American Myths</u> New York:
        MacMillan Publishing.

   1976 "Emotional Child Abuse." in <u>Winning is Everything and Other
        American Myths</u> New York: MacMillan Publishing.

   1979 "The Myths of Early Competition." in D. Stanley Eitzen
        <u>Sport in Contemporary Society</u> New York: St. Martin's
        Press.

Zucher, M.
   1965 "A Question of Balance." <u>Sports Fitness</u> June: 61+.

Course Outline
for
Women and Sports
by
Joan Ferrante Wallace, Department of Sociology
and
Joan Catherine Whitman, Department of Philosophy
Northern Kentucky University

Texts:

Women and Sport: From Myth to Reality (1978) edited by Carol Oglesby

Out of the Bleachers: Writings on Women and Sport (1979) edited by
    Stephanie Twin

I. Historical Background

    A. The birth of the American Sportswoman is a 20th century
phenomenon.
    B. During the last century changing females sport roles correspond
to the changing role of women in general.
    C. Biographical sketches provide insights about social forces
affecting women athletes since 1890.

        1. The years 1890-1919 are considered to be a period
            of Idealization. Women's dress was conservative
            and feminine and women were allowed to participate
            in some sports (Coffey, 1965). The most important
            sports events for women took place in women's colleges.
            Francis Willard's experience with the bicycle typifies
            the atmosphere (Willard, 1895).

            a. Francis Willard wrote the first book on bicycle
                riding in 1895.
            b. Bad press was given to women who had succeeded
                in bike riding. Bike riding was not in keeping
                with the ideal image of women. Consequently,
                little support or encouragement was given to
                those who attempted to learn.
            c. Francis Willard was an exception. She both
                succeeded at bike riding and bike maintenance.
                The mastery of the bike was also a mastery of
                herself.

        2. The years 1920-1929 are years of Emancipation. There was
            more leadership for women. Women had a greater desire to
            participate in sport, and less restrictive clothing facili-
            tated increased participation in sport (Coffey, 1965).
            Still, women athletes were expected to fail, as exemplified
            by the case of Gertrude Ederle, who in 1926 became the first
            woman to swim the English Channel in a record breaking

time--a time two hours ahead of then men's record
(Gallico, 1964).

a. Clothing for women swimmers was reduced to one
    piece, which in addition to making swimming less
    restrictive, also emphasized the shape of women's
    bodies.
b. Women athletes, such as Ederle, were said to have
    a "lack of beauty," indicating that they did not
    fit into the female image.
c. After failing to swim the English Channel in April
    of 1926, Ederle attempted the feat again in August
    of that year. Expecting her to fail, the London
    Times preprinted the front page announcing her
    failure.
d. Her success in August was a tribute to women
    athletes. Yet, despite her accomplishment, Ederle
    became a swimming instructor and was all but forgotten.

3. The years from 1930-1943 were the Socialization period
    (Coffey, 1965). Clothing was designed to accentuate the
    "feminine" female body. Femininity in sports was vital.
    During this period athletic feminism arose but was quickly
    laid to rest (until the 1970's).

    a. Alice Sefton, in a 1937 issue of the Journal, noted
        that beauty should be the by-product of sport
        participation.
    b. Ethyl McGary, a former Women's Association Olympian,
        spoke out against the male "do or die" style of
        competition.
    c. Athletic stars of the period such as Mildred Babe
        Didrikson, Annette Rogers and Helen Stephens (all
        1932 and 1936 Olympic track stars) are examples of
        outstanding women athletes. Yet, little attention
        was given to their achievements until recently.

4. The years 1944-1965 were the period of Participation.
    In general, women were entering the workforce and getting
    physical training in the armed services. This "partici-
    pation" spread to other segments of the society including
    sport.

    a. Intramural programs were enhanced, and more equal
        sport programs for men and women were beginning to
        develop in some of the schools.
    b. Althea Gibson, a tennis player, typifies the
        struggles of women athletes, especially black
        women (Gibson, 1958).

        --Tennis gave her self-discipline and purpose. It
changed her life.

231

--Even as a child living on a North Carolina cotton farm, Althea Gibson was an independent thinker.

--She was a "tomboy" as a child and was encouraged by her father, who wanted her to be a prize fighter (for self protection).

--"Act like a lady, play like a tiger" was her motto.

--She was subjected to racism. She was the first black player to break the color barrier in the USLTA after having protested her initial rejection by the tennis association.

4. The years 1965 to present can be considered years of Emergence for women. Katherine Switzer, Willye B. White, and Bev Francis are only a few women who have succeeded in athletics.

   a. Katherine Switzer was suspended from the AAU for participating in the 26-mile Boston Marathon in 1968. She was the first female to run in it.

   --She was ignorant of the fact that women could not run in the race especially since she had been running 10 miles a day with men.

   --She notes that she was once considered a "freak" but is now considered "chic."

   --Her actions elicited social changes that affected other female athletes.

   b. Another athlete of this period is Willye B. White, a track and field star from the mid-50's to the mid-70's (Jordan, 1975).

   --She fought the obstacles of racism and agism.

   --She participated in the Olympics five times.

   --She was aware of the stigma--"Being a female athlete is always being two different people."

   --She was considered a freak for being like a "man."

   c. In the 1980's Bev Francis, an Australian body-builder, served as an unprecendented role model for women (Steinem, 1985).

   --Her strong masculine appearance was repulsive to both judges and other body builders.

--She was trained by male bodybuilders.

--Her presence brought into serious consideration
the stature of females and their mythical limitations.

--Her "unprofessional" treatment by judges of comparative
body building contests underscored the sex-discrimination operative
in sports--that men and women are evaluated by completely different
standards.

II. Myths and Realities About the Female in Sports (Gates, 1979, Twin,
1979).

A. Myths are any real or fictional stories, recurring themes, or
character types that appeal to the consciousness of a people by embodying
their cultural ideals or by giving expression to deep, commonly felt
emotions.

1. Women are the weaker sex.
2. Women who participate in sport become "muscle" bound.
3. Women are less coordinated than men.
4. Women have less muscle power and stamina than men.
5. Menstruation prevents women from participating in sports.

B. Each of the myths outlined above can be countered by objective
findings.

1. More males die in utereo than females. More diseases
affect males than females. Life expectancy for females
is higher than males.
2. Women have only small amounts of testosterone, which
means they can not develop "masculine" muscle bulk.
They can increase strength dramatically without
appearing muscle-bound.
3. There is no evidence that there is a difference between
neuromuscular efficiency.
4. Women's performances in running and swimming, for
example, are improving faster than men's. Women hold
the speed records for swimming the English Channel in
both directions.
5. Top performances are possible at all stages of the
menstrual cycle.
6. Complications in pregnancy are less frequent in women
who have participated in sports.

C. The overriding myth concerning the sportswoman is that the
male anatomy is inherently better suited to sport.

1. An unknown amount of difference in performance is
socially induced (Hudson, 1978).
2. If the male physique is better suited to most sports,
it is because males developed sports to suit their
physique. But if women had been the historically

233

dominant sex, competition emphasizing flexibility, balance, and timing might have dominated (English, 1978). 3. Since sport standards are male, the woman in sport is compared with men--not with other women--hence she is viewed as inferior. Perhaps the goal should be the attainment of perfection within the limitations of each physical type (Scott, 1974).

III. Female Socialization into Sports

    A. The family is very influential to the athletic career of females (Greendorfer, 1978).

        1. Parents elicit more motor behavior from their sons than from their daughters.
        2. Family attitudes are one of the most significant factors accounting for female athletic participation. It seems females need approval and support from parents to offset negative feedback about their involvement in sport.
        3. Parents channel their children in the direction of sex-appropriate sports (e.g., boys: football or baseball; girls: gymnastics or cheerleading).

    B. The organization of play and sports in educational institutions perpetuates the cultural constructs defining sex-appropriate sports behavior.

        1. Boys and girls participate in different kinds of games, and consequently, each gender learns to move in a different manner (Lever, 1978).

            a. In comparison to girls' play and games, boys' play and games are characterized by interdependent roles and structure (explicit goals, rules).
            b. Girls' play, on the other hand, tends to be characterized by low interdependence of roles (e.g. such as turntaking) and low structure.

        2. Segregation of play and games by gender at an early age accentuates and helps transmit a value system concerning masculinity and femininity.
        3. There are greater numbers of sports available to males than to females.

    C. The media (e.g., TV, newspapers, magazines) influences conceptions about sex-appropriate sports and behavior.

        1. Media coverage of females and male athletes mirrors stereotypic versions of men's and women's sport roles.
        2. The media reflects and reinforces the sport options available to both sexes.

3. In comparison to the media coverage and attention given to the male athletes, the amount of coverage given women is very little.

    a. Because of their greater visibility role models for females tend to be male (Greendorfer, 1978).
    b. The greater attention given to the male reinforces a perception that males have a "better" gender role.
    c. Role ambivalence may result because women have a psychological need to act in ways traditionally appropriate to their sex, but they are attracted to the greater social benefits that men receive.

IV. Female Athlete as a Social Anomaly (Felshin, 1974)

A. There is a normative incongruity between the role expectations of the position female and the role expectations of athlete.

1. The adjectives "passive," "gentle," "delicate" describe society's stereotypic view of acceptable female behavior.
2. Qualities socially defined as necessary for successful participation in competitive sport include assertiveness, competitiveness, physical endurance, and ruggedness.

B. A state of cognitive dissonance exists for those who occupy the position of female-athlete and for those who come in contact with female athletes (Festinger, 1957).

1. If we assume that dissonance is an unpleasant state, action may be taken to reduce it.
2. To achieve consistency or consonance efforts are undertaken to change and to make the discrepancy between the two roles plausible.

C. Responses to this state of dissonance vary depending on the individual's relation to the female-athlete.

1. Spectators or audience reaction to female-athlete (Snyder, et. al., 1975).

    a. Sports characterized by bodily contact, application of force to some heavy object, face-to-face competition in which bodily contact appears or the projection of body through space for long distances receives little support from the public.
    b. Sports involving grace, flowing movements, flexibility and aesthetics receive more support from the public.
    c. The chances of gaining public approval are greater if the athlete is physically attractive.

2. The media's reaction to the female-athlete (Hiestand, 1982).

    a.   The media has tended to give the female athlete limited exposure.

    --Women's sport receives only one percent of total sports coverage. This is mainly in the Olympics and World Games as well as scattered coverage of golf and tennis.

    --Major sport magazines such as Sports Illustrated give little coverage to women's sport.

    --When covering female athletes, usually there is some mention of physical appearance or indirect statements about level of the athlete's femininity.

    b.   There are almost no female sport broadcasters, reinforcing an image that females know little about sports.

    --Jane Chastain became a football commentator without adequate preparation.

    --Phyllis George was part of a broadcast team for a pre-game football show. She was, again, poorly trained by the network.

3. The female-athletes' reaction.

    a.   Women athletes aware of "masculine" stigma protect their femininity by exposing an apologetic; that is, they emphasize their femininity by (i) dressing in appropriate ways, (ii) not taking sport seriously, (iii) by pursuing acceptable sports, etc.
    b.   Another way to relieve cognitive dissonance is to attribute successes to factors external to the self (e.g. luck or low ability of opponents). This is a subtle way of saying I (a female) had nothing to do with athletic success.
    c.   While female athletes acknowledge the stigma attached to athletic behavior, they also acknowledge positive feelings toward their own body. In essence, the perceived advantages outweigh the perceived discrepancy.
    d.   Women get caught up in the femininity game--they criticize athletes among them that are not feminine.

V A Case of Dissonance: Women Body Builders

    A. Issue: The case of female body builders vividly underscores the issues faced by women athletes.

    1. Do sex role expectations obstruct the full realization of female sport potential? (Derieux, 1985)

a. The number of women participating in this sport has helped the public see that muscles are not a symptom of masculinity.
b. However, female weightlifters are encouraged to emulate the feline muscule line of body building champs like Rachel McLish rather than the heavily muscled body of Bev Francis.
c. Confining muscle development in feline parameters is equivalent to deciding to run the 100 yard dash in a time defined as feminine.
d. The role confusion female body builders experience may be operating even in sports defined as "feminine" such as tennis, golf or gymnastics—the consequence in all cases is the development of female athletic potential within the parameters of socially defined femininity.

B. Issue: To be commercially viable must athletes fit a model of femininity acceptable to the public (Gaines & Butler, 1983)?

1. Women's body building is almost totally represented by slim, graceful, pretty women with muscles that do not show unless they are flexed.
2. In an effort to make the sport commercially viable, women with muscle bulk are not winning the contests nor are they endorsing the major body-building products.

VI. Women as Spectators: The Case of Cheerleaders (Bernikow, 1973).

A. Cheerleaders are both spectators and spectacles.
B. Cheerleading encourages stereotypical female roles.

1. Cheerleaders wear revealing clothes.
2. Team support is the focus of the cheerleader.

C. Although cheerleading leads to glory for the individual cheerer, the role entails worshiping the ones for whom she is cheering.

D. Overall, women in cheerleading are lead to believe that they have status, are independent, and have certain freedoms, yet these advantages are tied to the men who make their cheering position possible.

VII. Inequality in Athletic Programs (Coakley, 1978)

A. In comparison to men's programs women's athletic programs are inadequately funded.

B. Facilities and equipment disparities are often the result of funding differences. To compound this, however, women are often given the use of facilities and equipment when men do not find them convenient to use.

237

C. Fewer equipment coaches are hired for women's teams than are for men's teams.

D. There are also substantial differences in the quality of transportation to away games, daily food allowance and accomodations.

E. At all levels, men have a greater number of alternative sports to participate in than women do.

F. Media coverage (e.g., T.V. and newspaper) of female sport events is considerably less than that for male sport events.

VIII. Setbacks for Women in Sport

A. The failure of coed sport programs, especially among the young, has contributed to continued training inequalities as well as emotional tension between the sexes (Monagan, 1983).

    1. There is a lack of equal training from the start.

        a. Boys have a two-year start in athletic competition.
        b. As a consequence, athletic development is different for male and female adolescents.

    2. Studies indicate that children would rather not participate in sports at all than to participate in coed sports.

        a. Participation in coed sports yields confusion, fear of lack of competence, and sexual identity crisis.
        b. A coed setting seems to increase competition.
        c. Girls sense boys' hostility towards them.
        d. Male athletes drop out of coed sports in protest.
        e. Girls threaten the integrity of boys. Fear of ridicule and failure are likely consequences.

B. Title IX has not been written or implemented in the manner in which it was intended and has thus failed to contribute to equality between the sexes in the realm of sport.

    1. The exact meaning of the term "equal opportunity" in Title IX is not specified. Hence Title IX is open to broad interpretation (Hogan, 1976).
    2. The document as written left the means of achieving equal opportunity open.
    3. The underlying message is "the money is yours if you can get it."
    4. Not all athletic programs receive federal assistance and thus are not subject to the stipulations of Title IX.

5. Too much grace time to enact Title IX was given to schools.
6. Some schools are simply not conforming to the Title IX policies and standards.

C. Setbacks in equality for women in the sport environment have been accompanied by overall setbacks for women.

1. The decline of the women's movement has left women without a unifying set of goals or focus.
2. The Equal Rights Amendment failed to pass.
3. The general problems of women in the mainstream of male dominated society are still interpreted as "personal" rather than institutional.
4. The work-home conflict has not been satisfactorily resolved.
5. There were pressures on women to adapt to male values in home, work and play. At the same time women were struggling to establish an identity as powerful as the males yet distinct.
6. The lack of male support for the women's movement contributed to its decline.

Bibliography

Bernikow, Louise
    1973 "Confessions of an Ex-Cheerleader." pp. 155-161 in Stephanie
        Twin (ed.) <u>Out of the Bleachers: Writings on Women and Sport</u>
        New York: Feminist Press.

Coakley, J.J.
    1978 "Women in Sport: Separate or Equal." pp. 243-273 in <u>Sport</u>
        <u>and Society: Issues and Controversies</u> St. Louis: C.V.
        Mosby Press.

Coffey, Margaret A.
    1965 "The Modern Sportswoman." pp. 277-286 in J.T. Talamini and
        C.M. Page (eds.) <u>Sport and Society</u> Boston: Little Brown
        and Co.

Derieux, Robin
    1985 "The Weight Room: Building Strong Friendship." <u>Ms. Magazine</u>
        October: 72-74.

English, Jane
    1978 "Sex Equality in Sports." <u>Philosophy and Public Affairs</u>
        7 (Spring): 54.

Felshin, Jan
    1974 "The Triple Option for Women in Sport." <u>Quest</u> 21 (Jan):
        36-40.

Friedan, Betty
    1985 "How to Get the Women's Movement Going Again." New York
        <u>Times Magazine</u> November 3: p. 26+.

Festinger, Leon
    1957 <u>A Theory of Cognitive Dissonance</u>. Stanford: Stanford
        University Press.

Gallico, Paul
    1964 "Gertrude Ederle." pp. 142-155 in Stephanie Twin (ed.)
        <u>Out of the Bleachers: Writings on Women and Sport</u> New York:
        Feminist Press.

Gates, Barbara and Nan D. Stein
    1979 "Teaching Guide" to accompany <u>Out of the Bleachers: Writings</u>
        <u>on Women and Sport</u> New York: Feminist Press.

Gibson, Althea
    1958 "I Always Wanted to Be Somebody." pp. 130-142 in Stephanie
        Twin (ed.) <u>Out of the Bleachers: Writings on Women and</u>
        <u>Sport</u> New York: Feminist Press.

Greendorfer, Susan
    1978 "Socialization into Sport." in Carol Oglesby (ed.) <u>Women</u>
        <u>and Sport: From Myth to Reality</u> Philadelphia: Lea & Febiger.

Hiestand, Deborah
1982 "Women in Sport in the United States: 1945 to 1978." in Reet
Howell (ed.) Her Story in Sport: A Historical Anthology of
Women in Sports New York: Leisure Press.

Hogan, Candace Lyle
1976 "Shedding Light on Title IX." pp. 173-181 in Stephanie Twin
(ed.) Out of the Bleachers: Writings on Women and Sport
New York: Feminist Press.

Hudson, Jackie
1978 "Physical Parameters Used For Female Exclusion From Law
Enforcement and Athletics." In Carol Oglesby (ed.) Women
& Sport: From Myth to Reality Philadelphia: Lea & Febiger.

Lever, Janet
1978 "Sex Differences in the Complexity of Children's Play and Games."
American Sociological Review 43 (August): 471-83.

Mathis, Sharon
1978 "Body Image and Sex Stereotyping." in Carol Oglesby (ed.)
Women and Sport: From Myth to Reality Philadelphia:
Lea & Febiger.

McHugh, Mareen C., Mary E. Duquin and Irene H. Frieze
1978 "Beliefs About Success and Failure." In Carol Oglesby (ed.)
Women and Sport: From Myth to Reality Philadelphia: Lea
& Febiger.

Monagan, David
1983 "The Failure of Coed Sports." Psychology Today March
pp. 58-63.

Scott, Jack
1974 "The Masculine Obsession in Sport." in Barbara J. Hoepner
(ed.) Women Athletes: Coping with Controversy Washington,
D.C.: AAHPER.

Steinem, Gloria
1985 "Coming Up: Unprecendented Women." Ms. July: 84+.

Twin, Stephanie
1979 Out of the Bleachers: Writings on Women and Sport. New York:
Feminist Press.

Willard, Frances E.
1895 "How I Learned to Ride the Bicycle." pp. 103-114 in Stephanie
Twin (ed.) Out of the Bleachers: Writings on Women and Sport
New York: Feminist Press.

Course Outline
for
The Black Athlete
by
Joan Catherine Whitman, Department of Philosophy
and
Joan Ferrante Wallace, Department of Sociology
Northern Kentucky University

Preface: We are very disappointed with the literature concerning the
black athlete in American society. With the exception of a few works
(Edwards, 1969, 1971, 1973; Loy and McElvogue, 1970; Ashe, 1985;
Halberstam, 1981 Yetman and Eitzen, 1971; Hare, 1971), the accounts of
the black athlete at all stages of the sport career are superficial.
We acknowledge the general lack of substantive research in the field
of sport in general, but the work on the black athlete--both male and
female--is especially limited. Accounts of the black female athlete
are almost nonexistent. We have done our best to organize this
literature. Unfortunately, in many sections of the outline we can
offer only broad generalization about some aspects of the black athlete's
career. Moreover, in a number of areas we can only report about the
lack of information.

Text:

The Breaks of the Game by David Halberstam (1981)

Film:

The Hard Road to Glory by Arthur Ashe (1985)

I. Historical Background

[Note: Historical data throughout this outline is taken primarily from
two sources: the film The Hard Road to Glory (1985) by Arthur Ashe and
the book The Games They Played by Douglas A. Noverr and Lawrence E.
Ziewacz (1983).]

    A. In the United States, the existence of black sports heroes
dates back to the early 19th century.

    B. The experience of blacks in sports since the 19th century mirrors
the social and political climate.

    C. Biographical sketches provide insights into the problems black
athletes have faced in our society since the early 1800's.

    1. The 1800's

--While black athletes existed, the first "hero" wasn't publicly recognized
until 1810 when Tom Molineaux fought Tome Cribbs, the English World

Champion, and knocked him out after 23 rounds. Cribbs supporters claimed Molineaux had weights hidden in his gloves. Consequently, Cribbs was given two minutes, four times as many as usual, to recover. The fight resumed in the 24th round and went until the 42nd, at which point Molineaux was declared the winner.

--While boxing was popular for black athletes, black jockeys also succeeded in the early 1800's. In pre-Civil war days, most towns had horse tracks. In addition to riding for their owners, blacks were permitted to race their own horses on weeknights. Monkey Simon was a great jockey from Nashville, Tennessee. Issac Murphy, winner of three Kentucky Derbys, was another well-known black jockey who earned over $20,000 a year racing horses. However, the emergence of organized labor and the closing of northern tracks to black jockeys contributed to the eventual extinction of the black jockey.

--Blacks participated in baseball until the end of the 1800's. In 1889 Major League Baseball banned blacks from participation until 1945 when the Brooklyn Dodgers signed Jackie Robinson.

--Bike racing was also popular in the late 1800's. Two important black cyclists were Nelson Bails (Olympic winner) and Major Taylor (winner of two world titles).

    2. Early 1900's

--Boxing became popular again in the early 1900's. In 1903 Jack Johnson became a highly visible and controversial sports figure. Johnson was nicknamed the "Restless Hunter." Two of the better known white boxers-- Tommy Burns and Jim Jeffries--refused to box Johnson for many years. In 1910 Jeffries agreed to a fight with the black boxer and Johnson won. Riots broke out after Johnson's victory and 13 people were killed. Booker T. Washington believed that the incident, along with the fact that Johnson's dating of white women was so widely publicized, caused irreparable damage to the black race.

--Henry McDonald, a running back for the Rochester Jeffersons, and Doc Baker, a halfback with the Akron Indians, were black professional football players in the early 1900's. Fritz Pollard won notoriety at Brown from 1914-1916 and was the first black to make 1st team All-American. In addition to playing for four different professional teams after his college career, Pollard became the first black player-coach at Akron and Hammond.

--Track and field were sports in which blacks were permitted to excel. In 1923, H. P. Drew tied the world record for the 100 yard dash (9.6 seconds). In 1924, DeHart Hubbard entered the Inter-Allied Games in Paris and jumped 26 feet in the long jump, nearly a foot beyond the previous record. Hubbard won a gold medal in the 1924 Olympics.

3. The 1930's and 40's

--In 1935 Jesse Owens, representing Ohio State in the Big Ten Championships, set three world records and equaled a fourth in one afternoon.

--The performance of black athletes at the Berlin Olympics brought into serious question myths of Aryan superiority. Jesse Owens set an Olympic record for the 200 meter dash; Mack Robinson took second place in the same event. Archie Williams won the 400 meter race. Other black stars of these Olympics included Archie Williams, Jimmy LuValle, Johnny Woodruff and Cornelius Johnson.

--The successes of blacks in track and field in the 1936 Olympics helped open opportunities in other sports. A major breakthrough for blacks came when Branch Rickey signed Jackie Robinson with the Brooklyn Dodgers in 1945.

--In boxing, Joe Lewis joined the East-West All Star League and, after losing once to the German Max Schmeling, defeated him convincingly in less than one round. His efforts were applauded by the United States and his victory symbolized an important political statement.

--In 1942, Joe Louis joined the army and was instrumental in desegregation efforts. At one point he was refused entry to a movie theater. He complained, and the officer who enforced the rule was relieved of his command. His influence also facilitated the admission of blacks into Officer's Candidate School.

--Alice Coachman of Tuskegee became the first black woman to win an Olympic Gold Medal. In the 1948 Olympics she took a gold medal for the high jump.

4. 1950's

--Advancements for blacks increased throughout the 1950's especially after the 1954 Brown vs. the Board of Education Supreme Court decision.

--A number of racial barriers in sport were overcome in the 1950's. The racial barrier of the NBA was broken. Arthur Ashe became the first black male to enter the U.S. Open and Wimbledon. In 1956 Ed Temple became the first American Black coach for a black women's track team. In addition, Althea Gibson became the first black female tennis champion.

5. The 1960's

--The 1960's were years of advancement for blacks in sport but will also be remembered as years of protest. During these years the Olympics provided an arena for black stars.

--In the 1960 Olympics Wilma Rudolph won the 100 and 200 meter dashes and "anchored" the 400 meter relay team to victory (Noverr and Ziewacz, 1983).

244

--Cassius Clay (later Muhammed Ali) was the gold-medal winner in the light
heavyweight division. He became a controversial figure during the mid-60's
when he joined the Black Muslims and adopted Islamic beliefs. He rejected
his American identity and claimed he was a black man. He was stripped of
his boxing title when he protested the draft during the Vietnam War.

--In 1966 Bill Russell became the first black head coach in professional
basketball. Two years later, Emmet Ashford became the first black
umpire in the American League.

--Perhaps the most memorable events of the 1960's took place at the 1968
Olympics at Mexico City when two black athletes, led by Harry Edwards,
raised their fists as a sign in protest during the United States National
Anthem.

      6. The 1970-80's

--The 1970's and 80's gave blacks greater recognition in sports. Still,
prejudices existed.

--David Halberstam's book The Breaks of the Game provides excellent insights
into the situation of the black athlete in professional basketball. Some
professional basketball players profiled by Halberstam include (1) Kermit
Washington, a player victimized by the press when he got in a fight and
smashed the face of a white player named Rudy Tomjanovich. The press
unfairly portrayed Washington as the instigator and replayed the fight
scene an unnecessary number of times. (2) Kareem Abdul-Jabbar, a player
who refused to play for the U.S. Olympic basketball team to protest the
unfair treatment of blacks in America; (3) Moses Malone, the first player
to turn professional out of high school; and (4) Billy Ray Bates, who
played for Kentucky State, a black college, and faced a number of special
difficulties making the transition from a black college to the professionals.

II. Myths and Realities About the Black Athlete

    A. There are a number of myths about the physical abilities of black
athletes as well as myths about the extent to which sport provides an
avenue of upward mobility for blacks (Kane, 1973; Michener, 1976;
Edwards, 1973). These myths include the following:

        1. Blacks have genetic traits favorable to sport (e.g.,
        longer limbs, smaller calfs, double-jointedness, etc.)
        2. Blacks have a greater psychological capacity to
        relax under pressure.
        3. An unintended consequence of the practice of selective
        breeding during slavery was the creation over time of a
        superior physical specimen.
        4. Sport is one area in American society where blacks
        experience equality.
        5. Sport participation offers blacks both educational
        and economic mobility.

B. Each of the myths outlined above can be countered by more objective findings (Edwards, 1973).

    1. The range of differences among blacks and among whites with regard to physical traits is much greater than any differences between the two groups. Even if there are differences, can they explain variations in athletic performance? (e.g., same position athletes come in a variety of shapes and sizes).

    2. Black athletes, because of the unique pressures on them, are more vulnerable to the stresses of sport. In comparison to successful white athletes, successful black athletes are more serious, concerned, uptight, and have a more controlled orientation toward their sport career.

    3. Slaves that survived the best were the most shrewd rather than the most physical. Moreover, the black race can hardly be considered pure, considering the amount of miscegenation that took place. Finally, the survival of the fittest explanation overlooks the shorter life span of the black.

    4. Blacks experience considerable inequality in sport (see Section V. of this outline).

    5. More talent is aborted on the playground than can be calculated and as a result the black community is left impoverished.

C. Widespread acceptance of these myths by both the white and communities has a number of negative consequences.

    1. The hard work and effort of black athletes is negated because it is perceived that their abilities are simply natural.

    2. Position segregation—blacks concentrated in positions characterized by fleetness of foot, muscular agility, and a capacity for quick turns in air and whites concentrated in the central leadership, "thinking," playmaking positions—is justified.

    3. Sport becomes an opiate for the black community.

    4. A perception by black youth that sport is the avenue of mobility causes them to channel all their energies in a single direction. The result is that the black community has plenty of athletes but not enough teachers, doctors, etc.

III. Socialization into Sports: The Character of Early Experiences

A. There is almost no research in this area. Most research about the black athlete's sport career focuses on the transition from high school to college (recruitment), college and pros.

B. The information that does exist is at best a series of generalizations.

1. Black culture both encourages and pushes its youth into athletics much more than white culture does its white youth.
2. The media is very influential in communicating sports (and entertainment) as the avenue of success.

    a. Achievement through athletics appears to be the surest avenue of success.
    b. Black role models in high prestige non-sport positions are all but invisible to black youth.

3. Many black youth are mislead by the well-publicized success of a few black stars and channel all their energies in the direction of sport.
4. For many young blacks, sport achievement is emphasized to the neglect of educational achievement during junior high and high school.

IV. The Career of the Black Athlete

    A. The Transition From High School to College

        1. Most knowledge about the transition from high school to college comes from indirect sources.

            a. The media informs the public about the signing of outstanding black athletes. From such accounts we can gain some glimpses of what the transition is like.
            b. National scouting services prepare profiles of high school athletes. These are purchased by college coaches who use them to select players.

--The scouting reports include the following information about each player: grade point average, height, weight, relevant statistics and race.

--The questions are why is race included on the scouting reports and why isn't information about playing ability sufficient?

        2. We know little about the decision-making process for either race. Some areas that might be of interest include the effects of a potential college team's racial composition on the decision, the effect of the coach's race on the decision, the athlete's perception of playing time.
        3. Within the sport of basketball, for example, there are approximately 200,000 high school seniors. There are only 12,000 college scholarships (new and returning) given each year. Research is needed on the social and psychological effects to those who fail to make the transition.

B. The College Career

   1. Acceptance of a college athletic scholarship may be
   the first step to a truncated career.

      a. Colleges often use the black player as a performer
      without taking responsibility for his educational
      experience.
      b. A large number of blacks terminate their college
      career without a professional contract and without
      the skills for a job. Except for occasional accounts
      by the media, we have almost no knowledge of what
      happens to black athletes after their college career
      ends.

   2. Most college environments are predominantly white.
   Such colleges import black athletes into a situation where
   there are few black co-eds and almost no blacks in the
   surrounding community.
   3. Too often, the publicized salaries are illusionary
   or fake.
   4. Evans (1974) found that black recruits for college
   tend to be better players than their white counterparts.

      a. Blacks have more high school varsity experience
      than white counterparts.
      b. In comparision to white recruits, blacks had won
      more awards during their high school careers.

C. The Professional Career

   1. In proportion to their numbers, black athletes are
   overrepresnted in the professional sports of baseball,
   football, basketball, and track and field. They are
   underrepresented in such sports as swimming, gymnastics,
   skiing, skating, cycling, golf and tennis.
   2. The statistical possibility of landing a paying job
   in professional sports is bleak. It is estimated, for
   example, that approximately 5,000 basketball players end
   their college career each year. Only 54 land a professional
   contract.
   3. To break into the pros a black must be more outstanding
   than his white counterparts (Calhoun, 1981).

      a. If filling a position comes down to a black and
      white of equal talent, the white will generally get
      the position.
      b. Since professional teams are supported by white
      audiences, "bench" positions are more often filled
      by white players than black players.

D. Post-Professional Career

   1. At the end of his professional career, even the successful
   black athlete faces unusual difficulties.

      a. After their professional careers, few black
      athletes become managers or coaches.
      b. The conspicuous case of the black who becomes
      a sports announcer obscures the hundreds of cases
      of men who are left with nothing.

   2. If they have no special abilities apart from their
   sports skills, life after the pro-career becomes especially
   painful.
   3. An interesting case of problems faced by the black athlete
   forced into retirement is the case of Bill Robinzine, a professional basketball player who committed suicide in 1982 when
   a knee injury brought his career to a sudden end (Shapiro, 1982).

V. Social Inequalities at the College and Professional Level

   A. Racial discrimination in sport is manifested through stacking;
   that is, central, "thinking," leadership positions are disproportionately held by whites while non-central, reflex, physical,
   speed positions are disproportionately held by blacks.

   B. The most documented form of discrimination is stacking (Loy and
   McElvogue, 1970; Eitzen, 1972; Medoff, 1977).

   C. In each of the three major sports--football, basketball and
   baseball--stacking has been documented.

      1. In football, whites tend to be concentrated in the
      positions of quarterback, center, and guard and linebacker.
      2. Even in basketball, in proportion to the number of
      whites who play at the college or professional level, whites
      tend to be concentrated in the positions of point guard and
      center.
      3. In baseball, whites tend to be concentrated in the
      infield positions (including pitcher and catcher).

   D. Black athletes are systematically removed from positions of
   leadership as they move from high school to college to the
   professionals (Eitzen and Sanford, 1975).

   E. A number of hypotheses have been advanced to explain stacking.

      1. Coaches may believe that blacks are better suited for
      non-central positions and whites are better suited for the
      leadership positions.
      2. Blacks are socialized to play the non-central positions.

3. Genetic reasons might be involved if the physical attributes of blacks just happen to match the physical characteristics of non-central positions (unlikely explanation).
4. Role models for blacks occupy non-central positions so phenomenon of discrimination is accidentally perpetuated.

E. There are a number of negative consequences that result from these discriminatory practices.

1. There is loss of income since 3/4 of TV, radio, and newspaper spots go to players in central positions.
2. There is a loss of media coverage since central positions are emphasized more by sport commentators.
3. Because non-central positions tend to be more physical, athletes in those positions generally have shorter careers than athletes in central positions.
4. Athletes in central positions are more likely to continue their athletic careers through coaching college or professional sports.

VI. The Media

A. The media has always affected the public's perception of athletes.

B. Since the fame of Jack Johnson from 1908-1915, the media has often been influential in creating an image of the black athlete. The inter-racial exploitation of the Johnson-Jeffries fight gave not only black athletes a bad name, but the black race in general a bad reputation.

C. A number of blacks have been connected to controversial political issues on both national and international levels, made even more controversial by the media itself (e.g., Jesse Owens, Joe Louis, Cassius Clay [later Muhammed Ali], Lew Alcindor [later Kareem Abdul-Jabbar], Tommie Smith and John Carlos, to name a few.)

D. Often race, not talent, seems to be the focus of news stories, which hurts more than helps blacks. Good examples are the cases of Kermit Washington (Halberstam, 1981) and Carla Dunlap (Steinem, 1985).

VII. Setbacks for Blacks

A. The plight of the black athlete has not received the public exposure and coverage that warrant the situation.

B. The experiences of blacks in the labor market encourage youth to perceive sport as the solution to their predicament.

1. Unemployment is high, especially for black youths. The 1981 unemployment rate for blacks between the ages of 16 and 19 was 41.5%. For blacks as a group the unemployment rate is 25 percent.

2. Inequalities in rates of joblessness are repeated in unequal earnings for those who have jobs.

   a. Blacks persistently earn less than whites and are greatly overrepresented among workers who occupy the lowest positions.

   b. Blacks, despite important advances, remain substantially underrepresented in the best jobs.

   c. In 1980, the job category with the highest proportion of blacks was garbage collector; the one with the highest proportion of black women was maids and servants.

C. There are more poor blacks in 1981 than in any year since 1965, and the black poverty rate is roughly triple the white rate. The implication is that there are more blacks vulnerable to the mystique of sport.

D. The economic shift in U.S. society from a manufacturing economy to an information and service economy means that the job situation could get worse for blacks since manufacturing provided a substantial number of solid jobs for blacks.

VIII. The Black Female Athlete

A. "To the extent that sport provides an escape route from the ghetto at all, it does so only for black males (Edwards, 1973)."

B. Due to a combination of racism and sexism in sport, the black female athlete is essentially invisible.

C. Despite a number of successes in sport, the black female athlete has received little financial reward or publicity.

1. Alice Coachman of Tuskegee Institute was the first American black female athlete to win a gold medal in the 1948 Olympics. Although blacks were supported by Americans in the war against Nazism, the black male received most of this attention.

2. Althea Gibson, the first black player to break the color barrier of the USLTA after protesting her initial rejection, typifies many of the struggles (Gibson, 1958).

3. Willye B. White, a five-time Olympic track and field star, fought against racism, sexism and ageism. She was considered a "freak" for being like a man. She was painfully aware of the female-athlete dichotomy (Jordan, 1975).

251

4. In 1983 Carla Dunlap won the Caesar's World Cup for Bodybuilding. She has received little media attention. In addition, she has not been on the cover of any of the bodybuilding magazines (Steinem, 1985).

5. Lynnette Woodard became the first female Globetrotter in 1985. She captained the 1984 Olympic gold medal team. During her college career at the University of Kansas she attained the school's career scoring record, eclipsing the record of Wilt Chamberlain and Jo Jo White. She was hired to help the Globetrotters gain attention. She sees her position as vicarious act for all her sisters who can't make a living at their sport (Vecsey, 1985).

IX. Teaching Suggestions

A. Assign students the task of finding biographical material on early black athletes.
B. The most recent statistics on stacking for the three major sports can be figured easily by students. Unfortunately even the latest textbooks only include statistics up to the early 1970's.
C. Read profiles in sport magazines about black athletes in "white" positions (e.g., Warren Moon, Arthur Ashe, Dwight Gooden).
D. Conversely, read profiles in sport magazines about white athletes in "black" positions (e.g., Larry Bird, Bill Walton, Jerry Cooney, etc.)
E. Compare write-ups on black and white athletes. A good case study is the November 20, 1985 issue of Sports Illustrated and the November issue of Inside Sports. Both magazines profile the top five college basketball players for 1985-86 season. In addition, Sports Illustrated profiles the top 40 colleges and the outstanding players of each. The accounts of white and black athletes, (we promise), will make interesting class discussion. One example is the cases of Mark Price and Bruce Dalrymple at Georgia Tech (Newman, 1985).

1. Price (white) is portrayed as serious, intelligent, and religious. Of the two he is the leader. Price worked real hard to develop his basketball skills.
2. Dalrymple (black) is a "free spirited ghetto blaster" (page 24). "He likes to party and he likes women. You have to stay with him every minute." (p. 25). Dalrymple was born with a basketball in his hands.

Bibliography

Ashe, Arthur
    1985 The Hard Road to Glory

Axelrod, Phil
    1985 "Our Fabulous Five." Inside Sports December: 24+.

Calhoun, Don
    1981 Sports, Culture, and Personality New York: Leisure Press.

Curry, Elliott and Jerome H. Skolnick
    1984 America's Problems: Social Issues and Policy. Boston:
          Little Brown and Company.

Edwards, Harry
    1969 The Revolt of the Black Athlete. New York: Free Press.

    1972 "The Myth of the Racially Superior Athlete." Intellectual
          Digest 2:58-60.

    1973 "The Black Athlete: 20th Century Gladiators for White
          America." Psychology Today November: 43-53.

Evans, Arthur S.
    1979 "Differences in the Recruitment of Black and White Football
          Players at a Big Eight University." Journal of Sport and
          Social Issues 3:1-9.

Gibson, Althea
    1958 "I Always Wanted to Be Somebody." pp. 130-142 in Stephanie
          Twin (ed.) Out of the Bleachers: Writings on Women and
          Sport New York: Feminist Press.

Halberstam, David
    1981 The Breaks of the Game. New York: Ballantine Books.

Hare, Nathan
    1971 "A Study of the Black Fighter." The Black Scholar 3:2-8.

Kane, Martin
    1971 "An Assessment of Black is Best." Sports Illustrated
          January 18:73+.

Kirkpatrick, Curry
    1985 "Lights . . . Camera . . . Cheryl." Sports Illustrated
          November 20: 124+.

Loy, John W. and Joseph F. McElvogue
    1970 "Racial Segregation in American Sport." International Review
          of Sport Sociology 5:5-24.

Medoff, Marshall
    1977   "Positional Segregation and Professional Baseball."
          International Review of Sport Sociology 12:49-56.

Michener, James A.
    1976   "Sports and Upward Escalation." pp. 144-172 in Sports in
          America New York: Random House.

Newman, Bruce
    1985   "Opposite Sides of the Track." Sports Illustrated
          November 20: 20+.

Noverr, Douglas A. and Lawrence E. Ziewacz
    1983   The Games They Played. Chicago: Nelson-Hall.

Shapiro, Michael
    1982   "Life and Death of an Athlete." The New York Times
          Biographical Index October: 1382-1383.

Steinem, Gloria
    1985   "Coming Up: Unprecedented Women." Ms. July: 84+.

Twin, Stephanie
    1979   Out of the Bleachers: Writings on Women and Sport. New
          York: Feminist Press.

Yetman, Norman R. and D. Stanley Eitzen
    1971   "Black Athletes on Intercollegiate Basketball Teams: An
          Empirical Test of Discrimination." in Norman R. Yetman and
          C. Hoy Steele (eds.) Majority and Minority Boston: Allyn
          and Bacon.

Vecsey, George
    1985   "The Newest Globetrotter." New York Times October 13.

ABOUT THE EDITORS

Douglas A. Noverr and Lawrence E. Ziewacz are authors of <u>The Games They Played:</u> <u>Sports in American History, 1865-1980</u> (Nelson-Hall, 1983), "Violence in American Sports" in <u>Sports in Modern America</u>, edited by William J. Baker and John M. Carroll (River City Publishers, 1981), and "Sports in the Twenties" in <u>The Evolution of Mass Culture in America</u>, edited by Gerald R. Baydo (Forum Press, 1982). They are also co-Area chairperson of the "Sports" section of the American Culture Association and the Popular Culture Association as well as contributors of articles to the forthcoming <u>Biographical Dictionary of American Sport</u>, edited by David L. Porter (Greenwood Press).